NAPOLEON'S MEN

Napoleon's Men

The Soldiers of the Revolution and Empire

Alan Forrest

Hambledon and London
London and New York

Hambledon and London

102 Gloucester Avenue
London NW1 8HX (UK)

838 Broadway
New York
NY 10003–4812 (USA)

First Published 2002

ISBN 1 85285 269 0

Copyright © Alan Forrest 2002
The moral right of the author has been asserted

A description of this book is available from
the British Library and the Library of Congress

Typeset by Carnegie Publishing, Carnegie House
Chatsworth Road
Lancaster, LA1 4SL

Printed on acid-free paper and bound
in Great Britain by Bath Press, Bath

Contents

Illustrations

Text Illustrations

Introduction

All wars are personal, in the sense that they are personal to those who fight in them. They produce moments of passion and exhilaration with which few peacetime experiences can compare; but they also leave a terrible debris in their wake, tearing families apart and leaving a lasting legacy of regret, fear, illness and depression that goes on to haunt so many former soldiers throughout the rest of their lives. Veterans of modern wars are encouraged to remember, by their families and friends, and by others interested in what they underwent. And because they are so much more literate than the soldiers of previous wars, many of them take the opportunity to write about their experiences, whether to share their triumphs or to confound their demons. As a result, we know more about them and about their lives in the military than we can possibly hope to know about the soldiers of previous generations, who too often remain mute, existing in history only as names or regimental numbers, devoid of the feeling and individualism which words alone can express.

Napoleon's Men is an attempt to fill that void for the French soldiers who fought in the Revolutionary and Napoleonic Wars – wars which involved millions of men over a period of more than twenty years, and which, for the European world of the late eighteenth and early nineteenth centuries, can be realistically compared in scale to the world wars of the twentieth century. Of course many of the soldiers who fought in them, whether for France or for Prussia, Austria or Great Britain, lacked the literacy and the ability to express emotion which we have come to associate with those who fought in the mud of the Somme or who faced General Giap's guerrilla fighters in Vietnam. But what is astonishing is not how badly they wrote but rather that they wrote at all, driven by a desire to communicate with their families, to seek reassurance by keeping in touch with the outside world. They wrote in their tens of thousands – something that cannot be said of previous generations, or of earlier European conflicts. From previous wars, of course, from the *Iliad* onwards, there survive occasional records of military experiences, usually those of generals, infrequently of officers, very rarely of other ranks. But the French Revolutionary and Napoleonic Wars produced for the first time a mass army drawn from the population at large, the product of requisitions and conscription which fell upon all, regardless of their social position or their educational attainments. They may not have served willingly – not all of them, at any rate – but that merely ensured that they would reflect more fairly the feelings of society at large. It also meant that this was not an army of the poor and under-educated, and that not all lacked literary skills: they included in their number not just artisans and shopkeepers, peasants and labourers, but a considerable sprinkling of students, teachers, lawyers, clerks, insurance agents and public officials. Many also had a level of political awareness unparalleled in previous generations. They had lived through the French Revolution and had been educated to think of themselves as citizens, men with rights and with opinions. As a result this was not a silent army, one about whom our knowledge must necessarily remain limited. For the first time we have a substantial body of personal information, written by the generality of soldiers as well as by their chiefs. From their accounts we can assemble a portrait of eighteenth-century soldiering, of an army that we can know in a detail that would have been unimaginable in previous periods of warfare.

My focus in this book is on the soldiers themselves: on their experiences of army life and their emotions when faced with years away from their homes in the strangely unfamiliar environment of the military. It differs from most other studies of the Revolutionary and Napoleonic Wars by offering no narrative of the period, unless by that is meant the collective narrative of the men who took part. Instead, what I present here is a view of the war years from below, as they were seen by those who spent a large part of their youth in the service of the Revolution and of the Emperor. How did they view the army and the profession of soldiering? How did they respond to the challenge of battle, to the long spells of boredom and drudgery, to the emotions of fear and passion that were unleashed by active engagement? How did they react when faced with what was for many a severe and unwelcome test of their masculinity? Some, of course, became overnight heroes, and must have counted themselves lucky. But this is not a book about heroism. Rather it is about the contrasting reactions of ordinary soldiers to the conditions of warfare at the end of the eighteenth and during the early years of the nineteenth century, their fears and anxieties as well as their pride and their moments of intoxicating triumph.

They expressed the whole gamut of human emotions in the course of their long, wearying campaigns, not least that sense of adventure which soldiers have always shared and the wide-eyed wonderment of travellers faced with new experiences and alien cultures. Of course, there was nothing new in this. Young men from time immemorial had chosen to join the army to get away from poverty and tedium, family quarrels and judicial retribution; indeed, one of the attractions of soldiering had always been the opportunity to escape; that sense of freedom that came with the open road. And soldiers had always travelled, abandoning their farm or their village to respond to the call of arms in distant lands. The Ancient Greeks who served under Alexander the Great in Persia and the Swedes who followed Gustavus Adolphus across the plains of central Europe, to say nothing of the Crusading armies in the Holy Land or the Spanish and Portuguese forces who opened up Latin America to conquest, all had been excited by their adventures, just as all had wondered at the lands they discovered in the course of their campaigns. A large part of the identity of old soldiers, once they had left their regiment and returned, often uneasily, to civilian life, rested precisely on the fact of having travelled, of having seen interesting and exotic things, of having had experiences that were not available to the vast majority of the population. They had a reputation as the tellers of tales and the bringers of wonderment, even if many of their tales were deemed to be tall and the stories they told of doubtful veracity. Yet few had ever travelled on the scale of the generation who fought for the Revolution and Empire. The French armies barely stopped travelling, covering huge distances over many years, their soldiers moving inexorably from snow-capped Alpine passes to the hot plains of Castile, from the vineyards of Italy and the Rhineland to the deserts of Egypt and North Africa. Some had fought beneath the Pyramids, others in the sugar-islands of the Caribbean. And if it all ended disastrously in the snows of Russia, those who returned came back with a wealth of travellers' tales about exotic landscapes and cultured capital cities, strange diets and novel crops. A whole generation of young men who would in other circumstances have ventured little beyond the confines of their native village was suddenly exposed to the wonders of an entire continent.

If the war is seen through the eyes of the French troops, it is also told, as far as is possible, in their own words, in the language they used to describe their experiences. Of course these words are not without their problems, for many expressed themselves with extreme difficulty, and in the heat of a military campaign few had the time or leisure to maintain a consistent or coherent record. But write they did, just as the young men who fought in other wars of the modern era – whether in the Crimea, in the American Civil War, or in the world wars of the twentieth century – showed a quite unquenchable appetite for writing and communicating with the outside world. These writings are of very different kinds. Some were the words they wrote down at the time in diaries and journals or turned to later in their memoirs when they looked back on their military careers. They might be written for themselves or to show to others when the war was over. But the vast majority of their writing was much more ephemeral and was not intended for the public gaze – the words they wrote to their families and loved ones in the hundreds of thousands of letters that were faithfully carried by the military posts back to the towns and villages of France. These letters form the major source for this book, and they provide precious insights into the most immediate concerns of the young soldiers. They ask after the health of parents and express fears for the harvest; they talk of generals and battles and military glory; they tell of wounds and spells in hospital; they report those moments of joy when they met friends and brothers and enjoyed a drink or a meal in a wayside inn; and they record their everyday miseries and deprivations, the drill, the poor food, the cold and hunger and lack of sleep. They also contain significant silences, on the large areas of military life which the troops appeared to eschew or found it impossible to discuss with others. Taken singly, these letters tell the stories of individual soldiers, revealing what was on men's minds at particular moments or what it was that they wanted their families to hear. Collectively, the many hundreds of letters that form the basis for this book tell much more than that. They allow us to reconstruct the daily life of the troops, to understand what most affected ordinary Frenchmen and to reflect on their thoughts, their fears and their morale, and their responses to the very masculine culture of military life.

Works of literature they are not. Many were hastily penned by young men who often had only a modest education, or who consigned their writing to others, to men better schooled than themselves. But if they are poorly written, ungrammatical and banal in the sentiments they express, they also have the benefit of spontaneity and a lack of guile; indeed, they have a hauntingly honest quality which diaries and published memoirs lack. Besides, if we are seeking out the feelings and emotions of ordinary soldiers, they are the most significant source available to us. Unlike the Great War, this generation of conflict did not produce poets or novelists; and it left posterity with no visual or photographic record. These letters, however flawed and imperfect they may be, constitute the best mirror we have of the thoughts of serving soldiers, the most useful source for measuring their reactions and emotions and for comparing the rhetoric of their political leaders with everyday experience in the ranks. Of course they had drunk in much of that rhetoric and they shared in the culture of the army, the relief and joy when a battle was won and victory seemed in sight. That is only to be expected. But the letters also reveal another side of soldiering which the ideological language of Jacobin and Napoleonic speeches too often overlooks – the fears and anguish, and the sheer, unremitting tedium of life in the regiments. These are not glorious or heroic matters, and too often they are quietly overlooked in the histories of these wars; yet they are crucial to military morale and go far to explain the fevers and depressive illnesses suffered by the troops. Historians of twentieth-century wars, and most especially of the Great War of 1914–18, have long understood the importance of gloom and depression in soldiers' lives, the *cafards* of the trenches of the Somme and Verdun. But they were in no sense the prerogative of twentieth-century soldiers. As these letters make clear, they were widely experienced by the men sent to the Peninsula and on the Moscow campaign.

What the soldiers of the Great War did have was a power to communicate that was far more expressive than that of their less educated forebears. They were often older, too, more wise in the ways of the world. And among them were men of letters of true literary distinction who could express eloquently what the men of 1792 or 1809 could only falteringly grope towards, the open analysis of their feelings and emotions. Yet it is difficult to avoid the conclusion that they were saying much the same thing, albeit in words that were innocent of literary artifice. They were proud to be soldiers, proud, possibly, also of the cause in whose name they fought. But the majority of them did not enjoy life in the army, and they craved the day when they would find a release from it. Among twentieth-century novelists are many who have expressed the mixed and often contradictory feelings that beset the soldier, the kinds of feelings to which these young Frenchmen were a prey. Whereas they were told to feel pride and honour, they too often admitted to other emotions, to homesickness and loneliness, boredom and fear, reactions which they half understood, and which left them confused and miserable. It is a condition familiar to all armies, one which the Canadian novelist Robertson Davies summed up memorably in the context of service with the Canadian Corps on the Western Front in 1915:

> I was bored as I have never been since – bored till every bone in my body was heavy with it. This was not the boredom of inactivity; an infantry trainee is kept on the hop from morning till night, and his sleep is sound. It was the boredom that comes from being cut off from everything that could make life sweet, or arouse curiosity, or enlarge the range of the senses. It was the boredom that comes of having to perform endless tasks that have no savour and acquire skills one would gladly be without ... But I was not discontented with soldiering; I was discontented with myself, with my loneliness and boredom.

The young soldiers who followed Bonaparte would have recognised that boredom and understood it as their own. They would also have understood the novelist's description of fear, the kind of fear which affected them after their first taste of battle and which they found so difficult to admit to, both at the time and in later life. As Davies analyses it, it too was a complex of emotions:

> In France, though my boredom was unabated, loneliness was replaced by fear. I was in a mute, controlled, desperate fashion, frightened for the next three years ... I think there were many in my own case: frightened of death,

of wounds, of being captured, but most frightened of admitting to fear and losing face before the others. This kind of fear is not acute, of course; it is a constant, depleting companion whose presence makes everything gray. Sometimes fear could be forgotten, but never for long. [1]

For Marianne

Acknowledgements

This book has been a long time in the making, too often put to one side as I completed other writing commitments or found myself deflected by the demands of university administration. Initially my interest in soldiers' writings arose from chance discoveries in departmental and municipal archives and in the pages of local historical journals, often while looking for quite different things, and at that stage I saw them principally as a means to an end, as illustrations of men's feelings and of the texture of everyday life in the regiments. Only gradually did I become aware of their richness and variety and conclude that I should study them as documents in their own right. It has been a rewarding experience. Analysing the content of these letters and later discussing them with academic colleagues at seminars and conferences has helped me to appreciate their value as ego-documents, personal testimonies that provide explanations of military motivation and routes into men's minds and souls.

A glance at the bibliography will show that the quest for soldiers' writings, and especially of their letters home to their parents, has taken me to the four corners of France, and occasionally beyond. The quest was not always easy. Such letters are seldom catalogued in discrete series in archives; more often – since they had in their own right no clear administrative function – they are included in the series to which they related at the time of their insertion, which could be either civil or military, depending on whether they dealt with policing or desertion, or legal, the result of a claim for land or for an inheritance. Tracking them down often proved difficult, and would have been impossible without the active help of archival staff in widely dispersed departmental archives, from the Finistère and Pas-de-Calais to the Basses-Pyrénées (as it was called by the Revolution; it has now been more decorously renamed Pyrénées-Atlantiques) and Savoie. Indeed, one of my first steps was to write to every departmental archivist in France asking whether, by good fortune, they had any such letters in their collections. My heart-felt thanks go to those – in some three-quarters of the *départements* – who took the trouble to reply and to investigate on my behalf, often providing precious call numbers and, in some instance, photocopies of their finds. These replies convinced me that there was, indeed, material there in manuscript form to supplement printed materials in journals and justify a larger-scale project. So, too, did the files of the Ministry of War, the *Service Historique de l'Armée de Terre* at Vincennes, where handwritten copies of many local letters – some of them now, sadly, lost in the original – exist in series Xw, the product of an unusual exercise in military history conducted in another age as part of officer training. These particular officer cadets were asked to visit local archives and libraries throughout France and to copy every document they could find concerning the army during the revolutionary period. They did so assiduously, and amongst the piles of paper which resulted are the texts of several hundred soldiers' letters, painstakingly copied from their original scrawl into legible copperplate. They, too, a generation of young men who doubtless went on to serve as officers in the French armies and to experience their own range of thrills and emotions in war, are due a word of appreciation for their efforts.

A more pressing debt, however, is to the living, to those friends and colleagues who have helped further this research and have encouraged me to bring it to fruition. In this country I have had long and fruitful discussions of parts of this work with a wide range of fellow-scholars, historians of both modern France and of warfare, often in the context of seminars and colloquia. In particular, I should like to mention Michael Broers, Malcolm Crook, Charles Esdaile, David Hopkin and Hew Strachan. In the United States I have enjoyed valuable exchanges with Michael Fitzsimmons and John Merriman, and was fortunate to be asked to give a keynote address on soldiers' writings to the annual conference of the Consortium on Revolutionary Europe in Charleston, South Carolina, in 1999. My thanks go to the organisers, and especially to Owen Connelly, both for inviting me to what was an excellent conference and for permission to draw extensively on the text of that address while preparing Chapter 2 of the present volume. Similarly, various of the ideas that have been incorporated elsewhere in the book were first tested on audiences at international colloquia, most notably at the Rudé Seminar at Canberra in Australia in 1996, and at Revolutionary and Napoleonic gatherings in Alessandria in Italy, Louvain-la-Neuve in Belgium and La Roche-sur-Yon in France. My appreciation is again due to the organisers of those events, in particular to David Lovell, Vittorio Scotti Douglas, Marcel Watelet and Jean-Clément Martin. The author and publishers are grateful to the following for permission to reproduce illustrations: Archives Départementales du Cher (p. 35); Archives Départementales de la Corrèze (p. 43); the Louvre/Bridgeman Art Library (pl. 12).

I also owe a debt of gratitude to those friends who have drawn my attention to sources, particularly to individual letters or letter collections which have found their way into the present research; who have generously shared their own research findings; and who have been *compagnons* on the rather tortuous *route* that has led to this publication. Bruno Ciotti, Steven Clay and Philippe Raxhon have all provided precious references to archives of letters in France and in Belgium; Chuck Walton has helped disentangle the intricacies of the military postal service; and Jean-Paul Bertaud has been a source of wise counsel all along the way. At Hambledon and London, Tony Morris and Martin Sheppard have provided both careful guidance and enthusiastic support; this is a much better book in consequence. More than any, though, my thanks go to my family: to Rosemary and Marianne, who have for too long had to live vicariously with the men of the revolutionary and Napoleonic armies and with my recurrent absences in libraries and archives. They must have begun to feel that this is their book as much as mine. Even Zaki, the family cat, has played his part, providing company through long hours of writing, and clearly empathising with the view so often expressed in the soldiers' correspondence, that the most important things in life are not glory or victory, but those ordinary creature comforts like food and warmth, security and companionship. It may not be a very heroic view; but who is to say he is wrong?

1

The Armies of the Revolution and Empire

Though war is not the immediate subject of this book, it provides its inescapable context – a costly and exhausting war which engulfed France and the French people for the best part of a quarter of a century, and in whose cause a generation of young Frenchmen would volunteer and be conscripted, fight and desert, enthuse, despair and be sacrificed. That they fought well and bravely is not in question: for proof we need look no further than their conduct at Valmy or Jemappes, Marengo or Jena. France demanded and obtained an inordinate level of sacrifice from that generation, from those young men unlucky enough to reach their eighteenth birthday between 1792 and 1814. It is their experience which is our concern here, their commitment and motivation, the fears and doubts that they expressed in the name of the French Revolution and the First Empire. Why did they answer the call to defend the *patrie en danger* with such seeming alacrity, or accept conscription into Napoleon's legions? What motivated them to fight in battle after battle, without apparent thought for their own survival, when glory had lost some of its initial glitter and they understood the grim realities of warfare? How did they react to the rigours and discipline of army life, the forced marches across Europe, the boredom of winter camp, the cold fear they experienced on the battlefield? And how did they respond, these young Bretons and Gascons, Flemings and Auvergnats, to being removed from their families and their villages, almost certainly for the first time in their short lives, to play their part in the great revolutionary crusade against the tyranny of kings? That they suffered is not in doubt. They often admitted to feeling desperately homesick, cut off from their parents and their culture, prone to attacks of weariness and lassitude – that raft of nervous and depressive illnesses which contemporaries described as *mal du pays*. They suffered, too, from deprivations of a more mundane kind, from a lack of warmth and sleep, food and drink, boots and clothing. Too often supply trains were delayed, pay failed to come through, and men were left to forage for their own sustenance. How far did these deprivations affect their morale and motivation, or their belief in the cause for which they were fighting? And how deep was that belief? The soldiers of the Revolution, in particular, are often presented as young men fighting for a political cause, for the ideals of liberty, equality and fraternity which they bore on their escutcheon. But were they? Or is this, too, little more than political rhetoric, one of the many fictions of the revolutionary years which would be embroidered by nineteenth-century republicans and passed down to posterity?

The declaration of war in the spring of 1792 was one of the critical moments of the French Revolution, one that dramatically affected both the course of the Revolution itself and the political history of Europe in the years that followed. It transformed government priorities and helped increase the sense of fear and paranoia which was to characterise so much of revolutionary history, particularly in Paris. It bore a heavy responsibility for destroying any possibility of political pluralism, for increasing the influence of the radical sections, and for expediting the resort to Terror. In the economic sphere it deprived France of a large part of its agricultural labour supply, undermined the progress of industrial development, and destroyed much of the prosperity of the Atlantic trade. Across the European continent it awakened dormant nationalist aspirations insulted by France's attempts to impose a cultural and ideological hegemony. It was no doubt unavoidable that the pursuit of victory brushed aside many of the Revolution's other objectives, most particularly in the field of social provision and public welfare, while the constraints imposed by a war economy further reduced the scope for achieving civil liberties. With the passage of time, indeed, the increasing emphasis on the needs of the war effort risked dominating the entire political agenda, as victory became an end in itself and as a more professionalised army quickly evolved its own distinctive loyalties and priorities. Unfairly, perhaps, many Frenchmen already saw the Directory as a regime beholden to the successes of its armies, its politicians increasingly despised and the eyes of the nation turning to the military for achievement elsewhere. Indeed, long before Napoleon seized power on 18 Brumaire, France had been transformed, from a nation fighting for the integrity of its frontiers and its institutions, into an imperialistic power whose principal objective was to seize land from its neighbours and establish political control across much of continental Europe.

In theory, of course, revolutionary war was like no other, the product of foreign threats and patriotic insurgency, as the French people responded to the government's clarion call to defend the *patrie en danger*. Faced by the threat of an imminent Austrian invasion in 1791, the young men of France rallied to the nation's cause, the nation's and the Revolution's, since both French territorial integrity and the political gains made since 1789 were imperilled. They were, in the official language of the time, the language so consistently promulgated in decrees and proclamations, 'volunteers' who had offered their youth and, if necessary, their lives for the defence of France and its revolutionary principles. Their beliefs and selflessness stood in stark contrast to the desperate poverty of those who had composed eighteenth-century European armies, who frequently were too downtrodden or too marginalised to pursue any other form of career. Like the National Guardsmen who had responded to the crisis of 1789 and 1790 by coming forward to defend their towns and villages against attack from supposed 'brigands', the first volunteers were honoured by their communities and became symbols of the generous spirit of the young. Army reform followed, and with it the rights of active citizenship. Suddenly, France's soldiers were treated with unprecedented respect, allowed to vote, and encouraged to participate in public celebrations and festivals. A new age appeared to have dawned in which soldiers had a different status, a different outlook, a different relationship to society and the state.

But did they? Historians of the Revolutionary Wars have increasingly come to question the ideological nature of the conflict and to place these wars in the context of an eighteenth century scarred by commercial, colonial and dynastic squabbling between European states.[1] Official language seldom reflected day to day reality, and there is little evidence to support the notion that the soldiers themselves thought of this war as being so very different from the many conflicts which had littered the European landscape throughout the eighteenth century. Some, it is true, echoed the patriotic sentiments of the politicians or shared their ideological commitment to liberty and equality. They, like their leaders, were spurred by the seemingly ideological attacks of their enemies, in

the Declaration of Pillnitz and the Brunswick Manifesto, to defend their
Revolution against outside attack and to fear a counter-revolution in the
name of kings and despots. But occasional quotations rich in patriotic
rhetoric should not be allowed to deceive us. Few of the men who
answered the first call for volunteers in 1791 were prepared for the lengthy
struggle that was to follow: many, indeed, thought of their service as
lasting for one campaign season, and were fully prepared to return to
their villages once the summer was over. Some, one might suggest
cynically, even volunteered in 1791 precisely because war had not been
declared and soldiering was still more about demonstrations of patriotic
commitment than about risking life and limb on the battlefield. For if
the call was generously answered in 1791, with most areas of the country
providing an excess of volunteers (in some eastern departments the
battalions were three and four times oversubscribed), there were many
fewer willing to serve when the step was repeated in the following year,
once war had been declared and that risk had become a reality. Some
regions of the country even admitted that their people were naturally
reluctant to offer themselves, arguing that the needs of agriculture or a
lack of military culture had created a widespread revulsion for soldiering.
In these circumstances it became clear that the revolutionaries could
not hope to defend France in the spirit of its own rhetoric, with a citizen
army of patriotic volunteers burning to defend the gains they had made
since 1789.

The call for volunteers was therefore abandoned as an insufficient
means of raising the large infantry battalions France needed, with the
consequence that by the spring of 1793 the voluntary principle had
already given way to a degree of coercion. Departments were called
upon to provide quotas proportionate to their populations, as the
government called for a *levée des 300,000* to offset the ravages of the first
months of fighting. The term 'volunteers' was stubbornly maintained,
along with the ideal that in the best of all possible worlds men would
continue to come forward voluntarily, but few were deceived. Besides,
the law did not presume to lay down how soldiers should be found; it
merely insisted that communities meet their recruitment targets, stipu-
lating that 'in the event that the voluntary enrolment does not yield the
number of men requested from each commune, the citizens shall be
required to complete it at once, and for such purpose they shall adopt,

by plurality of votes, the method which they find most suitable'.[2] In practice, the manner of their recruitment was seldom voluntary, as local authorities turned to various forms of balloting and imposition in increasingly desperate efforts to fill their quotas. A few, it is true, could do so with apparent ease, principally in those departments of the north and the east where men had for generations been accustomed to defend their homes and their farmsteads against invasion from across the Rhine. But in many departments, especially in the more historically recalcitrant areas of Brittany, the Massif Central and the Pyrenean foothills, recruitment remained sluggish, and local mayors were forced to draw lots, or pay for replacements, or – in a curious perversion of equity known as *scrutin révolutionnaire* – to call on their fellow-villagers to nominate the most courageous and most revolutionary to march in their name. This was rightly seen by many as an open invitation to deceit and evasion, and there were many cases where the process aroused bitter resentment, with villagers volunteering the sons of their most hated rivals, or callously nominating outsiders and men marginal to the community – seasonal harvesters who happened to be passing through on the day of the ballot, men drawn from marginal communities or living as shepherds on isolated hillsides, those who been banished from their parental home after an argument, or those who had been consigned by society to hospitals and poorhouses, or by magistrates to prison.[3] It was an instance where words like 'patriotic' and 'republican' could cover a host of social and moral peccadilloes.

The *levée en masse* of August 1793 marked a clear step in the direction of conscription, though conscription of an exceptional, one-off variety born of military emergency rather than a systematic annual exercise. The decree began with these famous words: 'Henceforth, until the enemies have been driven from the territory of the Republic, the French people are in permanent requisition for army service.' In theory the decree placed the whole population, young and old, male and female, on a war footing. 'The young shall go to battle, the married men shall forge arms and transport provisions, the women shall make tents and clothes, and shall serve in the hospitals, the children shall turn old linen into lint, the old men shall repair to the public places to stimulate the courage of the warriors and preach the unity of the republic and the hatred of kings.' And in each district the battalion that was raised was

to be united under a banner bearing the patriotic inscription, 'The
French people risen against tyrants'. The levy, it was explained, was
general, though in practice it was the young, unmarried citizens or child-
less widowers from eighteen to twenty-five years, who were expected to
defend the frontiers.⁴ The law was designed to avoid the abuses of the
previous March, including the perceived unfairness of a system where
anyone with money could buy themselves out of personal service by
finding a man willing to fight in his stead. It did not, however, eradicate
another source of unfairness, since the young men who left for the
armies in the autumn of 1793 often faced a long and arduous assign-
ment. For the law failed to define the length of each man's service: the
conscript was to stay in the army until the end of the war, until peace
was declared, and throughout the Directory it was on these conscripts
of 1793 that the burden of the war continued to fall. Only in 1799, with
the Loi Jourdan, did France see the introduction of systematic conscription, with the annual levy, *classe* by *classe*, turning into a necessary rite
of passage for each succeeding generation as they reached their twentieth
or twenty-first birthday.⁵

Nevertheless, the language of liberty was doggedly maintained, the
revolutionaries cherishing above all else the belief that theirs was a new
kind of army, an army that was truly representative of the French people,
and whose success and tactical formation were based on the idea of the
masse, of the combined force of the people in arms. It was certainly a
far larger army than those which had served the Bourbons during the
Ancien Régime, though the army which Louis XVI had at his command
on the eve of the Revolution cannot be dismissed as insignificant: in
1789 the line army consisted of 121,000 infantrymen, 33,000 cavalry, and
seven regiments of artillery – in all, some 170,000 men, excellently armed
and equipped.⁶ But numbers were not everything, and historians have
increasingly come to question whether the combat capacity of the
revolutionary forces was very much greater than that of the old line.
Following the *levée en masse*, for instance, we know that the French
could muster around three-quarters of a million men; yet the size of
armies in the field remained stubbornly static. The significance of the
levée en masse, however, extended far beyond the size of units or
the sense that French battalions were more representative of the nation
than those that had served Louis XVI. It became a powerful symbol

of national unity and patriotic endeavour, a symbol which would be respected by future generations of Frenchmen and would inspire them in hours of need or of national emergency – in the Revolution of 1848, for example, or during the Franco-Prussian War of 1870, or again in the years following the Dreyfus Affair when France was once more girding her loins for war.[7] It proclaimed the volunteer spirit of the French people while accepting the right and duty of the state to organise the country for war; and it envisaged the mobilisation of all the people, regardless of age and gender, to contribute to that war effort.[8] It would also have a wide international resonance that extended far beyond its country of origin, influencing military thinking throughout much of nineteenth-century Europe and helping to mobilise opinion in large areas of the Third World – in China and Vietnam, for instance, and on all sides during the Algerian War – where peoples sought both a symbol of their nationhood and a practical form of military organisation to fuel their struggle against a colonial or imperialist power.[9]

The *levée en masse* was unique in that it made no concessions to wealth or to regional identity. Unlike previous levies and most of the conscriptions that followed – the only exception being the very first conscription, in 1799 – service had to be carried out in person. All were equally liable, and no provision was made for the more affluent to buy themselves out by finding men willing to serve in their stead. Politicians followed Maximilien Robespierre in praising the integrity and virtue of troops born of the people and united in defending the nation; the soldiers, he argued, were intrinsically good precisely because the people from whom they sprang were good. But did the *levée*, as the revolution-aries claimed, produce a new kind of army? Did French soldiers fight differently because they enjoyed civil rights, because they could vote, could discuss public affairs, and could even join political clubs and popular societies? French revolutionary historians, from Jean Jaurès to Albert Soboul and Jean-Paul Bertaud, have argued that they did, that there was a commitment, a self-belief and *élan* about the Revolution's volunteers which went far to compensate for their lack of tactical knowledge and experience in battle, and which contributed mightily to early victories. They had as their inspiration the classic work of Clausewitz *On War*, which claimed that with the Revolution conven-tional warfare had changed for ever. 'War had again suddenly become an affair of the people, and that of a people numbering thirty millions, every one of whom regarded himself as a citizen of the state ... Henceforward, the means available ... had no longer any definite limits.'[10] It was a message which the crowned heads of Europe could not easily afford to ignore.

Others, however, see the age of mass armies as being more a Napoleonic than a revolutionary creation. Charles Esdaile, for instance, on examining the average size of the armies deployed in battle during the Jacobin months, found that their strength was actually lower than that of Frederick the Great's armies in the Seven Years' War, at around 49,000 men. There is little evidence here to support the idea of a revolutionary *masse*. Rather, he argues, it was Napoleon who first had the capability to send large armies into the field, and he shows that at Jena, Austerlitz, Friedland and Wagram the average size of French forces had risen to over 80,000.[11] This was not simply a question of manpower. For if the Revolution had large numbers of men in uniform following the *levée en masse*, it did not have the capacity to deploy commensurate numbers in the field. And with the passage of time the 750,000 would steadily diminish, through death and injury in battle, through desertion, and through the fevers and infections which spread like wildfire through the military wards of hospitals. If there were three quarters of a million men under arms by the end of 1794, that number had fallen to less than half a million by autumn 1795, to just over 400,000 by July 1796, and to little more than 325,000 by 1799. Crucially, there were no serious attempts to replace them before the Loi Jourdan of the Year VI, which prescribed the first regular annual conscription for the spring of 1799. It came just in time, as the depleted ranks of the armies bore poignant witness. Desertion was rampant and morale poor, while damaging rivalries further undermined military effectiveness. In the words of the general inspection report of 1801, 'the officers are apathetic. They know their trade fairly well, but they are sullen and without spirit. And the non-commissioned officers are even worse. The majority is ignorant, pretentious and slack. These men between twenty-five and thirty-five act as if they were eighty'.[12]

The introduction of conscription marked a significant change in political thinking, since initially the revolutionaries had quite specifically rejected it. In December 1789, Dubois-Crancé had urged the National

THE ARMIES OF THE REVOLUTION AND EMPIRE

Assembly to introduce a 'conscription' – and the word was used – that would include all active citizens 'from the second person of the Empire [the words were chosen carefully to exclude only the King] to the most modest *citoyen actif*. Moreover, he had insisted that everyone must be equally liable to serve; there could be no exceptions, he warned, no provision for replacements, or everything would be lost.[13] But the Assembly had thrown out the idea, and had argued that generals needed willing soldiers, not ones who served reluctantly or through coercion. And throughout the Revolution politicians would continue to maintain that theirs was not a conscript army, even when the evidence suggested that effectively it was. The *levée en masse* was conscription in all but name, yet the authorities insisted that it was purely an exceptional measure introduced to resolve a short-term national emergency. Indeed, it was not repeated. The Directory had no rolling programme of recruitment for the armies, with the consequence that it was those young men unfortunate enough to be twenty or twenty-one in 1793 who bore the brunt of its defence. They often found that *congés* were unobtainable from commanders who needed their presence and their experience, and that their service lasted not for one or two campaigns, but until peace was made. With the passage of time, many came to identify evermore closely with the army and to regard themselves less as civilians serving for a short period in uniform than as professional soldiers, men who have made a career in the military and who had few aspirations to return to the farm or workshop.

Annual conscription was first introduced in 1799, and it remained in force throughout the Empire. Those affected were young men aged between twenty and twenty-five on the first day of Vendémiaire each year, who would be arranged into classes according to their age, with the youngest most liable to be taken and the oldest only really in danger in years of national crisis. Jourdan himself had foreseen that in normal circumstances reaching the age of twenty-two without seeing active service would be the equivalent of a *congé absolu*, though Napoleon's more and more costly wars in eastern Europe and the Peninsula would by the end of the decade be devouring virtually all those deemed fit to serve. The process was driven by the needs of the military, which varied greatly from year to year in accordance with the progress of the war, for the last thing the army needed was a large number of untrained

surplus conscripts to feed, clothe and train. It had little to do with the
ideological commitment to equality beloved of revolutionary orators.
Thus the demands of the recruiting officer were particularly heavy
in 1807 and 1808, lighter in 1809 and 1810 when peace seemed to be in
prospect, then utterly savage from 1811. Indeed, in September 1813 even
the Prefect in the Ariège was driven to protest about the demographic
damage which conscription at this level was wreaking. 'I am taking
everyone', he complained; 'there will be no one left from the years 1813
and 1814 capable of procreation and maintaining the population.' [14] Local
autonomy and discretion in the conscription process were rapidly
abolished, with control taken out of the hands of municipal councils
and passed to the more dependable *conseils de recrutement*, and, though
in 1800 there was no provision for buying oneself out, in all subsequent
years substitutes were again authorised. Napoleon, after all, shared the
view of his senior officers that it was better to have soldiers who had
both some capacity and some appetite for military life; and he accepted
that the reluctant sons of the bourgeoisie could make a more useful
financial contribution than they could through active service. Napoleon's
approach remained consistently pragmatic. He had no interest in egalitarian theories of citizenship and equality before the law. His main
concern was to ensure that the conscription process ran smoothly and
that the army was assured its regular intake of manpower, his desire
being to make conscription into something automatic that would be
borne without resentment, less of a curse than a simple rite of passage
as young men attained the age of manhood. Given the vast scale of
desertion and avoidance in many areas of the country, and the need to
persuade communities in Holland, northern Italy and along the Rhine
that they, too, must play their part in sustaining imperial arms, this was
always a difficult task, with the policy only enforceable by persistent and
often brutal policing. And yet, with the passage of time, even conscription began to become a habit. Despite a handful of major scandals and
intermittent village riots, by 1811 – twenty years after the first call for
volunteers – the evidence would suggest that this most difficult of
Napoleonic objectives had been largely attained.

By Brumaire, of course, the *patrie* was no longer in danger and war
had little to do with revolutionary ideology. In 1790 the revolutionaries
may have promised to liberate the other peoples of Europe, but by

1795 their goal was already territorial conquest, the creation of a buffer of friendly states to France's east, and beyond that, expansion into Germany, Italy and central Europe. It was not only political territory that lay before them: it was also rich granaries, orchards and vineyards, and prosperous trading cities. French armies looted and pillaged, both at the level of individual gain – Saint-Just once famously remarked that pillage posed a greater threat to their morale and discipline than ever desertion did – and at that of state aggrandisement.[15] For the rapid extension of the war and the annexation of the land of France's neighbours – whether in the form of sister republics like the Batavian or the Helvetic or as *départements réunis*, annexed to the *Grande Nation* – brought added costs which could only be met through imposition and requisition. In 1795 around one third of Belgium's food crops were seized to help feed the army, while paintings and other valuables were shipped back to Paris, often to adorn the newly-created national museum in the Louvre. French troops who may originally have been inspired by the patriotic call to save their Revolution from destruction soon came to savour the joys of victory and conquest. Paradoxically, the fact that the French courts demanded conclusive proof of guilt in cases of looting led to the abandonment of many prosecutions, against Belgians and Italians as well as Frenchmen, with their acts of plunder left unpunished.[16] Their generals in turn enjoyed the prestige and acclamation that went with victory. They also took advantage of the greater independence that was theirs as the armies marched farther away from French soil, farther from political surveillance and interference. In Italy, especially, Napoleon profited from his new authority, taking advantage of the Directory's unpopularity at home and its indecisiveness in policy matters, to drive home his victory over the Austrians and impose the Treaty of Campo Formio on them in October 1797 with only the minimum of political consultation. By February of the following year French troops were in Rome; in May Bonaparte left for Egypt, accompanied not just by his troops but by a scholarly army of naturalists, archaeologists and classicists eager to add to France's cultural imperium. The way was clear to advance his own political ambitions through the military putsch that was Brumaire.

By this time the whole French economy was geared to the pursuit of war, and domestic ambitions were largely predicated upon military

success. Napoleon's personal temperament was that of a military leader,
eager to push home his next victory, and incapable of envisaging that
there might be a case for compromise or concession. While this might
be invaluable on the battlefield, in the diplomatic arena it could stand
in the way of rational agreement. In particular, it goes far to explain
France's inability to draw maximum advantage from its very strong
diplomatic position in 1802 and the resultant resumption of hostilities
after a brief period of truce. For scarcely had peace been concluded at
Amiens than Napoleon was already dreaming of his next adventure,
convinced of the superiority of his armies and of his own invincibility,
and seeing in every peace settlement a source of future humiliation.[17]
So the peace lasted no more than fourteen months before France faced
new combinations of powers in still further coalitions. As for her
soldiers, they faced ever-broader horizons as they pounded their way
across the continent. By 1805 they had accompanied Napoleon to Milan
and Vienna, and by 1806 he was in Berlin. Those years saw French
victories over the Austrians at Ulm, over the Austrians and Russians at
Austerlitz, and over the Prussians at Jena and Auerstadt. In 1807 the
French defeated the Russians again at Friedland and signed the Franco-
Russian alliance at Tilsit. By that year French hegemony had spread
across much of continental Europe. France consisted of 130 departments
as against the original total of eighty-three, and many of her neighbours
had been forged into satellite kingdoms and principalities ruled over by
Napoleon's brothers and by others loyal to the French imperial throne.
French soldiers had been triumphant on land, sweeping all before them;
the supremacy of Napoleon's land forces was not in doubt. It was only
at sea that France remained vulnerable, leaving Britain unconquered
and the Royal Navy unchallenged after their routing of the French and
Spanish fleets in 1805 at Trafalgar. For the French navy this was a major
disaster. Of the thirty-three vessels with which Villeneuve had set sail,
only nine returned to port, while the Admiral himself, taken prisoner
and roundly abused by the Emperor, committed suicide on his return
to France.[18]

Bonaparte's *Grande Armée* had, it seemed, continental Europe at its
mercy, led by a commander of genius who understood the benefits of
speed and surprise, and who had a rare gift for motivating his troops.
His presence on the battlefield, Wellington once remarked, was worth

40,000 men. But gradually he became the victim of his own insatiable ambition, making the crucial mistake of opening two new fronts in Russia and the Peninsula even as his enemies were learning from their earlier defeats and were launching their own programmes of military reform. If in the years up until 1807 French soldiers had enjoyed the fruits of victory, thereafter the tide began to turn. The Continental System, introduced in the previous year, did not succeed in its avowed purpose of checking Britain's commercial ambitions or of destroying the country's appetite for war. And in Spain the stream of military successes began to dry up. Here French troops encountered not only fierce resistance from the enemy army but also, on a scale unparalleled elsewhere in Europe, popular resistance by villagers, peasants and entire communities. Spain was the land of *petite guerre* and guerrilla warfare, of ambushes and kidnaps, all conducted in a mountainous terrain which made it difficult for regular troops to counter-attack. War here was unlike any other, and many of the troops felt themselves abandoned to lawlessness, to a warfare that knew no rules in a country where anyone, man, woman or child, was a potential adversary. The French were slowly worn down by the deadly attacks of guerrilla fighters who then vanished into the local countryside, cutting off stragglers and undermining morale.[19] But it would be a mistake to ascribe French failure in the Peninsula to guerrilla tactics alone. Popular resistance continued as long and as effectively as it did because it was sustained by the campaigns of Wellington's army. The inability of the French generals to overcome their personal rivalries and win a decisive victory over the British was an essential precondition of Spanish resistance.[20]

In 1812 the Emperor made what proved to be his most costly blunder, when he sent an army of 600,000 against Russia, the famous *Grande Armée* that was destroyed both by the Russian winter and by a much smaller Russian army at Borodino and the Berezina.[21] Like the Spaniards, the Russians presented their campaign as a 'people's war', the resistance of ordinary Russians to an imperial invader from the west. What is clear is that Napoleon had miscalculated badly, and also that his own battle skills were failing him. As the remnants of his army straggled back to France, their morale in tatters, he knew he was on the defensive. He would try once more to rally his marshals, and drained France's man-power to do so. By August 1813 Napoleon could mobilise 700,000 men, the Allies 800,000. At Leipzig the opposing armies would be vast, with the battlefront extending for sixteen miles and the battle itself a huge bloodletting on all sides.[22] The armies regrouped to lick their wounds, but Leipzig was a strategic turning-point, a notable Allied victory which showed that the Emperor could be defeated on the battle-field. It suggested that the Napoleonic imperium was now nearing its end. Above all, he was seen to be fallible, capable of making tactical errors on the battlefield, of throwing away a winning position. The Allies pressed home their advantage at Waterloo, a battle where chance may have played its part – the bad weather, the late arrival of Grouchy for the French, the timely intervention of Blücher and the Prussians whom Grouchy had been instructed to neutralise, all of which Napoleon himself identified as critical – but it spelt defeat, surrender, and exile, bringing to an end a military and political adventure that had straddled the years of the Revolution and Empire and had brought France close to world dominance.[23]

The extent of Napoleon's military debt to the Revolution was, of course, considerable. It was the Revolution which had helped to change the popular image of the army and had abolished many of the ordin-ances and regulations which had tied the officer class so tightly to the landed aristocracy. It had opened careers to talent, providing rapid promotion to the able and the ambitious, a process further expedited by the death and emigration of serving officers during the Revolutionary Wars. Napoleon himself was, quite spectacularly, a beneficiary of this new world of opportunity. The revolutionary régime had abandoned the old provincial character of French regiments and, with the *amal-game* of Year II, had created a truly national army, capable of building on both the bravado of the new volunteer units and the experience of the men inherited from the American War. Regiments, indeed, were themselves cast aside as being too big and unwieldy, and were replaced by a new unit, the *demi-brigade*, which combined one battalion of regular troops with two of volunteers. Tactically it aimed to increase manoeuvrability in the field, adopting and complementing the ideas of eighteenth-century military reformers like Guibert in the sphere of infantry tactics and Gribeauval in the deployment of artillery. Overall, it renewed the officer ranks, rejuvenated the army and abandoned much suffocating protocol, providing a series of structural and organisational reforms which allowed the battalions to operate more efficiently. By the time of the Directory, the staff officer had emerged as a figure of real authority and competence in an army that was increasingly professional in its outlook. The troops were far more likely to think of themselves as soldiers, rather than as civilians who had been temporarily extracted from civil society, and their units had come to act as a focus for loyalty and even affection.

The result was an army of 196 *demi-brigades* of infantry, each with a company of artillery attached, plus units of light artillery, engineers and cavalry. The role of the infantry was crucial, deployed in lines and columns which could move speedily and take the enemy by surprise; it was the infantry which assumed the main burden of combat throughout the 1790s. And while the revolutionary cavalry was widely regarded as mostly mediocre, its artillery was not. The artillery had always been less feudal and more technocratic in character, even under the Bourbons; it was here that men of high ability and mathematical prowess – men like Lazare Carnot – had sought and had attained command, and the revolutionaries put greater trust in them.[24] During the 1790s the numbers of artillery more than doubled, while horse artillery were added for the first time; it was also the period when France first established separate sapper battalions. It is perhaps no accident that Napoleon himself made his name as a general of artillery, nor that he continued to place great trust in cannon as a weapon in war.

These were significant changes, but they did not constitute great technical innovations in the nature of warfare. Rather, as a mature Clausewitz reflected after 1815, they were the result of political determination and administrative flexibility, of the will to make the system work. It was, Clausewitz argued, those qualities which distinguished the French armies from those of their European opponents, and particularly from the Prussian army for which he spoke. He analysed the situation a decade after the defeat of Napoleon:

> The tremendous effects of the French Revolution abroad were caused not so much by new military methods and concepts as by radical changes in policies and administration, by the new character of government, altered conditions of the French people, and the like. That other governments did not understand these changes, that they wished to oppose new and over-whelming forces with customary means: all these were political errors ... In

short, we can say that twenty years of revolutionary triumph were mainly due to the mistaken policies of France's enemies.[25]

If Clausewitz is right, then it was this suppleness of approach, combined with a firm determination to push home reforms whatever the cost, which turned around the Revolutionary Wars and led to French domination of much of the European continent. It was this combination which Napoleon was uniquely able to build upon during the wars of the Consulate and Empire.

This book is not, however, about military tactics or Napoleonic generalship, far less about campaigns and diplomacy, though reference is necessarily made to them in the writings of the period. It is about the men who fought in the name of the Revolution and Empire, the officers and NCOs and simple soldiers who volunteered or who were conscripted, and who then fought and suffered in the cause of France. They came from almost every section of society, which is one of the reasons why their experience is so fascinating. They included some of the best-known figures of their generation, since Napoleon had every interest in promoting his most successful generals and in rewarding them with the great offices of state. Indeed, the high status which he reserved for the military is often seen as one of the essential underpinnings of the entire Bonapartist system. The figures speak for themselves. Of around 300 prefects appointed between 1800 and 1815, fifty-three came directly or indirectly from a military career, of whom twenty were generals and the other thirty-three high-ranking officers.[26] Of the men promoted to the Legion of Honour – some 32,000 by 1814 – only around 5 per cent were civilians.[27] And when Napoleon handed out titles – in all some 3600 were conferred by letters-patent between 1808 and 1814 – 59 per cent of them went to the military.[28] There was, in short, a decidedly military culture to the Napoleonic governing class.

Even more exclusive were the men at the pinnacle of the military hierarchy, the marshals of France, of whom there were never more than sixteen at any one time. The title was an honour with which Napoleon rewarded his generals for their brilliance, their loyalty, and their political commitment. Once again, origins and social background were unimportant compared to talent and service to the state, and if most marshals came from predictable bourgeois families, rooted in administration and the law, there were significant exceptions. A few were sons of Ancien Régime nobles, while several others came from genuinely popular roots and helped substantiate the myth that every soldier carried a marshal's baton in his knapsack. Thus Augereau was the son of a domestic servant, and the estimable Lannes the son of a peasant family from Lectoure in Gascony, who had been working as an apprentice dyer before enlisting in 1792, at the age of twenty-three, in the second volunteer regiment of the Gers. Lannes, indeed, can almost be taken as the paradigm of the revolutionary soldier, who on the very day of his enlistment had been elected to the rank of *sous-lieutenant* by his comrades.[29] Both ended their careers as marshals, ennobled by Napoleon as dukes of Castiglione and Montebello.[30] They were part of a very characteristic Napoleonic elite, faithful servants of the state who enjoyed the fruits of their eminence, being showered with honours, titles and lands and offered manifold opportunities for plunder and self-aggrandisement.

The marshals' lot must have seemed terribly remote to the infantry-men who made up the bulk of the soldiers in Napoleon's armies, the *grognards* who followed him from Ulm to Friedland, who suffered the indignities of ambush in the Vendée and in Spain, and who marched across an entire continent to Moscow in 1812. They, too, are the subject of this book, their ambitions, their sense of achievement, their fears and illusions. Their sheer numbers, their youth, indeed, their very ordinari-ness all serve to make them a difficult group to assess, and may help explain why the treatment that follows may often seem impressionistic, based on individual boasts and declarations, complaints and grievances, expressions of hope and despair. They came from all social groups and every area of France, peasants as well as artisans and shopkeepers, men of property alongside landless labourers. In that sense conscription did produce a nation in arms, even though, in these wars as in so many others, rural Frenchmen showed less interest in soldiering and peasants were more likely than townsmen to seek escape by buying a *remplaçant*. Similarly, not all regions of the country were equally represented. Some had no tradition of fighting and proved difficult recruiting grounds. Others had too many men who were short and rather stunted, or who failed to qualify on medical grounds because of a particularly high incidence of fever or pulmonary disease. In 1808 Hargenvilliers estimated that the average level of recruitment for France as a whole was one conscript for every 138 inhabitants. But that figure concealed wide divergences, from the heavily urbanised Seine and Rhône, departments dominated by the urban centres of Paris and Lyon (at one in 209 and 212 respectively), to the deeply recalcitrant departments of the Centre and the Massif Central, most dramatically the Yonne (at only one for every ninety-seven). It also concealed wide discrepancies between years, as the needs of the armies were wildly different across time. All things considered, it would be difficult to claim that the geographical representation was in any sense an equitable one, or that, for the young, conscription was ever other than a harsh and cynical lottery.[31]

Moreover, if the soldiers who defended the Revolution in 1792 and 1793 could with some justice claim to represent the people they were defending – the claim that they were 'the people in arms' – foreign troops continued to play a significant part in the country's defence. The Constituent Assembly continued to honour the special status of foreign regiments in the French army, while, if the various legions were disbanded under the Republic, even the Jacobins were pragmatic about foreigners and distributed any remaining soldiers amongst the regular army units.[32] There was little desire to deprive France of the manpower which mercenaries represented, especially in time of war. By the time of the Consulate and Empire a large proportion of the men fighting for France were not French by birth but the product of conquest across a continent. For just as the French demanded booty and food from the territories they occupied, so they increasingly demanded soldiers to help fight their European war of conquest. The result was a highly professional and polyglot army whose loyalty was less to France than to the person of Napoleon. The most extreme example of the internationalisation of the military is the *Grande Armée* which the Emperor mustered for his assault on Russia in 1812, a huge force numbering some 611,000 men. Scarcely a third of them can be classed as French, if by that is meant men emanating from lands that had been French before 1789. Around 300,000, it is true, came from what was now France – 200,000 from the national territory proper, and a further 100,000 from the annexed departments – men who were by birth Belgian, Dutch, Swiss, German or Italian. The others included 130,000 Germans from the Confederation of the Rhine, 90,000 Poles and Lithuanians, 27,000 Italians, and some 9000 Swiss, to say nothing of around 50,000 troops provided by France's involuntary allies, Austria and Prussia.[33] The Imperial Guard, of course, had always been highly international in its composition. Under Bonaparte, the nation-in-arms of the French Revolution was rapidly extended into a whole continent-in-arms, a continent whose soldiers formed part of the tribute due to the military prowess of the Emperor. They fought out of duty, and they were rewarded for their dedication and military prowess and their professionalism in battle. The ideological commitment so much vaunted by the revolutionaries was already a distant memory, a full generation in the past.

The dramatic increase in the size of the French armies was, of course, quickly matched by France's enemies, forced by Napoleonic victories to adopt new tactics and to reform their own military establishments. As a result, battles became mass engagements in which armies suffered unprecedentedly heavy casualties. Figures remain confusingly imprecise as men lay unaccounted for on the battlefield, but the lists we have are tragically suggestive. At Eylau, for instance, France lost around 15,000 dead with a further 20,000 wounded; at Wagram 17,000 dead and 50,000 wounded; at Leipzig over 20,000 dead and a further 55,000 wounded or unaccounted for. In 1815 in the combined battles of Ligny and Waterloo between 30,000 and 45,000 were killed or wounded.[34] Still more tragic were the casualty figures from Napoleon's ill-fated attack on Russia in 1812. Here the odds against survival were overwhelming: of the 140,000 soldiers who set out back from Moscow, 120,000 died before they reached the frontier, while the entire Russian campaign cost the French armies some half a million men.[35] In all, it has been estimated that France probably lost some 1,400,000 soldiers during the whole period of the Revolutionary and Napoleonic Wars, the majority of them, it is true, dying not on the battlefield or as a result of enemy action but less heroically, of fevers and diseases, pneumonia and gangrene, in their camps and billets, or in the beds of French military hospitals. Others again passed their final months in enforced exile, in the degrading surroundings of a prison or prisoner-of-war camp. With the passage of time, the scale of these losses became increasingly clear to the troops themselves, who increasingly expressed their despair in the face of endless marches and fatigues, and their pessimism about ever getting out of the army or returning to their villages and families. Their despair was generally stoical and seldom gave way to anger directed against either their generals or the Emperor. Indeed, their loyalty to the Revolution and especially to Napoleon is both striking and impressive in the face of such dreadful adversity. For the degree of their suffering cannot be overestimated, however much it may have been assuaged by the grant of civil rights during the 1790s or by the honours lavished on them by their Emperor ten years later. Their generation had had a terrible burden to bear. For the young men of Revolutionary and Napoleonic France, indeed, these twenty years of conflict were a demographic catastrophe without precedent in modern European history, one that is comparable only to the First World War itself.

2

The Soldiers and their Writings

The Revolutionary and Napoleonic Wars may form the backcloth to the present study, but neither they nor – except indirectly – the soldiers who fought in them are its real subject matter. For this is a book less about men than about the writings they left behind during their long years of service, those narratives of army life which have survived for posterity. They are necessarily a rather random sample of the mass of letters, memoirs, diaries and reminiscences which were produced during these years, whether by officers confidently discussing their new careers or by conscripts writing home to inform their families of their lot. They vary enormously in style and literary value, in forcefulness and confidence of expression. Some are works of literary precision discussing in great detail the passion and anguish of military life, others little more than form letters through which callow eighteen-year-old soldiers told their equally anxious relatives a little of what was happening, quite bewilderingly, around them. In style and content they reflect a wide gamut of experience, reflecting military rank and social class, attitudes and levels of literacy. Yet they all have a value for historians trying to assess the morale and motivation of the young men caught up in European war. Indeed, they constitute the most immediate conduit we have to the thinking and mentality of those involved, and the most personal, in that they reflect the experience of individuals rather than the goals of army administrators or the public self-image of political leaders.

For that reason they are often refreshingly non-judgemental, stubbornly reluctant to distribute praise or blame. Almost invariably, indeed, personal narratives are just that: they tell a story, the story of an individual's experience or his later memory of it, along with occasional reflections on that experience, either at the time or in succeeding years. Recently the American historian Samuel Hynes has asked just how much

we can hope to learn from narratives of this kind. Are they to be taken
as anything more than the accounts of individuals, as acts of personal
commemoration, the commemoration of army life with all its fears and
dangers, its loyalties and heightened consciousness? Can we, indeed,
generalise from them in any way that might help recreate a national
memory of war? Hynes, it should be emphasised, is talking about the
twentieth century and largely about the Anglo-Saxon world – the wars
of 1914 and 1939, those of Spain and Korea and Vietnam as they affected
the British and American troops who fought in them. He is discussing
a time and a culture which have experienced a particular need for the
national commemoration of war and its sacrifices without precedent in
previous generations, a desire to mourn and express the grief of communities as well as of individuals, an urge to create and nurture collective
memory through museums and film archives, war memorials and acts
of public remembrance. These all form part of our shared heritage, part
of a much broader, European collective memory, a collective grief and
act of mourning, 'sites of memory' which faced the past rather than the
future.[1]

There are no such memorials to the soldiers of the French revolutionary and imperial campaigns. Yet their memoirs and diaries, their letters
and *carnets de route*, are also a contribution to a wider commemoration
of war, albeit on a personal, individual scale. For they are more than
just the stories of individuals, random and disparate. They have a
more general value, too. Hynes, talking of the vast array of personal
memoirs and correspondence penned by soldiers in the First World
War, describes their value in these terms:

> We can say that each example tells the story of one man in actions involving
> many, and that each speaks in its own individual voice, which is not the
> voice of history, nor of collective memory. We might add that the span of
> time in a narrative is not historical either, but personal, that few personal
> narratives begin when a war begins and end when it ends, but tell only that
> part of the whole story that is a man's personal war, and show no interest
> in the military idea of closure in victory or defeat. Indeed, in personal
> narrative the War, as a global historical reality, scarcely exists, only men
> exist, and act, and sometimes die, and when they do, they do so *personally*.[2]

Thus their narratives, however simplistic and incomplete they may be,
however partisan and unrepresentative, form a useful complement to

official histories in that they allow us to distance ourselves from the concerns of policy-makers and to understand something of the priorities and mentalities of those who spent the best years of their lives in the service of the Revolution and Napoleon.

Not all narratives, of course, are written with a common purpose. In particular, the evidence of memoirs and reflections published after the event may be very different from that of personal letters, hastily composed and despatched in time to catch the next post. Memoirs allow for so much more conceit and literary flourish; they may be seen as a man's own memorial to the years he had spent in the army, and that memorial is often carefully scripted. The message conveyed may be that which he believes in retrospect, once the heat of battle is past and often after several decades of civilian experience have intervened. And the passage of time in the quickly shifting political landscape of the early nineteenth century – from Consulate to Empire, Hundred Days to Restoration, years charged with the new power of the printed word so encouraging to state propaganda – meant that received wisdom on the Revolutionary and Napoleonic Wars changed apace. Unlike the more ephemeral day to day correspondence of the troops, memoirs were usually written to be historical documents, to be read and digested by future generations, perhaps even by future generations of historians. Those of generals and senior officers – and there are relatively very few memoirs written by ordinary infantrymen, though the few that do exist have gained widespread notoriety – were almost always written with clear intent, to try to ensure that the writer would enjoy a respected place in history. Facts are carefully sifted, judgements offered with the benefit of hindsight, analysis effected with just a hint of conscious self-justification. Only too often soldiers' memoirs – like those, so much more blatant, of political leaders – were created precisely because the individual worried about his place in the national memory and sought to put the record straight before he died. Some did so discreetly, pointing up their own contribution to winning a battle or devising a strategy. Others were openly boastful, rewriting the history of their times as they would like them to have been. Of these none took greater liberty with the truth than Napoleon himself, who whiled away the long days of his exile on Saint Helena pouring out to Las Cases his insights into and confidences about the years he had lived through and describing the prescience he had shown in the face of so many threats and dangers. The resulting *Mémorial*, first published in 1823, provides both a colourful account of the Emperor's last frustrating years in captivity and a text-book case of rewriting history in order to justify oneself to succeeding generations.[3]

Memoirs, in other words, necessarily lack spontaneity. They are the product of mature reflection, with all the advantages and shortcomings which reflection implies. Some were written in exile, from London or Brussels or Liège, by men who had suffered for their republican faith and who had an axe to grind with the Bourbon authorities after 1815.[4] Many are infused with a sense of wonder and nostalgia at the awe-some world with which the writer had been thrown into contact. They describe what were for many of those concerned the most exciting and exotic moments of their lives, times which had allowed them to escape from the mundane demands of village life and to explore foreign cities, encounter exotic cultures, hear the contrasting cadences of unknown languages, and dream of conquering a continent. Such experiences almost demanded the use of colourful idioms, the resort to superlatives. Others were written so long after the events they describe that memory could only be a distorting mirror, the product of leisure, of retirement, and of fifty or sixty years of political conflict which helped etch and nuance any lingering impressions they might have of the Revolution and Empire. From the 1820s on, popular memory of the revolutionary years had been reshaped by the publication of volume after volume of Girondin memoirs, through which an idea was peddled of what was good and bad about the 1790s, of where just distinctions could be drawn between liberty and terror. The imperial years, too, became rapidly en-shrouded in nostalgia, with a rich effusion of tracts, etchings and popular prints recalling the glorious exploits of the Emperor and bringing a heroic image of the Napoleonic legions into the humblest peasant cottage. With the best of intentions, it was difficult for those looking back to ignore the images they saw all around them, to avoid looking back at the war years through the prism of complex layers of memory.[5]

There is no reason to suppose that military memoirs would be any different. With the vogue for publishing memoirs from the Napoleonic campaigns, in particular, which swept France during the Second Empire, it was perhaps unavoidable that the story they presented should have incorporated current myths and reflected the memories of old men looking back on the events and achievements of their youth. One of these, Jean Marnier, who was over eighty when his *Souvenirs de guerre en temps de paix* were published in 1867, was honest enough to admit in his preface that such a work could never aspire to be definitive, and that he had been driven to record his own impressions by reading the memoirs of others. He had enjoyed a long career, and parts of it were beginning to grow dim as his memory of events started to fade; indeed, there can be no doubt that the tone of his writing is not untouched by nineteenth-century romanticism. He had been a pupil at the Ecole Spéciale Militaire at Fontainebleau in 1803, before joining the army proper the following year and setting out on his Europe-wide adventure, and he acknowledged that in these circumstances all he could really hope to do was to look back into remnants of his past and record his memories. As he very modestly phrases it, 'I can do no more than draw upon some of the jottings I made at the time'.[6] He would, in other words, tell the story as he recalled it, without any attempt at analysis or theorisation, his version of events as they appeared through the filter of half a century of existence, half a century of politics, two revolutions and two contrasting restorations. The writing of memoirs after the passage of such a long period of time and in the wake of such conflicting onslaughts of political propaganda – Legitimist and Orleanist, Republican and Bonapartist – can only be seen as an exercise in reconstituting one man's memory of the past.

If Marnier is touchingly modest in the claims he makes, war memoirs as a genre are not well suited to such modesty. Looking back, the soldier or army officer often found it hard not to be dazzled by the exciting times he had lived through, and by the sheer glory of the events he had witnessed. This was not merely the natural temptation to boast and exaggerate one's personal contribution, or to set the record straight for posterity. It was a product of the context of war, of a war which had thrown ordinary men into direct contact with great events for the first and only time in their lives. The army, after all, had torn them from the farms and villages where otherwise they might well have passed their entire existence, to take them across provinces and whole countries of which they had known nothing. It had associated them with national events and politics, with the *Grande Nation* and a Napoleonic empire which at one time had threatened to stretch from the Urals to the Iberian Peninsula. At times, of course, that experience was fraught with discomfort and danger, and many of the soldiers who bivouacked in the Alps or on the plains of central Spain dreamt of little beyond the distant prospect of returning to their homes. The reality of soldiering could be painful, their day to day existence marked by hunger, boredom and despair. But with time that perspective changed, so that by the 1820s or 1830s their years in the army had often been transformed into the most interesting and formative of their lives. It was not, it should be stressed, that their personal contribution had been so very crucial, that they had made great decisions or personally affected the outcome of the conflict. It was rather the simple fact of having been there, of having been part of a great event or associated with a great victory, of having experienced war and the things which war had done to them and their fellows. Again it is pertinent to consider Samuel Hynes's verdict on the memoirs produced during the First World War and on the burning desire of so many soldiers, once they were safely back in civilian life, to record their memories and to consign their experiences to writing:

> It's easy to see why men remember their wars. For most men who fight, war is their one contact with the world of great doings. Other men govern, sign treaties, invent machines, cure diseases, alter lives. But for ordinary men – the men who fight our wars – there will probably be only that time when their lives intersect with history, one opportunity too act in great events. Not to alter these events – no single soldier affects a war, or even a battle – but simply to be there, *in* history.[7]

It is equally easy to see why men felt the urge to write about their wars at the time, why they were struck by the need to communicate with others, why, even in a society that had limited access to literacy, they felt drawn to put pen to paper. They did so not just because they felt they had something to say, some experience that might be of interest to others. They were also filled with a pressing desire for news of the outside world, a desire that was only increased by the state of semi-permanent ignorance in which they lived. In the Revolutionary Wars as in others in the twentieth century, soldiers were consistently and quite deliberately kept in the dark about what was happening around them – the progress of battles, the extent of casualties, the news from other fronts. News was carefully rationed and bad news censored in the belief that this was the most effective way of preventing demoralisation. At the most banal level this lack of information implied nothing very sinister: it stemmed from the imperfect knowledge that even military commanders could assemble about progress on the battlefield: there were inevitable delays before the extent of gains and losses could be assessed, and rumours spread like wildfire among the troops. But soldiers also felt excluded from news, deliberately deprived of information, both information about the progress of the war and news of political developments back in France. The strategy of concealing disasters and minimising reverses may, ironically, have had the opposite result from that which was intended. Uncertainty and non-communication sapped the morale of the troops – troops who had recently been told that they enjoyed all the rights of citizens in the French *cité* – and this often widened the gulf which existed within the army between officers and men. This did not, it is true, occur on the scale of the First World War, when the sense that news was being deliberately withheld sapped army morale and undermined confidence in the commanders.[8] But the desire to write was sufficiently obvious to suggest a sense of regret and deprivation among the soldiery.

Memoirs are relatively rare among military writings and they do little to record immediate responses to events. They were penned with deliberation and sometimes with considerable literary artifice with the express purpose of being read by others, by people of whom the writer knew little, who might not even have been born at the time of the events he described. In this respect they are quite unlike the vast numbers of letters that were written by soldiers during these years of war, spontaneous outpourings scribbled on the spur of the moment in those brief periods of leisure that could be snatched by the campfire or in the bivouac. These were essentially private documents which had no place in the public domain. A few, it is true, were more official in character – letters written during the Revolution by avid republicans to their clubs and popular societies, mayors and sections, written, in other words, to make a point about their patriotism or about the conduct of their officers, a point that was intended to be read by those in public life. But these must be seen as exceptions. The vast majority of soldiers' letters were highly personal documents, sharing their experiences and confidences with mothers and fathers, brothers and friends. They were

not intent on voicing an opinion on the political events of the day or
on adopting a public posture. That they have survived at all is largely
a matter of chance, piles of letters lovingly preserved as a last memory
of a son or husband who would never return, abandoned in nineteenth-
century village attics to be rediscovered by later generations, often when
they, too, were faced with military call-up on the eve of 1914. It was
then, in the upsurge of patriotism that characterised the pre-war world,
that families sought to incorporate them in the public record, either by
publishing the texts in a local historical journal or by depositing them
in their town library or the local archive.

Some private letters, it is true, entered the public domain much earlier,
when they were produced as evidence before revolutionary or Napoleonic authorities. Under the Jacobin Republic, for instance, letters from
men at the front were submitted to the town hall as soldiers sought to
benefit from the sales of national lands; they claimed their share of land
in the village, as the law entitled them to do, naming someone else – a
relative, or a lawyer, or someone more literate than themselves – to act
on their behalf.[9] Others were produced by men's relatives during the
Empire as evidence that a son or brother was indeed still with his unit
and had not – as was rumoured – deserted his regiment or returned
secretly to live in clandestinity in his native village. By the early years
of the nineteenth century such evidence had become necessary if parents
were to avoid the unwelcome attentions of the gendarmerie and were
to escape heavy fines or the threat of having troops billeted on their
cottage or farmstead.[10] From our standpoint, of course, the crucial thing
is that in these ways private letters fell into the hands of the authorities.
Once a letter was in the public domain, it might be kept as evidence,
be attached to notarial documentation or thrown into a police file.[11]
And conscientious archivists up and down France did what archivists
are trained to do, filing and cataloguing them for posterity, thus ensuring
that personal correspondence which would normally have little place
in the public sphere is now to be found among the administrative and
judicial papers of the departmental and municipal archives. In some
departments, indeed, including a number where the administrative
record has suffered from fire or war damage over the years, archivists
have made a point of collecting as much personal material as possible
from local families in a bid to compensate for the losses they had

sustained, with the consequence that in departments like the Oise and the Pyrénées-Atlantiques there are now substantial bundles of soldiers' correspondence – numbering several hundred letters in each case – from the period of the Revolutionary and Napoleonic Wars.[12]

Although of the letters that survive a higher proportion were written by officers than by ordinary conscripts, writing was by no means the monopoly of the officer class. Many of the letters were written by simple artisans and peasant boys who had drawn a low number in the ballot or who had been passed as fit for conscription. Indeed, it is the very ubiquitousness of personal correspondence across these long years of war (complementing the evidence of occasional journals and *carnets de route*, like those of the *canonnier* Bricard [13] or the *dragon* Marquant), [14] which makes letters so valuable to anyone seeking to know more about the attitudes of ordinary soldiers, their grievances and pressing concerns, as well as those surges of enthusiasm on which so much of military morale came to depend. For, unlike many of the memoirs produced during and after the wars, they cannot be dismissed as the work of a military elite, of men more motivated than their fellows by patriotism or the prospect of promotion, or of an officer class holding privileged information denied to the mass of the troops. They reflected the views of the most reluctant conscripts as well as career officers, who were as different in 1800 as they would be in 1917, when a rather clearer distinction would be drawn between 'comrades' and 'chiefs'. Comrades were those – and it mattered little whether they were junior officers, NCOs or ordinary soldiers – with whom the war was lived in all its messy deprivation, those who shared the same experiences of battle and the same sufferings during forced marches and long months of inactivity. Almost by definition, they excluded the high command, the senior officers who established strategy and barked their orders from a distance. In the mind of Captain Rimbault, himself a serving officer in the Great War, this was a distinction that was understood by all who fought in the army, reflecting their day to day experience and social acquaintance. It was also a very precise distinction. 'To have a knowledge of the war', he wrote, 'you must have lived through it at a rank not above company commander. Only a man who has lived night and day in the trenches understands modern warfare. Comrades include everyone from the company commander to the simple *poilu*. The rest are *chefs*.'[15]

These letters allow us to explore the fundamental psychology of the 'citizen-soldier' so lauded in the official despatches for his qualities of patriotism and civic virtue. This official discourse is hard to sublimate when we are considering the mentality of the troops themselves. The soldier, in Robespierre's idealised vision, was of the people from whose ranks he had emerged, and it followed that he was therefore good and virtuous, the representative and standard-bearer of the *peuple souverain*. He was a citizen first and his citizenship, it was implied, informed everything he did, including his motivation as a soldier. This made him very different from the troops of traditional European armies, the hirelings of kings and emperors. In the words of the *Feuille Villageoise* on the eve of the outbreak of war, the French soldier defined himself by his citizenship and his membership of the nation, and the respect which he enjoyed reflected that honourable standing. 'He is a citizen, treated and respected as such, at all times, in all places, and by all. The military laws which govern him are, just like the civil laws, rooted in the Rights of Man.' [16]

But did the fact of being a citizen change the way an individual fought, or, more fundamentally, the way he thought? It has long been assumed that it did, and that the revolutionary *demi-brigades* fought with an enthusiasm and a devotion that belied their lack of experience and skill, and enabled the armies of the Republic to triumph. Indeed, the root-and-branch military reforms undertaken by the revolutionaries were justified by the notion that only an army that was fully committed to the ideals of the Revolution could be expected to fight in its name. What they inherited was not only impossible to justify politically; it was, in the eyes of a Robespierre or a Dubois-Crancé, incompatible with good discipline and effective soldiering. The troops, they argued, were forced to watch the principles to which they were committed desecrated before their eyes. 'It is calmly accepted that the officers should rape and plunder and publicly flout the laws of the Convention, while the men in the ranks must show them the most unwavering respect, the most blind and unquestioning submission.' [17] The safety of France and of the Revolution demanded, they insisted, that such behaviour should cease, and that discipline should be a matter of acceptance and consent rather than of imposition. But should the role of ideology be taken for granted – as it has overwhelmingly been in French republican historiography – just because it was central to the political discourse of the revolutionary years? Or should we question its value to troop motivation, even dismissing it as empty and largely irrelevant, as several historians have recently done? After all, there were striking continuities between the last years of the Ancien Régime and those of the early Revolution. Both the technology and the strategic ideas used during the 1790s had been evolved under the Bourbon monarchy by men like Servan and Gribeauval, army officers who were among the greatest military reformers of their day. Indeed, it would have been rash and highly irresponsible to do otherwise, since there was a science to strategy and the application of technology, and revolutionary generals knew that they would be lost unless they adhered to the tactical advice conserved in the rule books of the Ancien Régime.' [18] Once more we are presented with the challenge of trying to understand the mind-set of the French soldier at war.

Without the personal correspondence of the soldiers we have surprisingly little evidence against which to assess the official discourse, and much of what we do have is itself part of that discourse – reports on *esprit public* by the generals and by deputies sent on mission to the armies; declarations issued in the military press; and occasional petitions to popular societies or letters to revolutionary sections in their home towns – all opinions which were intended for public consumption and which their authors knew would be submitted to the eyes of officialdom, all documents which should therefore be seen as belonging in the public sphere. Private letters sent to parents and loved ones are of a very different order, especially since the censorship of letters sent back to France from the armies was still fairly light, and certainly in no way comparable to the far more intrusive controls set up by the military postal service, the *Contrôle Postal*, during the First World War, which both limited the range of expressed opinions and created heightened fear and mistrust among the troops. In the Revolutionary and Napoleonic Wars, by way of contrast, little in the texts suggests that the men were made constantly aware of the attentions of the censor, far less that their criticisms of those in authority were artificially muted.

That is not to say, of course, that the words they wrote should be taken at face value. There are, in these campaigns as in any other, things that such letters do not and cannot do, and these limitations must be candidly recognised at the outset. Some of the omissions were

doubtless voluntary. Soldiers seldom express the depth of their feelings
or emotions, or the full measure of disgust, revulsion and horror which
characterise active service but which are virtually impossible to communicate to those who have not shared in it, the gut fears and terrors
which had to be reserved for one's comrades, for those who had been
there too. These feelings remained largely unspoken: they must be seen
as among the pregnant silences of letter-writing, the questions that are
generally passed over without comment and certainly without graphic
description. In part this may be explained by the lack of fluency of many
of these young men when they had to express themselves on paper, for
this was an army which still lacked much of the ease of expression that
came with more general education, the ready flourish that would be
found in the Great War or in the American Civil War. But more crucially
these omissions occurred, as they occur in any army, because soldiers
could not find the words to express what they have lived through, not
through any lack of vocabulary or facility of language, but because they,
too, were repelled by the horror of it all: the terrified neighing of
wounded horses, the smell of burned flesh and excrement, the groans
of the dying, aspects of the battlefield which they, like the Civil War
soldiers who followed them, could not bring themselves to linger over.[19]
These were the stuff of nightmares and flashbacks, pictures that drove
men over the abyss, images which they would take with them to the
grave. They were far too terrible to discuss in the cosy context of a
family letter.

Other omissions are better seen as involuntary. Soldiers could not
pretend to any overview of military operations, any comprehension of
the broader picture. A soldier can write with authority of his own
experience in one corner of a campaign, whether it be the barracks or
the battlefield; he can write of his own ambitions, his own feelings and
reactions to what he sees around him; he can talk of his comrades, his
fears and his losses; and he can relate his experiences to his family, to
his village, to the life he knew and had left behind. But he can say little
that is useful or authoritative about the army as a whole, little about
strategy, little of the advantages gained or conceded. These are matters
which only the commanders, whose business it is to inform themselves
of the general picture and to take account of the numbers dead and
missing in each encounter, can assess with accuracy. The soldier, indeed,

can only learn of these things from others: he has no access to reliable statistics of his own. Hence the figures which he so often cites, whether in letters, in diaries or in memoirs of the individual campaigns, necessarily reflect the information he has been given by his superiors or by the political leadership through the medium of the military press.

In such figures there was always a strong element of propaganda, deemed necessary for the maintenance of morale among the troops as well as in the civilian population. Strikingly, there were few official admissions of failure during the 1790s, few moments when the French *état-major* would publicly acknowledge that battles had been lost, that ground had been ceded to the enemy, or that it was the French who had suffered the greater loss of life. The soldiers themselves were encouraged to read in the emerging military press – often in papers specific to individual armies, like those of the Pyrenées-Orientales or the Côtes de Brest – highly coloured reports of glorious victories chalked up on other fronts and of the frightful casualties suffered by France's enemies, all of which were supposed to persuade them that with a little more effort the war would be over, and that only by imposing their victory could there be any promise of peace. Under the Directory, with the armies absent from France for lengthy periods, the role of the military papers became even greater. If their ideological message was blunted, the official optimism about casualties and the outcome of battles remained unashamedly undimmed. With Napoleon, indeed, the habit of routinely issuing implausibly rosy casualty figures became ever more firmly institutionalised, both in the general press in Paris and through the publication of a series of highly propagandist newspapers for both a civilian and a military audience.

This flow of newsprint began in 1796 when Bonaparte was a young general with the Army of Italy, and it continued through the Egyptian campaign and in the months up to Brumaire. All his titles were written by professional editors, men who were well disposed to Bonaparte, of course, but who maintained sufficient independence to avoid accusations of simple propaganda at a time when he was making increasingly caustic comments on the Directory. The papers had the dual purpose of reassuring the troops while building up Bonaparte's reputation as a hero, a patriot, and a leader of genius who understood his men and was trusted by them. From Italy he produced the *Courrier de l'Armée*

d'Italie and its sister-paper, *La France vue de l'Armée d'Italie*, as well as
the tellingly named *Journal de Bonaparte et des Hommes Vertueux*; while
from Egypt came the *Courrier d'Egypte* as well as more specialist papers
aimed at the scientific community.[20] Nor did the practice cease once he
became Emperor. The *Bulletin de la Grande Armée* – known more
familiarly and less respectfully as the *Menteur* – was reprinted in the
official press and issued in simplified illustrated versions throughout
provincial France, usually in the form of wall posters and hand bills.
The *Bulletin* deliberately set out to deceive. If we take the notorious case
of the battle of Eylau – the subject of the fifty-eighth *Bulletin* – the
extent of the deception becomes clear. The battle could hardly be termed
a victory for the French, at least not in any material sense. Their armies
lost close on 30,000 men to the enemy's 25,000. But it was imperative
that it be presented as a victory, partly in order to sustain army morale,
but partly also to maintain the supposed 'contract' on which Napoleonic
rule was founded. Hence the deeply misleading figures that were circulated about the battle: according to the *Bulletin*, France lost no more
than 1900 men killed and 5700 wounded, the official figures released to
the army itself.[21] To the extent that they took them literally and quoted
them in their letters home, the troops can be seen to have played their
part in spreading the good news which the government sought every
opportunity to impart into the community.

It is true that only a small proportion of these letters have survived
– some tens of thousands, perhaps, out of the millions that were handled
by the military post during the Revolution and Empire. But that does
not necessarily reduce their value, at least for the social and cultural
history of the French armies. There is, as we have seen, something very
random and reassuringly unpremeditated about the ways in which they
survived which allows us to view them as a fairly representative sample.
As a result we have at our disposal thousands of letters which were
written by young men caught in one of the rare moments of their lives
when they felt the burning need to commit their thoughts to paper.
This is no mean source for the end of the eighteenth century, at a time
when such riches are rare, and when it is difficult to gauge the first-hand
responses of people from artisanal or peasant backgrounds. After all,
we are not talking here of a hugely literate society, certainly not if we
compare France to some of the Protestant states of northern Europe:

Décadi 10 Ventose ; an V. (N° 9.) Mardi 28 Février 1797.

JOURNAL
DE BONAPARTE ET DES HOMMES VERTUEUX.

Annibal dormit à Capoue :
Mais Bonaparte actif ne dort pas dans Mantoue.

Nouvelles d'Italie. — Conquête de la Marche d'Ancône, de l'Umbrie, du pays de Pérugia et de la province de Canorino. — Arrivée à Paris du général Augereau, avec soixante drapeaux. — Prise de Rome. — Proclamation du général Bonaparte, concernant les prêtres réfractaires. — Cinq cents bouches à feu, 43 pièces de campagne, quantité d'obusiers, et plus de 17 mille fusils pris à Mantoue. — Quatre-vingt-dix-neuf bouches à feu et plus de 23 mille bombes, grenades, etc., pris à Ancône. — Inquiétude de la cour de Vienne, sur les mouvemens des troupes de la Porte ottomane. — Détermination de l'empereur de Russie. — Résolution qui annulle les élections de Saint-Domingue. — Arrêté qu'il sera présenté un travail sur le sort des enfans nés hors le mariage, l'adoption, le divorce, etc. — Rapport et projet de décret sur les douanes.

Le Prix de l'abonnement est de 9 livres pour trois mois : 18 liv. pour six mois, et 36 liv. pour l'année.
On s'abonne à Paris, chez DEBAUDRE, Directeur du Journal, Montagne Geneviève, ci-dev. collège Navarre.
AUBRY, Libraire & Directeur du Cabinet Bibliographique, rue Baillet, N° 3.
DENTU, Libraire, Palais-Egalité, Galerie de bois, N° 240.
Et au Bureau, chez HUGELET & LEFEVRE, Imprimeurs, rue des Fossés-Jacques, N° 4, au 3°.
Les Lettres et l'Argent doivent être AFFRANCHIS.

NOUVELLES ÉTRANGERES.
ARMÉE D'ITALIE.
ARTICLES OFFICIELS.

Bonaparte, général en chef de l'armée d'Italie, au Directoire exécutif.

Au quartier-général de Macérata,
le 27 pluviose, au 5.

Citoyens Directeurs,

Nos troupes seront, j'espère, ce soir, à Foligno, et passeront la journée de demain à se réunir à celles que j'ai fait marcher par Sienne et Cortone.
Loretto contenoit un trésor d'environ trois millions de livres tournois : on nous y a laissé à peu près la valeur d'un million. Je vous envoie la Madona avec toutes les reliques ; cette caisse vous a été directement adressée, et vous en ferez l'usage que vous croirez convenable : cette Madona est de bois. .
La province de Macérata, connue plus communément sous le nom de Marche d'Ancône, est une des plus belles et, sans contredit, une des plus riches des états du pape.

Il n'y a rien de nouveau dans le Tyrol, ni sur la Piave.
Vous trouverez ci-joint l'inventaire de l'artillerie trouvée à Mantoue et à Ancône.
Ci-joint copie d'une de mes lettres au cardinal Mattey.

Du 30 pluviose, au quartier-général de Tolentino.

Nos troupes se sont emparé de l'Umbrie et du pays de Pérugia ; nous sommes maîtres aussi de la petite province de Canorino.
. Signé BONAPARTE.

PLACE DE MANTOUE.

État des principaux effets d'artillerie existans dans la place et dans la citadelle de Mantoue, à l'époque du 17 pluviose, an 5.

Pièces en bronze.

Pièces autrichiennes depuis le calibre de 36 jusques et y compris celui de 16, 126. Pièces depuis le calibre de 15 et au-dessous, 175, Mortiers en bronze, 56. Pierriers, idem, 2. Petits mortiers à grenades, 40. Boites et passerons pour barques du luc ; 7. Pieces en fer du calibre de 12 et 6, 81.
Pierriers en fer. 4.
En tout 500 bouches à feu.
Pièces de campagne pour la défense de la place et des ouvrages avancés, 43. Obusiers de campagne, id. 16. Fusils pour infanterie, artillerie, pionniers et cavalerie, dont 5,000 environ en état. 17.115.
Une quantité considérable de pieces de rechange ; bois et autres objets pour la réparation des armes.
Pistolets, dont 1000 en état, 4484.
Une grande quantité de bois, etc. pour idem.

The *Journal de Bonaparte et des Hommes Vertueux*, 28 February 1797. The journal was one of several newspapers which General Bonaparte published in Italy and in Egypt to keep French opinion informed of his triumphs.

in Sweden and much of Scandinavia governments had pursued veritable
literacy crusades, with the consequence that by 1800 virtually the entire
population was able to read.[22] In France the growth in literacy across
the eighteenth century had been at best erratic, varying widely from
region to region. The most rapid development had taken place in the
north and east, while large parts of the Massif Central and the rural
south west remained relatively unaffected by the spread of print culture.
In Provence, too, the period was one of 'cultural stagnation', with the
graph of literacy remaining largely static and the printed word making
only a limited impact in country areas.[23] As yet access to education is
not something that could be taken for granted, at least beyond the larger
towns and cities.

    That is not to say, of course, that literacy was wholly restricted to
the towns, or that conscripts from rural backgrounds were necessarily
underprivileged and unlettered. The growing success of popular
tracts and wood prints, and especially of the low-cost pamphlets of the
Bibliothèque bleue which were increasingly distributed by pedlars on
their tours of fairs in rural areas, suggests that in the course of the
eighteenth century a new rural clientele for popular tales and simple
works of piety was developing in many areas of the country. For if
Troyes was still the leading centre of production for these works, it
did not enjoy a monopoly. The distribution of popular literature was
becoming increasingly regionalised, and important print shops had been
established in Avignon, Besançon, Caen, Limoges and Rouen.[24] An
appetite for fiction, in particular, was being created in country districts
previously starved of stimulation, and from the often contemptuous
reports provided by the Abbé Grégoire's regional correspondents during
the Revolution we know that popular works – often fairy-tales or works
of sorcery, but extending to simple works of religion, novels and popular
histories – were circulating widely in country areas. In the opinion of
more sophisticated townsmen, they were corrupting and infantilising
peasant taste. This does not mean that the average peasant would have
been capable of reading a continuous text in French, though some
clearly did; in the words of the Bordeaux lawyer Bernadau, 'those
country people of this district who know how to read like reading,
and, all else lacking, they read the *Almanach des Dieux*, the *Bibliothèque
bleue*, and other poppycock that the pedlars carry annually into the

countryside'.[25] Some bought almanacs from Jewish pedlars who came to their village; others gained access to tracts when they visited local fairs and markets, still subject to regulation by the intendants until 1789.[26] Others again, less confident or barely literate, read in groups, often in country inns, sought pamphlets written in *patois*, or had stories read to them. Or they turned to the work of imagists, at a time when the cheap, single-sheet prints known as *images d'Epinal* were circulating more freely in the countryside and could be bought for a few sous at the local market. They were also extending their range of themes, especially during the Empire, from traditional religious images to ones drawn from politics and from the military.[27] Many of the families who sent their sons to war under the Revolution and Empire would have been familiar not just with the literature of the *Bibliothèque bleue* but, even more commonly, with the brash, luridly coloured images of soldiers in bright uniforms – of infantrymen and drummer-boys as well as high-ranking officers – which had become a standard part of the repertoire of Jean-Charles Pellerin and other popular imagists of the day.[28]

It remains true, however, that large numbers of the young men in the battalions were not able to read or write, while many others would never previously have had occasion to write a letter. In village society, with the extended family living in close proximity, there was little reason to write, and little incentive to study to learn the skills required. The Revolution certainly talked of providing primary education for all, secular and freely obtained, in pursuit of its dream of a more enlightened population, but that remained a dream, far removed from the reality of rural life. As far as the young men of the requisitions were concerned, it was something for the future, a goal to which others, following in the footsteps of Lakanal, might aspire. At the time of the Revolution literacy rates for France as a whole remained low, the greatest increases over the eighteenth century being recorded to the north of a line from Geneva to Saint-Malo, with, for men only, an extension to the south described within an arc from Lyon to Bayonne. Conscripts were unlikely to constitute a significant exception to the trend, although the absence of accurate literacy figures during this period makes any very specific conclusions difficult. What can be said is that even in the years after 1830, when we do have usable figures, the percentage of conscripts able to sign their names did not pass above 52 per cent. And when it comes to the more sophisticated skills needed to write a letter, to choose things to say and express them in French, there is still much that we do not know with any certainty. What is clear, on the evidence of a much later census (that of 1866), is that the coefficient of correlation between the ability to sign one's name and the ability to write is rather higher than is often supposed: a recent assessment of this evidence places the figure at the very high level of +0.91.[29]

On this basis we may conclude that, at the most generous estimate, somewhere under half of the troops may have been able to sign or to read and write at a fairly basic level. Officers and NCOs were, of course, far more likely to be able to write than were the men in the ranks, which means that their thoughts and reactions are always likely to be over-represented when compared to those of ordinary infantrymen. This was not, it must be emphasised, an educated army by the standards even of the mid nineteenth century. Its level of literacy was very much lower, for instance, than that of the next mass armies in modern history, the three million soldiers who fought in the American Civil War, whether for the Union or for the Confederacy.[30] And that in turn has implications for the quality of what we have to read. There were relatively few French soldiers in this *fin de siècle* able to write with the confidence or the fluency that characterised the men of later periods; too often their prose can seem rather stilted and wooden, restricting the range of emotion and intensity that they can express. But equally, literacy levels among the mass of the population had increased markedly since the wars of the Ancien Régime, a fact which, along with the much wider recruitment base of the revolutionary and Napoleonic battalions, means that these are the first European wars for which a study of this kind can usefully be undertaken.

We know from the internal evidence of the texts that many of the soldiers either were unable to sign or were barely able to scrawl a few lines of reassurance to their parents. They did not approach their task with any confidence. Indeed, one of the stranger aspects of the unprecedented festival of letter-writing thrown up by the conscripts' experience of war is that very often neither the writer of the letter nor its ultimate reader was literate: mothers and brothers back in the village often needed to seek out a local interpreter, someone like an innkeeper, or a blacksmith, or a priest, so that they could have news of their loved

15 mai 1813 besanson

JE VEILLE AU SALUT DE L'EMPIRE.

Mon chere pere et Ma chere mere

je suis arivé en bonne santé grace a dieu je desire que vous
portie de meme bien je ai été en route en prison quelque fois
et en sortant de la charité je mieux porte je ne pas pue vous ecrire
comme je vous l'avois promis et en arivant a besanson nous
avons etez mis en liberté nous fesons l'exsisis deux fois par
jours et nous somme bien abillé et nous fesons l'exsisise 9 fois par
jours et je suis bien content de partir pour la russie je vous
assure bien mes chere parant que je ne vous ferez plus
de chagrin et que je ferai bien mon service mes deuse camerad
sont toujour avec moi ils se sont rendu de suitte je suis du
trante septieme regiment de ligne premie bataillon cinquieme
compagnie repondemoi de suitte a besanson je puis neore le
recevoir donnemoi des nouvelle du pays je finis en vous
embrassant de tout mon coeur et suis avec respect santé
la plus sincere Mon tres cher pere et ma tres tendre mere
je salut bien tout mes
parant et ami et tout
ceux qui demanderont
domes nouvelle

Votre tres humble
serviteur et fils
michel quaquin

'Je veille au salut de l'Empire'. Soldiers were encouraged to buy sheets of paper illustrated with a patriotic symbol. The writer is leaving for Russia after serving a prison sentence for desertion. (*Archives Départementales du Cher, Z559*) one. And equally often the text would have to be dictated to one of the few men in the regiment able to read and write, who would become a public writer for the others – an *écrivain public* in the manner of those still commonly to be found at fairs and country markets; the others would pay for his services, sometimes in cash, more generally by buying him a drink, and a crisis would ensue if he was laid low with fever, or was wounded or killed in battle. Often – though it was not an invariable rule – this was a task that fell to non-commissioned officers, to those with a little more education and *savoir-faire* than the rest, who both had higher levels of literacy than the ordinary infantrymen and who had a valuable awareness of what the army would and would not tolerate in terms of criticism and complaint. Indeed, it is noticeable that letters written by *sous-officiers* and other authorised scribes are often more careful in the opinions they proffer, avoiding any criticism of the officer corps and any reference to army positions and troop movements.[31] They had diplomatic skills and some political sensitivity, and they were good servants of the army as well of the individuals on whose behalf they wrote.

The psychological value of their contribution was recognised by the military authorities, and it was not restricted to that of cultural inter-mediaries between the army and the village, important though that undoubtedly was. For letters were the source of most of the dependable news that came to families about their sons' and brothers' lot – not only the letters sent directly by their relatives, but those passed from hand to hand in the village, from family to family, neighbour to neigh-bour. Such letters were intended to be read by more than one recipient, since they talked of friends and cousins and fellow-villagers encountered in the regiment, bringing news of the doings of whole units of local boys: who had achieved some notable exploit; who had seen an elder brother or cousin in transit or at a particular garrison point; who had fallen sick or been wounded in battle; or, most tragically, who had died of their wounds or of infection. Nor should we see letter-writing as a one-way process. Soldiers expected to receive news from home – of the harvest, the crops and the cattle, of younger brothers and the following year's levy for the armies. This was more than a matter of idle curiosity: their morale and good health were intimately tied up in the maintenance of such links with their families and with the assurance that there was still a place for them in civilian life. They needed letters, especially from wives and loved ones, if they were to be mentally fit for action and effective as soldiers. The degree of that need might vary, but there is no doubt that it was felt by the vast majority of soldiers, especially when they were stationed beyond France's frontiers. It is well expressed in one letter sent in 1800 by a general in the Army of Italy to his wife back at home in France:

> Past mail and future mail, that is my life: the rest is nothing but vegetation. More than anything, absence underlines the sheer inanity of the present. Really it constitutes nothing more than a dividing line between the past and the future. The past is the letter that has been received, and it must lead to the future which is the letter to come; and when the road lasts more than four days, it seems really long.[32] *

Indeed, the absence of any news from home was one of the most commonly cited explanations given for that curse of the revolutionary and Napoleonic armies, nostalgia or *mal du pays*, a severe form of homesickness which could affect whole battalions and which was recognised by medical opinion as a serious and debilitating illness. Those suffering from it developed all the physical and mental symptoms of melancholia, and their level of resistance to other ailments was so seriously undermined that even minor illnesses could become debilitating, and in some cases mortal.[33] Though the term was not used by contemporaries, it was a disease akin to clinical depression in the twentieth century, brought on by solitude and anxiety, by a sense of having been abandoned by family and friends; experience of active service brought symptoms of amnesia and apathy which deepened that depression and were similar to what today we would call shell-shock. The French revolutionary battalions were familiar with these illnesses, and with the listlessness and resignation which they inculcated. But medical science was incapable of providing a cure. Soldiers facing near-starvation in foreign lands looked to a letter to reassure them that they were still valued, that the extent

---

* Le courier passé, le courier futur, voicy ma vie: le reste n'est que de la végétation. Rien ne fait mieux sentir que l'absence, l'inanité du temps présent. Ce n'est véritablement que la séparation entre le passé et le futur. Le passé, c'est la lettre reçue, il faut qu'elle conduise au futur qui est la lettre à recevoir; et quand la route est plus de quatre jours, elle paroit longue.

of their sacrifice was recognised by those closest to them. A prolonged silence could so easily convince vulnerable young men that they had been abandoned, forgotten, cast off from the reassuring everyday routines that had given their lives shape. Even in an army that was not overwhelmingly literate, the sending and particularly the receipt of letters was crucial for maintaining their always fragile morale.

Letter-writing, in other words, was important to the army just as it was to individual soldiers; and the army could not afford to allow personal communication with the troops to be lost. Eighteenth-century governments were well aware of the therapeutic powers of correspondence in wartime, as, indeed, were the generals and the army high command, who encouraged soldiers to write to counter their boredom and re-establish their links with those for whom they were fighting. But in peacetime, when the soldiers were back on French soil, there was no need for a special military post: the soldiers were simply encouraged to use, and to pay for, the normal domestic postal service along with the rest of the population. It was only in times of war, after all, that the troops were organised into armies, and it was with armies, not individual units, that the postal administration was charged to deal.[34] Hence there was no special military post between the Peace of Paris in 1763 and the declaration of war in March 1792, leaving the revolutionaries to establish their own postal administration for the armies in the field. It was a task they addressed vigorously, since, like all modern armies, those of the Revolution and Empire understood the need to keep the soldiers in touch with their families, carrying news and letters, of course, but also occasional presents in the form of food, small sums of cash, or much-needed items of clothing. The task was one of some urgency as the war rapidly spread beyond France's own frontiers and the area that was already adequately served by a network of postal couriers. Laws were passed in rapid succession establishing the framework for a military mail service. In September 1792 the government appointed additional couriers, men elected in the Paris sections whose political allegiance was assured, to carry despatches to the armies and to return with news. In the following year further legislation provided guards for the military mails on the same basis as those defending the moneys to be paid to the troops, while in spring 1794, at the height of the Terror, the Committee of Public Safety took steps to ensure that no postilion was allowed to

A letter proudly written on notepaper bearing the letterhead of the Garde Impériale, 2 April 1812. Note the portrait of the Emperor and Empress. (*Archives Départementales de la Corrèze, 2F81*)

stop at the frontiers or refuse to carry mail to the armies. Some, allegedly, had already refused; the Committee decreed that 'those postilions who refused to continue their service as carters and leave for the army shall be regarded as suspects and shall be treated as such'.[35] Soldiers were to have the same right to a postal service as any other French citizen, and the law would defend that right by bullying and terrorising postal couriers when it deemed it necessary.

What this involved in practice was an extension beyond France's frontiers of the system of private postal couriers which operated for domestic mails, an extension that was operated purely for the benefit of the armies. The government took responsibility for the costs of moving mails to and from the armies, or at least for that part of the journey that transported them beyond the frontiers. The cost to the user was kept low. From 1794 mail was charged up to the French frontier only and was transported freely beyond the frontier; and for a brief period after 1796 post to and from the army and navy was carried entirely free of charge.[36] Cost was not, however, the only or even the major problem they faced as France's armies marched across Europe. Ensuring that they remained linked to the postal network was itself a significant challenge, and one that demanded a rational and somewhat complex administration. At first the revolutionaries did little more than adopt the traditional system which had been used by Louis XIV back in 1703, but, with the passage of time and the massive increase in the size of the armies, the postal administration was developed both in complexity and efficiency. Under the Directory a postal official or *waguemestre* was appointed in every battalion and every regiment, who had a legal responsibility for the security of all mails passing through his hands. If, as often happened, a regiment was divided for operational reasons, then each unit was equipped with its own postal bureau. In this way, it was hoped that the mails could continue to reach every soldier on active service. Similarly, a network of postal inspectors was created to regulate the service and ensure its smooth working.[37] Under Napoleon the degree of control was further augmented, with letters posted directly from each division passing through the general office of the corps and on to the *bureau général* of the *Grande Armée*, before being directed on to metropolitan France.[38] Postal directors had to inform themselves daily of the previous day's troop movements to ensure that errors were minimised.

And the whole system was tightly coordinated and supervised. In retrospect, what impresses is the sheer effort put into organising a mail service across a war-shattered continent, so that mail could be delivered to troops serving in Poland and on the steppes of Russia. In Egypt Napoleon took a personal interest in providing a mail service, even extending its benefits to the local population and advertising its services and charges in Arabic.[39]

A reading of government decrees and laws suggests that a great deal of time and effort was expended in perfecting postal services to the armies and in creating the much-vaunted *estafette* of the Napoleonic Wars. But, of course, huge logistical difficulties stood in the path of success. There was so much that could go astray, be mislaid or stolen on the long journey from a peasant cottage to the winter quarters of a distant regiment. Weather, mud, mountain ranges and winter snows all hindered the flow of mail, while enemy attacks often added to the problems posed by long distances and an inhospitable terrain. The poor quality of roads was compounded by the uncertainty of the destination, as the armies moved relentlessly on, passing from village to village, often from country to country, making it difficult for the mails to keep step. The *carnet de marche* of one young soldier, Aymez, who volunteered at the age of only sixteen in his Paris section of Buttes-des-Moulins, shows how unpredictable their progress often was. Between 20 May and 26 December 1796, for instance, he travelled a total of 1432 kilometres, covering eight kilometres one day, forty-eight another; winter snows and active service slowed his unit down, but in one month he marched a total of eighty-four kilometres.[40] In such conditions it is quite astonishing that so much did eventually get through, and that men stationed so far from home, in northern Italy and Holland, eastern Germany and Poland, could write back acknowledging the arrival of a welcome letter or parcel. Many, of course, did not, and the non-arrival of a hoped for letter from home could have a highly deleterious effect on morale, plunging the soldier into gloom and recrimination. It was thus doubly important for the armies that their mails got through.

The troops were well aware that there was something very hit-and-miss about postal deliveries. When a letter did arrive it was the cause of jubilation and high spirits, but inevitably there were many left disappointed, and others who suffered recrimination at the hands of their loved ones for leaving letters they had never received unanswered. This was one area of army life where all were truly equal, the commanding officer as likely to be betrayed by a break-down of communication as the humblest infantryman. The soldiers' feelings, and the sense of fatalism which this engendered, are touchingly expressed in letters sent to his wife by Choderlos de Laclos, then a *général de brigade* with the Army of Italy.[41] He was one of many French officers who made it a point of honour to write to his wife every day when that proved possible. But, once serious fighting began and his unit was constantly on the march, it was no longer realistic to think of posting letters from day to day. As he explained to her in a letter from the *quartier général* in Verona in Year IX, he has had to accept that from time to time there would be gaps of three or four days between his letters, 'since there are many days when there is no time to set up military post offices and when, as a result, letters cannot be sent, and also, quite often, I am just too far away from the point where the office has been established to get anything to it'.[42] Besides, army movements could disrupt the posts and letters fall into the hands of the enemy, incurring loss or severe delay. From Turin in the previous autumn he had described the circuitous route by which he had eventually received one of her letters:

> Since my last letter I have received one from you on which I was scarcely counting. It is dated 20 Prairial and addressed to the Army of the Rhine. A note, scribbled on the back, has allowed me to solve the puzzle. This note reads: 'taken, unsealed and sent back by the enemy'. So you see that you, too, have your share of the dangers of war.[43] *

Laclos was sufficiently informed of army movements to accept such disruption and he had the confidence and literary skill to explain them to others. For many ordinary soldiers, on the other hand, dependent on occasional letters for reassurance, it was a source of endless frustration and anxiety.

Soldiers did not only enjoy receiving letters; they also took pleasure

---

* Depuis ma dernière lettre, j'en ai reçu une de toi sur laquelle je ne comptois guère. Elle est dattée du 20 prairial et adressée à l'armée du Rhin. Une note, mise au dos, m'a donné le mot de l'énigme. Cette note porte: 'prise, décachetée, et renvoyée par l'ennemi'. Tu vois que tu as aussi ta part dans les dangers de la guerre.

in writing them. The importance of letter-writing – the need to consign thoughts to paper, to make one's voice heard by someone in the outside world – has been recognised by all the mass armies of modern times. It has grown with literacy, of course, but also with the scale of modern warfare; and it has increased in the mass armies of young conscripts and citizen-soldiers who characterise warfare in the modern world. Parallels can most readily be drawn with twentieth-century armies, or with the men who fought on both sides of the American Civil War, many of them young volunteers who enlisted, like the volunteers of the early years of the French Revolution, because they believed devoutly in the justice of their cause. They, too, started out for their regiment burning with enthusiasm, keen to right wrongs and defend the values of the communities they had left behind. And they, too, wanted to remain an integral part of those communities. They showed a seemingly insatiable thirst for personal contact, apparently enjoying the novelty of writing letters, describing novel experiences, unknown places, new friends and comrades. Some grabbed any possible opportunity to write home, to their mothers and fathers, wives and sweethearts, pillars of reassurance in a deeply unreassuring world. A few, we know, managed to keep up the routine of letter-writing every day, and almost all struggled to communicate, many in garbled prose characterised by poor spelling and warped grammar. But struggle they did. The postal services of the two sides carried millions of letters to and from the armies in a desperate bid to keep these vital lines of communication open. This represented, as Bell Irvin Wiley noted in his classic study of the Confederate army, an unprecedented 'tide of letter-writing' for the American South, which had never previously seen such a large proportion of its people uprooted from their homes at any one time. During the war, many who had never previously taken up a pen took to letter-writing, with the consequence that 'a large portion of the middle and lower strata of Southern society became articulate for the first time'.[44] Never was the desire to write, the need to communicate to the outside world, as painfully evident as it was in wartime.[45]

And so it was with the young Frenchmen consigned to the battalions of the Revolution and Empire. Such was the urge to communicate brought about by long periods of absence, an urge made deeper by the sheer strangeness of the experience of war and the terrible distance

which seemed to separate young men from their families, that people
who never previously would have considered literacy a useful or necessary acquisition now lamented their lack of education and openly
declared how much they would love to attain the freedom which reading
and writing conveyed. For if a man could not write or find someone
prepared to write for him, he was isolated, lonely and abandoned to his
own inadequate resources, a feeling of vulnerability which shows
through again and again in their correspondence. One young Savoyard,
from the mountain commune of Saint-Jean-de-Maurienne, reflected on
this need while he was suffering long months of illness in a hospital
bed: he has started to learn the rudiments of writing, he says, realising
at last what a benefit literacy can be and expressing the hope that he
will return home one day able both to read and to write.[46] Another
wrote home in 1809 to say that he bitterly regretted that he was unable
to read and write, and to share in what he perceived as the well-being
of those who could; he asked his parents to send him some money
so that he could receive instruction; knowledge, he realised, brought
incalculable happiness.[47] Similarly, the conscript son of peasants from
the Vosges rejoiced when he no longer had need of a third party in
order to communicate his feelings to them, something which he had
always found awkward and mildly embarrassing. For the army had
taught him to read and write, through the good offices of a corporal
from a neighbouring village who had befriended him and who had been
happy to give him some lessons during moments of repose. He made
no attempt to conceal the excitement which he felt at this achievement.
'I managed to read the last letter you were good enough to send me
without help from anyone', he wrote, and one can almost feel the pride
bursting from his carefully-formed words on the page.[48]

    Many young soldiers learned that in the army boredom was only
increased by illiteracy, as it greatly reduced the possibilities of contact
with others. Some realised that if their younger brothers were to follow
them into uniform it was imperative that they should be encouraged to
learn to read and write, and to persevere at school, even if the value of
such things might not be obvious to a young boy in a rural community.
One solicitous infantryman, Hubert-Joseph Jaminet, wrote home from
his unit at Hermalle-sous-Huy in Belgium, urging his brother to heed
his message since his needs in the army would be very different. 'Is my

brother Jean-Joseph yet able to read and write? Send him to school so that he can learn well! For a soldier who does not know his ABC is condemned to misery.'[49] The government increasingly listened to these pleas, and understood that literacy for many had become a searing need, the only path to solace and communication. Napoleon, in particular, sought to provide greater education in the regiments, introducing a modest initiative in schooling by which he hoped to raise literacy levels in the ranks. An instruction from the Prefect of the Hautes-Pyrénées in February 1808 shows how the scheme was to work with troops manning garrisons and in reserve companies behind the front lines. From the funds assigned to the reserve, money was allocated for a schoolmaster, knowledgeable in reading, writing, spelling and grammar, who was to give daily lessons to the soldiers and NCOs of the company, under the supervision of the captain and lieutenant.[50] In this way, it was hoped, letter-writing would be eased and troop morale lifted.

For some, it is true, their professed love of literacy was rather more calculated, their desire to read and write a means to a short-term goal. Reading might be equated with self-betterment and the possibility of promotion. Or the desire to study might be incited by the knowledge that demanding parents expected their sons to acquire the skills they would need in civilian life, instead of wasting their time in bars and taverns. A professed love of learning could be a way of ingratiating themselves into the affections of fathers still hoping for scholastic achievement when formal schooling had had to give way to soldiering. As one soldier wrote reassuringly to his father, a bailiff in Chambéry, even imprisonment in England had done nothing to interrupt his studies. He might be far away and safe from parental scrutiny, but 'my conduct is regular, and I dare to inform you that in a short time you will be able to appreciate the fruits of it, for I am continuing to pursue learning'.[51] Others had more immediate ambitions. An ability to write could, after all, lead to employment as a scribe for others, as a public letter-writer in the battalion who would be greatly in demand and who might be rewarded in money, or with small favours or free drinks. It was a way of buying popularity and status in the eyes of others. More importantly, literacy might even allow the occasional lucky soldier to avoid the full ardours of war. Louis Godeau, a former schoolteacher in the Loir-et-Cher, was one who believed that the book learning of his youth might now serve him well. His handwriting had been inspected, he told his family in 1794, and he had high hopes of being allocated a clerical job in the army. This he saw as an excellent move, since, 'apart from the fact that it is well paid, there is the benefit that I should not be exposed to fire or to physical blows; I should be safe, as it is in my interest to be, but safe in an approved manner'.[52]

The army, it would seem, had achieved what scores of eighteenth-century village schoolmasters could not. It had instilled in at least a proportion of its conscripts a desire for literacy and an appreciation of the value of the written word. But it could not instil fluency, or ease in expressing subtle emotions, and for that reason the letters which the soldiers wrote could express only stilted thoughts and half-formed emotions. Many of them were written in moments of great physical discomfort, moments snatched from guard duty or composed in the cramped surroundings of a hastily-constructed encampment. Many of them betray discomfort of another kind, too, as soldiers struggled to think of something to say or to find an appropriate formula with which to get started. Often the first paragraph follows a closely-observed model, possibly a form of words suggested by a friend or an officer or circulated in the unit as a guide for the uninitiated. For most of these young men, having no experience of writing letters, could become embarrassingly tongue-tied when the moment of composition arrived. Just how do you address your parents? Or send appropriate regards to aunts and uncles? Or admit to fears and anxieties without occasioning wholesale panic back home? Or – even more fundamentally – describe a way of life, a culture, an expectation that belonged only in the army and had little meaning for the civilian community? Writing letters in such circumstances could never be easy or spontaneous, even for those with some experience of what the practice of letter-writing involved. But many of these men, as we have seen, had none. They had had no occasion to write, or to turn to the writing manuals and *secrétaires* which circulated in provincial France, and which had been popularised by the *Bibliothèque bleue* during the second half of the century, but which were less concerned to instruct in the art of letter-writing than they were to nourish a certain rather fallacious social know-how.[53] The outpourings of the troops were little influenced by such questions of etiquette, beyond the most basic feeling for what was polite and decent. They were often poorly written and phonetically spelt, the handwriting almost touchingly laborious. At times they descended into the formulaic, and in many cases, whether because the writer lacked imagination or because he was overawed by the process of writing itself, the perspective offered never rose above the mundane and utterly banal. Works of creative literature they most certainly were not.

At their most basic these letters can be empty formulae, painstakingly copied from style sheets circulated in the ranks, repeating the same trite phrases and hackneyed greetings. In the archives of Savoy, for instance, we can read nearly two hundred letters written to their families by men from the department of Mont-Blanc who served with the *Grande Armée* between 1803 and 1815. Though this might seem a treasure-trove rich beyond most reasonable dreams, many of them are dull, repetitious, and almost completely bereft of any individual insight, the sort of letter that would result from the uncritical copying of an army style sheet. The most banal say little beyond inquiring after their parents' health and assuring them that their own is good, and that they have avoided the injuries and fevers which could be a harbinger of worse news to follow.[54] Or they consist of a copied introduction and conclusion, with a short piece of individual writing in the middle. Of course these can be frustrating documents to toil through. They are often naive and rather dull. Yet in a rather perverse way their very naivety gives them a special value to the historian of mentalities and social attitudes, trying to understand the feelings and responses of ordinary soldiers to the demands of army life and to the dangers posed by their involvement in war. They may have dumbed down their feelings, but they discussed them in terms which they knew their parents – and by extension, village France – would understand. They tended to avoid subjects that would cause hurt or distress, and to concentrate instead on what they felt would be expected of them: words of reassurance about their welfare and marks of affection and solicitude about what might be happening at home. Most crucially, they were the only form of communication which could be forged between two alien societies with quite different expectations and points of reference – between the frontier and the village, between the young soldier and the community he had been forced to leave behind.

Letters, unlike the more heroic medium of war memoirs, concentrate

heavily on the immediate experience of soldiers, on their own unit, the
men around them, the men with whom they shared so much more than
they would ever have had to do in civilian life. New loyalties sprang up,
to comrades and room-mates, units and regiments, and these loyalties
became all the more searing when friends were killed or maimed in
battle. Letters can be poignant, containing expressions of fear and regret,
admissions of human weakness, a sense of loss and pain. Some even
admit to feeling repugnance at the violence and the killing they see
around them. Often, of course, the day-to-day experiences they describe
are petty and banal, yet that very banality gives their accounts a degree
of veracity which otherwise they would lack. For their primary concerns
were so often far removed from heroism and glory – rather they were
matters of routine and training, shortage and deprivation, hunger, cold,
the lack of decent clothing during an Alpine winter, or of money with
which to pay off debts or cover the cost of basic necessities. And
boredom, especially perhaps that, the sort of gnawing boredom that
destroyed morale and made men in barracks and bivouacs long for a
return to action. These are hardly matters that contribute to the myth
of the revolutionary and Napoleonic armies, to the somewhat sanitised
memory of the *levée en masse* that would become a central part of the
iconography of the Third Republic, even if they do add weight to that
other reputation of the imperial troops, as *grognards* who grumbled and
groused their way across Europe, always complaining, never content
with their lot. Yet they are wholly consistent with the experience of
soldiers in most modern wars, begging comparison with the much more
voluminous records that survive, for instance, from 1914–18.[55] They are
not, of course, as varied or as sophisticated; yet in their own way these
letters of the 1790s and 1800s also offer a taste of history from below,
of the war as it was lived and experienced by the millions of young men
whose lives were upturned and often destroyed by it. They offer us, in
the words of one French soldier of the First World War, an insight
which no onlooker or journalist could offer, an insight into a world
which, though strange and unreal, could so quickly become ordinary,
the world of 'war as it was understood with the flesh'.[56]

3

Official Representations of War

If the letters and journals of ordinary soldiers present a confused and often unheroic image of the military, one far removed from the wide canvas of the high command and the military strategists, they also provide a healthy antidote to the highly propagandist picture that was being painted by the government and its agents. As in all modern warfare, the government saw it as its duty to inform the public of the progress of the war – a civilian public in the towns and villages of France as well as a military public in the various armies and battalions – and to control the flow of information in an attempt to maintain public morale. The new importance attached to public opinion in eighteenth-century France, the emergence of a literate public and the creation of a public sphere, served only to increase the intensity of this exercise and to exaggerate the influence which politicians ascribed to propaganda, to the provision of a wholesome official representation of the war effort.[1] Thus the revolutionaries were relentless in presenting an image of an army inspired by patriotism and dedicated to the political ideals of liberty and equality, an army of citizens united in its sense of purpose, committed to the goal of protecting the republic, of salvaging the public good. In similar vein, while playing down the more ideological values of the revolutionary years, Napoleonic discourse persistently emphasised the commitment to honour and the cause of the nation which was shared by the soldiers, those qualities of competence, dedi-cation, and loyalty to the person of the Emperor which they regarded most highly. Neither regime stopped to check on these responses; they were, it seemed, the spontaneous reactions of men who had been liberated from tyranny and who were fighting for their rights and for their nation. Their qualities were those of patriots and of warriors: their courage, their hatred of tyrants and of oppression, their openness and generosity of spirit.

The language used throughout the revolutionary period was, as we have noted, a language of citizenship, the single concept which, perhaps more than any other, was central to the Revolution's self-image. It was first stated in 1789 in the Declaration of the Rights of Man, which boldly declared the inviolability and inalienability of basic individual rights, before being integrated into the 1791 constitution and thus attaining the force of constitutional law. As a statement of principle it belonged primarily to the early part of the Revolution, from the debates in the National Assembly to the period of the Jacobin Republic; thereafter it faded to become part of a rather empty republican self-image, especially during the years of the Directory. But its power should not be under-estimated, especially in propaganda terms, and the image of France's soldiers fighting for a cause in which they believed, serving as citizens a regime which recognised and rewarded their sacrifices, would be an essential part of the mythology of the French Revolution. They were portrayed in somewhat stereotyped form: resisting the pull of their families, dragging themselves from the arms of wives and girlfriends, burning with patriotic pride and republican ideology to 'rush to the frontiers' to 'save the republic'. It is not only an image of duty and citizenship, two of the qualities which the Revolution most prized, but also, in keeping with the classical mood of the day, an image of heroism and self-sacrifice, of young men who accepted the call of their country and who willingly put the cause of the *patrie* above selfish ambition, above, indeed, the counter-appeal of filial duty on the one hand and personal affection on the other. The young republican of propaganda and legend was a man of steely resolution and virtuous rectitude.

This image would be reproduced not just in a thousand speeches but also, visually, in many paintings and popular prints, as art became established as a powerful vehicle for revolutionary ideology. Good examples are Berthaut's etching of *Les enrôlements volontaires au Pont-Neuf*, which eulogises the patriotism of the ordinary Parisian, and the touching painting in the Musée Carnavalet, once attributed to Watteau de Lille, entitled *Le départ du volontaire.*[2] In the young volunteer are concentrated all the passions of revolutionary youth – ardour and enthusiasm, patriotic devotion, outrage at the crimes of France's enemies, and dedication to the republican ideal. The institution of conscription with the *levée en masse* brought with it a less individual depiction of revolutionary patriotism, as paintings and etchings dwelt on the theme of mass enthusiasm, of the generosity of a whole people when called upon to save their country. One such painting, attributed to Gérard, captures the drama of the levy on the main square of a southern town, in which young soldiers scramble to enlist or embrace their wives and fiancées, women hug their loved ones while holding aloft babes-in-arms, and young boys bring swords, pikes and harness for the service of the army. The whole bustling scene, pregnant with classical imagery, presents a highly idealised, heroic vision of a country girding itself for war.[3] By 1793, indeed, it is notable how many pictures were concentrating on military themes, praising the valour of generals and portraying the heroic grandeur of a victorious army. Revolutionary iconography was now that of a country at war, and those qualities which the French discerned in their soldiers – courage, dedication, principle, gallantry – became major themes of the history paintings of the age.

In their most extreme form we can see the same themes in pictures of the child-soldiers so beloved of revolutionary propaganda, boys whose patriotism tore them away from their families and reinvented them as martyrs of liberty. Joseph Bara of Palaiseau and Agricol Viala of Avignon, both boys from humble backgrounds who died defending the Revolution against Vendean and Comtadin aggressors, became in death republican icons, offering future generations of France's youth an idealised representation of the citizen-soldier. Their deification, it is true, would not be complete until the later nineteenth century, when their stories would be admiringly recounted in every school textbook of the Third Republic. But even in 1794 the two boys had become enshrined in legend, praised by Robespierre in the Convention and, for a brief period, the subject of a revolutionary cult as paragons of self-sacrifice, teaching aids in patriotism and in the generosity of youth. Bara in particular, who at the age of thirteen charged with the republican cavalry against the Vendean rebels, and who, when captured, preferred a martyr's death to the ignominy of having to shout his support for the monarchy, came to represent the combination of patriotism and republicanism that the revolutionaries so much admired.[4] Images and medallions were produced in his honour and paintings recorded his sacrifice, while only the fall of Robespierre two days earlier stopped the national festival that was to be staged in Paris, choreographed by

the painter Jacques-Louis David, and the transfer of his remains to the
Pantheon. Because of his youth he was deemed a valuable role-model
for the young, for the next generation of boys on whom the revolutionaries would depend for their defence. In December 1793 Bertrand
Barère asked the Convention to commission an engraving of Bara to be
distributed to primary schools 'to provide a constant reminder to the
young people of France of the most perfect instance of patriotism and
filial devotion'.[5] His cruel death would live on in popular memory thanks
to David's famous painting, *La mort de Bara*, which depicts with a
touching tenderness the pathos of his murdered body, naked, fragile,
and somewhat androgynous, that of a child who had not yet evolved
into manhood, the vulnerable, butchered victim of Vendean treachery.[6]

David's painting is a good example of the use of art in the service of
the French Revolution, of art as political propaganda, as part of a
programme of education conducted at the behest of the state. In one
sense there was little new in this. Artists had long been commissioned
to paint canvases portraying the glory of the state or the high standing
of its rulers: Louis XIV had patronised artists and sculptors to enhance
his prestige, just as the medieval church had done to project a confident
image of western Christendom. But the Renaissance had given a spur
to the individualism of the artist, scorning submission to powerful
patrons and popularising the ideal of art for art's sake. These two conflicting views of the role of the artist jostled for supremacy during the
eighteenth century, and the Enlightenment increasingly preached a
didactic function, since art was seen as uniquely well placed to spread
moral and patriotic ideals to a wider audience. To a degree, therefore,
authors like Diderot and Mercier were already demanding in the years
before 1789 the sort of didactic art which would be at the heart of the
revolutionaries' educational project, and it is already possible to glimpse
in their writings something of that fundamental conflict of the revolutionary years, the tension between artistic freedom on the one hand
and government regulation on the other.[7] That problem remained important throughout the revolutionary years, as politicians clamoured for
artists to reflect the social purpose of the new regime. Only the level of
pressure would vary. During the constitutional monarchy the revolutionaries did little more than exhort artists to use their talents in the
cause of liberty and equality, and there were few concerted attempts to

put artists to work for the regime. It would be later, under the Republic, that politicians sought to employ artists directly in the revolutionary cause and came to see art as a major weapon of the republic of virtue.

The biennial salons of the *Académie de Peinture* provide us with a useful guide to both political patronage and public taste. Whereas the 1789 Salon, which opened just a few days before the proclamation of the Rights of Man, contained only about ten works with discernibly political themes, that balance would be dramatically reversed in the years that followed. Classical themes of heroism and stoical sacrifice abounded, as did historic scenes of the great moments of the Revolution – the meeting of the Estates-General, the storming of the Bastille, even the prison massacres of 1792. Among the Revolution's heroes, of course, were those who had opted to defend it, and in the 1793 Salon, reflecting what was in many ways the high point of the political revolution, the soldier as well as the political activist was given a place of honour in the roll-call of heroes. In that year exhibits included several paintings with duty and sacrifice at their core: most notably Colinion's *Portrait d'homme en Garde-National*, Mallet's *Le départ d'un volontaire*, and Lejeune's highly didactic *Un père arme son fils pour la défense de la Patrie, la Liberté et l'Egalité*.[8] By the Directorial years the theme of military glory had largely displaced those historical canvases which portrayed political triumphs or ideological allegories and which had consumed the energies of artists during the Jacobin Republic. In 1796, for instance, we see renewed interest in military subjects, whether the heroic paintings of battle scenes by Gros, the detailed studies of army life by Swebach, or the moving family dramas portrayed by Mallet and Van Gorp, as conscripts left for the front or returned in triumph to their families. In 1798 battle scenes were again in vogue, though on this occasion the Salon was notable also for its portraits of victorious generals like Berthier and Kléber, military leaders who had become the new heroes of the French republic. Generals were also the subject of the great historical canvases of that year, whether Le Barbier's moving tribute, *Les derniers instants du Général Marceau* or Thévenin's heroic commissioned portrait of *Augereau au Pont d'Arcole*.[9] The entries to the Salon provided a faithful reflection of France's new militarism, of the central position of the army and its leaders in the portrayal of contemporary history. But it is important not to exaggerate their influence. In both 1796 and 1798 history paintings constituted no more than a small minority of the entries; family scenes and portraits were much more numerous. Indeed, one of the best-known critics of the day, Chaussard, lamented the scarcity of patriotic subjects in the exhibits and the lack of political accountability among the rising generation of artists.[10] But where artists did elect to depict political scenes, it was the military rather than the civil sphere which focused their interest and attention. The France of the Rights of Man had by the time of the Directory given way to that of *la Grande Nation*; images of the legislator to those of the soldier.

The changing emphasis of revolutionary art faithfully reflected other changes in official discourse. The 'citizen-soldier' was an uncompromisingly republican ideal, that of a young man who, precisely because he was a citizen, could be called upon to fulfil his military obligations to the state. It was a concept which was developed with the abandonment of the old line army and the imposition of the *levée en masse*. Yet the identification of soldiering with citizenship was not dreamt up during the French Revolution: the revolutionaries were not noted for their intellectual creativity, and, like many of the ideas that gained wide credence during the 1790s, it was a concept that was already being discussed by enlightened authors and pamphleteers during the previous decades. Guibert, for instance, talked the language of citizenship in his influential *Essai général de tactique* of 1772, while Servan (himself a future Girondin and minister of war) published a celebrated tract on the need for soldiers to be citizens (entitled, appropriately, *Le soldat-citoyen*) in 1781.[11] Condorcet had discussed the need for soldiers to be citizens; so, too, had Diderot and numerous others. In short, there was already a debate on the status of the soldier, and by inference on the appropriateness of an army of hired men, recruited by their officers, including regiments of Swedes, Scots, Irish and other foreign mercenaries. Servan, indeed, had advocated an army drawn from the French population which would be fully integrated into civil society: for him, soldiers were first and foremost men of peace who would escape from the tedium of the camp to do useful work in the community, most notably agricultural work and land clearance that would be of direct benefit to the peasantry. For fighting and defence were only one part of their remit. In peacetime, especially, Servan's army would be engaged in manual labour – clearing fields, building roads, digging ditches and canals – and would constitute a vast pool of labour whose interest would be at one with civil society. By their work as much as by their defence of the people, Servan argued, soldiers would be citizens and would earn their place in French society. And unlike the mercenaries who served Louis XV or Louis XVI, they would provide France with a truly national army whose commitment to the cause of the people could not be called into doubt.

Even before the 'citizen-soldier', the Revolution had already accepted the analogous notion of the 'soldier-citizen', the soldier who, as a result of his exertions and his personal sacrifice, enjoyed the full rights of French citizenship and was entitled to the respect of his fellows. This was far removed from the unflattering image of the soldiery which had been so widespread during the Ancien Régime, when soldiering had often been seen as a career of last resort, the only outlet available to the younger sons of poor peasant families or to troublesome boys at odds with their parents or with the law. Too often the army recruit was someone who had been rescued from the poorhouse or was numbered among the more marginal miscreants in village life, those who had no patrons to defend their interests, no land to work, no jobs to occupy them. The reality of European armies during the eighteenth century may have fallen only somewhat short of Voltaire's notorious image of 'a million assassins organised in regiments and scouring the length and breadth of Europe'.[12] Indeed, better discipline in the garrison and on the battlefield had already gone a long way to achieving the rehabilitation of the soldier and his regeneration as an honest professional.[13] But his rehabilitation was not immediately reflected in popular perceptions or in folklore: here we will find, well into the nineteenth century, a persistent image of the soldier as a rogue, a *mauvais garçon*, a young man without roots or responsibilities who posed a threat to the more respectable tiers of European society. It should not surprise us if popular representations lagged behind social and institutional change: that is a norm rather than an exception. And, given the predilection of the troops for booty and plunder, and the unwillingness of their officers to put a stop to the practice, prejudice was bound to linger. Distrust and contempt remained widespread, especially among the towns and villages of border regions like Picardy and Lorraine. To convert this derogatory image into that of the patriotic republican would not be easy: it involved both the imposition of new regulations and discipline on the troops in

their relations with civilians, and a persistent and dedicated campaign
of propaganda by the revolutionary authorities to effect a sea-change in
popular perceptions.[14]

It centrally involved turning the soldier, the underprivileged, de-
meaned mercenary of the eighteenth century, into a citizen with rights
and self-esteem, a citizen of whom mothers and brothers could be proud.
This implied major changes in the army itself, a new system of discipline
based on consent and respectful of human dignity, a new relationship
between men and their officers which recognised the need for obedience,
necessarily, but which also implied a degree of mutual respect. Soldiers
could no longer be despised and bullied, or subjected to a wide range
of degrading physical and corporal punishments: they were – at least in
principle – men with rights and privileges, entitled to be treated with a
certain respect and dignity. Above all, perhaps, they were part of the
body politic, enjoying political rights including the right to petition,
the right to join clubs and popular societies, the right, even as serving
soldiers, to participate in the political process. They could attend
patriotic plays at the theatre and read radical newspapers like the *Ami
du Peuple* or the *Père Duchesne*. The army as an institution was expected to remain apolitical and to obey the orders it received from the
political leadership: the revolutionaries had no desire to create a military
force that would get involved in politics. But that did not exclude the
individual soldier from getting involved in revolutionary politics. For
his political rights were laid down, including the right to denounce his
superior officers if they abused their authority or betrayed the ideals of
revolutionary France. Under the Jacobins, indeed, men were encouraged
to keep their commanders under surveillance, since the officer class was
routinely regarded as politically suspect, the sort of men who, by political
choice or family tradition, might be tempted to side with royalists or
counter-revolutionaries against the cause of the republic. Some found
themselves denounced to the deputies on mission and the political
commissaires who increasingly accompanied the armies; some were
stripped of their commissions; a few, like Custine and Houchard in the
Nord, paid for their indiscretions on the guillotine.[15]

In practice, of course, this was not all about liberty or citizenship.
Much of the emphasis of Jacobin reform stemmed from a strong inherent
distrust of the officer class, from a belief that men born into privilege

were likely to betray their trust, to emigrate abroad, or to support the cause of monarchies and empires. And in 1789 there had been an understandable reluctance to disrupt traditional discipline in the army, lest mutiny and chaos should result. At the outset, indeed, it might be thought that the Revolution even acted rather reluctantly in this regard, hesitating to pass root-and-branch reforms, and giving rights to individuals rather than full political rights to the army as a whole. Concessions were made only slowly, sometimes in response to demands, at other times out of fear of mutiny. But with the passage of time the rights granted would be real enough. The nature of the individual's engagement was changed, so that he took his oath to the collectivity, to the state, rather than to the person of the king. And gradually the Assembly brought the soldier's civil status into line with his civilian counterparts, so that by February 1790 – as a consequence of a report by the *comité militaire* of the Constituent Assembly – they could, if they qualified through their tax payments, exercise their rights as active citizens, despite the fact that they might unavoidably be spending long periods away from their homes in the service of France. The committee laid down three principles which were to underpin military legislation throughout the revolutionary period. Soldiers would not lose their rights of residence as a consequence of their service. They would enjoy the same civic rights as others, whether as active or as passive citizens. And, after a defined period in the army, they would in any case be accorded the rights of active citizens.[16] Indeed, for the less affluent members of French society, those without property or social influence, army service could provide a viable route to political rights which would otherwise have been beyond their reach. Not that the route was without its inherent difficulties, since to qualify a man had to have served in the armies for sixteen years without reproach, which was itself an arduous requirement. But any soldier who survived that period of service would be rewarded with the rights of an active citizen, whether or not he qualified through property ownership or his tax contributions.[17] With the overthrow of the monarchy in 1792 and the creation of the Republic the distinction between active and passive citizens was abolished. Under the Republic the law simply stated that all soldiers who served in their unit until peace had been attained should enjoy the full rights of French citizenship.

If the soldier was to be a citizen in the full sense of the term, that implied, of course, that he should enjoy the same political rights as others, and especially the right to vote in both national and local elections. And that in turn raised the vexed question of domicile: just how could a soldier exercise his voting rights when his unit had marched half way across Europe? Indeed, should domicile matter in the unusual circumstances of the army? After all, a man could scarcely expect to vote in his home canton if he was on active service elsewhere, and the state had every interest in discouraging deserters and draft-dodgers from exercising their right to vote at home. The revolutionaries therefore decided that the troops could exercise their suffrage wherever they were on the day of the urns, whether within France's frontiers or beyond, provided only that they were not serving on garrison duty in their own canton. This last requirement may seem quixotic, but it was introduced with good reason, and reflected the Revolution's continued fear of pressure from those in positions of authority and of improper interference by the officer class. With the expansion of the military in 1793, an ever- increasing part of the electorate was composed of men in the armies, even if, for the most practical of reasons, the percentage who actually voted was often derisory and the impact of the soldiers' votes is easily exaggerated. This is particularly true at certain key moments when the electorate was called upon to accept a new constitution (as in 1793 or 1795). In the plebiscite of 1793, for instance, of over half a million men in France's armed forces only 7797 recorded their votes.[18] Those in camps and billets beyond France's frontiers were particularly reluctant to use the new rights they had been given, and there was no question at this stage of more sophisticated devices, such as votes by procuration. The right to vote, for most soldiers, may have been largely an empty gesture, though the very fact of having been given the suffrage and having been exposed to the hustings probably played a part in creating a strong republican sentiment in the ranks of France's armies, a sentiment that would survive even after the fall of Robespierre and the decline of Jacobinism in civilian life.[19]

If the citizen-soldier enjoyed the right to vote, he enjoyed other, more material rights which would have aroused the envy of the men who had served in the armies of the Bourbons. For there was a general recognition amongst political leaders, and particularly in the Jacobin Club, that blatant inequity could no longer be tolerated, that the fine words uttered in the name of the Revolution implied that there must be greater justice in the distribution of aid and assistance to those who suffered in its cause. Need, not status, had to be the basis for allocating pensions and other forms of relief. And veterans had suddenly become vociferous in demanding their rights, both for themselves and for their wives and families. In calculating pension entitlements, the revolutionaries took account of the degree of incapacity which men had suffered rather than the rank which they had occupied in their regiment, while widows were to receive a pension calculated in accordance with the number of years their husbands had served. It was no longer a system designed to sustain the privilege of the officer class. Thus the law of 8 February 1793 made the scale of pensions utterly transparent: men were to receive 15 sous a day where they had had to be invalided out of the army, 20 sous per day where they had lost a hand or arm in action, and 500 livres per year where they had lost the use of two of their limbs.[20] The same transparency was applied to the admissions policy of military hospitals. In the Ancien Régime, for instance, only officers had been admitted to the Hôtel des Invalides in Paris when, broken by years of service, they were forced into retirement. The revolutionaries, in contrast, insisted that the four hundred places in the Invalides be allocated in a way that would more fairly reflect the gravity of the wounds and the degree of incapacity incurred. Indeed, from 1793, those retired prematurely from the armies on account of their injuries might be offered a choice between a state pension and a place in the Invalides.[21] Citizenship could thus be demonstrated to mean equality to an unprecedented degree.

Or so the revolutionaries continually insisted. In practice, in this as in so many areas of revolutionary social provision, the best intentions of the legislators were often thwarted by the failure of the economy, by massive inflation and by a loss of confidence in paper currency. But we should not deride their efforts, since the period demonstrated an unparalleled commitment to caring for the wounded and the dependents of those who died. Like Carnot, many republicans felt that those able to remain in their civilian jobs had an added obligation to the men who served, to them and the families who were dependent upon them. The fact that during much of the period *remplacement* remained legal merely made the inherent inequity of the system more blatant: Carnot was not

alone in thinking that it was an affront to equality that the rich man
could be allowed to let the poor man die in his stead, on his behalf, as
a consequence of a money payment, while the circumstances of many
modest families were undermined by the scrimping and saving that had
been necessary in order to buy a son or a brother out of active service.
There was therefore a debt which society could not ignore. In all, the
Girondins introduced five major pieces of legislation on military pensions and assistance, and the Montagnards a further twenty during
their thirteen months in office. And it is significant that neither the
Thermidorians nor the Directory saw fit to repeal them.[22] The purpose
was plain – to alleviate the suffering of the sick and bereaved, and to
help those deprived of a livelihood by their service to survive with a
modicum of comfort. The means they proposed showed the extent of
their determination to repay that debt in so far as it was humanly
possible. The Montagnards, for instance, did not stop at voting extra
money for pensions and military hospitals; it was already clear, with the
extended scale of the fighting, that that could not be sufficient. They
found new ways of financing assistance schemes – by the sale of national
lands; with moneys seized from suspects; and by ensuring that the
harvest was safely brought in, in spite of serious manpower shortages
in agriculture. They also sought to devote more resources to education,
so that the orphans of soldiers might be schooled at the expense of the
nation.[23] If he were to be turned into a committed defender of the
Revolution, the citizen-soldier must be protected against the physical
dangers of war through adequate pensions and good-quality medical
care; and he must know that his dependents would be cared for should
he himself be lost in battle. Morale depended on it.

   The emphasis placed by the revolutionaries on providing for the sick
and wounded is proof of their commitment to egalitarian principles.
But it must also be seen as part of a complex and intricate exercise in
propaganda to persuade the troops that they were highly valued and
that their status as citizens was respected. The speeches delivered to the
armies on the eve of battle repeated the same uplifting message, as did
the fact of participating in one of the great revolutionary festivals devoted
to the sanctity of the republic or to the pursuance of victory. The message
might be subsumed into a wider text, but it was always there, that the
soldiers were an integrated part of society, standing shoulder to shoulder

with mayors and mothers, peasants and workers, teachers and administrators, their efforts as vital to the health and happiness of civilian France as those of any other social group. They were shown to have political importance, to be a crucial part of France's Revolution, guaranteeing the safety of women and children, the protection of revolutionary institutions, and the prosperity of agriculture even as they defended the frontiers of the *patrie*.[24] And they enjoyed the confidence and trust of those they were committed to defend. This was the message which deputies on mission to the armies consistently sought to impart to the troops on the frontier during 1793 and the Year II. Saint-Just, on his missions to the Rhine and the Nord, hammered home the message that army commanders must remain subordinate to the political leadership in Paris, and that a major aim of the war was to fuse together a united and organic army, inspired by republican ideals and virtues. The unity of the army, so necessary if victory were to be attained, was also a means of consolidating civil society for the period when the war would be over, for the defence of the 'one and indivisible' republic. Thus it was Saint-Just's declared goal to politicise the military, to do everything in his power to 'rally the armies to the cause of the people and the National Convention'.[25] His speeches, like those of many of his colleagues, were designed to give the troops a clearer sense of their place in the broader polity and a greater appreciation of their own worth.

Among the Revolution's political leaders none spoke with more passion about the rights of the ordinary soldier than Robespierre, and that in spite of his notable lack of enthusiasm for war and for the political risks it represented.[26] For Robespierre the issue was essentially a political one rather than a question of military strategy. The soldier, he believed, had a moral quality, a natural virtue which stemmed from the fact that he had emerged from the sovereign people whom it was his duty to defend. It followed that he must share the ideals and goals of the people, declared Robespierre, and since the people were naturally virtuous, so the common infantryman must be presumed to be virtuous too. This view balanced his natural fear of the privileged and his distrust of the officer class – noblemen who had betrayed before and who might at any moment be presumed to be about to betray again – and offered what he saw as a protection against the threat of Caesarism. But it meant that the ideal of the citizen-soldier was central to Robespierre's vision of a revolutionary army, and he preached this vision with passion and consistency. In particular, he insisted that the troops must remain in touch with the people, that they must continue to cherish their links with the civilian population and avoid the temptation of turning into a professional army, with all the loyalties and camaraderie which that implied. 'Carefully avoid', he urged the deputies, 'everything that could ignite in the souls of the *citoyens-soldats* such military spirit as cuts off soldiers from citizens and which yokes glory and self-interest to things that make for the ruin of citizens.'[27] Soldiers and citizens must think of themselves as one if the fabric of the Republic was to be maintained.

The same message was reinforced throughout the revolutionary years through the use of a wide spectrum of different media: symbols and insignia, statues and public art, buttons and uniforms, plays and caricatures, battle cries, military chants and songs.[28] All were intended to bring the concept of the citizen-soldier into the everyday life of the army and played a crucial role in cementing the image of an army that was like no other, fresh-faced, generous, and inspired by the ideals for which it fought. The individual soldier was portrayed as a volunteer, dedicated to the revolutionary cause even as the Revolution was committed to guaranteeing his freedom and his status. This was a novel image, one that had to be carefully nurtured and propagated, for eighteenth-century armies were unaccustomed to hearing their praises sung in this way. Rather they were accustomed to being treated with contempt and distrust by respectable society, to being accused of countless crimes and misdemeanours in the communities through which they passed, despised for their drunken, uncouth behaviour, and generally treated as thieves, brigands, and ne'er-do-wells throughout Ancien Régime Europe. In giving the soldier new status and self-respect, the Revolution was quite consciously starting a process of re-education to create an army in the image of the revolutionary nation. It would be a lengthy process, which involved breaking down many generations of prejudice and which would reach its apogee in the pedagogy of the Third Republic.

Of the various agencies of revolutionary education in the battalions, songs should perhaps be singled out as occupying a special place, because of their tunefulness, their easy rhythms, their simple lyrics of bravery and patriotism. Soldiers loved singing, whether to while away the long hours of a march or to amuse themselves around the campfire after the evening meal. And of the songs they sang an increasing number were overtly political in tone and content, relishing the liberty they enjoyed and stating their undying love of the *patrie*. They might be traditional songs inherited from the armies of Louis XV, or *couplets de circonstance* composed by the revolutionary soldiers themselves, simple jaunty airs adapted to the theme of the *carmagnole* or patriotic ditties penned by men of some musical talent and originality. The very flexibility of songs, the fact that they could be amended and extended, revised and caricatured, all helped add to their appeal, as did the sociability, the shared warmth and feeling of fraternity which singing could evoke. Some went on to have an even greater resonance. Increasingly soldiers sang adaptations of the two great military anthems of the Revolution, the *Chant du départ* of Marie-Joseph Chénier and the *Marseillaise,* the battle anthem memorably thrown together in a sleepless night by Rouget de Lisle to be performed before the mayor of Strasbourg in a scene that would be immortalised in every textbook of Third Republic France.[29] But there was no let up in the demand for songs or in the appetite of the troops for new compositions. Between 1789 and 1794 the number of new political songs published in France rose steadily each year: if there were 116 in 1789, the figure rose to 261 in 1790, 308 in 1791, 325 in 1792, 590 in 1793, and 701 in 1794.[30] And just as they sent bundles of political newspapers to the armies, Jacobin ministers of war recognised the value of singing and supplied the troops with song books to keep them entertained.

They also recognised the value of words, uplifting words that could raise the soldier's spirits, but also ideological messages that could serve to cement his cause to theirs. And if politicians and deputies on mission hammered home this message in speeches to the troops, it was more subtly communicated by the military press, those newspapers launched with the express purpose of informing and inspiring the armies. For, as citizens, soldiers had the right to be informed of what was going on beyond their own limited horizon: on other frontiers, for instance, in the National Assembly, and in the country at large. This right, it should be emphasised, was accepted long before the Jacobins came to power, since morale was so closely linked to military effectiveness and to success in battle. The relatively moderate *Argus du Département et de l'Armée du Nord* – the self-styled '*Ami Jacques*' – remained loyal to constitutional

monarchy until August 1792, but that did not prevent it from taking
the side of ordinary soldiers. The paper denounced defeatist attitudes
in others and heaped praise on the acts of courage and devotion performed by French soldiers; it deliberately played down the quality of
the enemy, and sought to impress upon its readers that fighting for
liberty in the way that only the French understood made the Frenchman
a far better soldier than the men who were ranged against him.[31] Other
papers went further. Lemaire's *L'Ami des Soldats*, again in the early
months of the Revolution, emphasised the soldier's debt to a government
that had abolished the privileges of aristocratic officers, and stressed the
unity of the French people, military and civilian alike; the men should
take inspiration from the National Assembly, 'where sit your brothers,
your parents, your friends'.[32] In that common cause, Lemaire urged that
they maintain their discipline and dedication, even to the extent that they
take care to obey those officers who have remained with the army and
who have, by doing so, shown their commitment to France.

Under the Jacobins, of course, such an exhortation verged on the
unthinkable. Virtue and patriotism had become the prerogative of
the volunteers and the troops of the line, while officers were regarded
with suspicion. The *Soirée du Camp*, for instance, Carnot's famous
military paper in the Year II, addressed itself uniquely to the ranks,
whom it personified in the fictional character of Va-de-Bon-Coeur,
a sergeant who had been born into the line army and who had lost a
leg in the service of his country. Va-de-Bon-Coeur was presented as
a trooper like themselves, a man without pretension or social ambition,
and bereft of the tedious pomposity of politicians. In a style reminiscent
of the Père Duchesne (on whom he was closely modelled), he talked of
girls and gaiety, patriotism and loyalty, and – his most compelling
attribute – he spoke to the soldiers in their own language, the language
of the campfire and the bivouac. His authority emanated from his long
years of service and suffering: he could speak to the young conscripts
as an equal, as a respected character with whom they could empathise
as a consequence of their own military experience.[33]

The power of words and music was complemented by the visual
impact of festivals and public celebrations, which often had military
themes – such as victories or heroism – but which would in any case
involve delegations from the armies as a symbol of their inclusion within

the body politic. Many of the festivals were almost liturgical moments, portraying values and moral lessons for the edification of local people, not least of those who were designated to take part. In 1793 and 1794 these would often have highly pedagogic themes, emphasising a common commitment to the ideals of the republic, and the armies were quite specifically included among the participants. They generally involved a procession, the performance of some military music, and they would end, almost traditionally, with dancing and alcohol, the classic consti- tuents of a village *bal*. These were frequent occurrences, and volunteers would be sought from the regiments to represent their comrades in the delegations assembled from each corps. In the Army of the Rhine, for instance, nine *fêtes* were celebrated in Strasbourg between July 1794 and the fall of Robespierre a year later, and in Colmar a further four. Most had clear ideological justifications, and all involved the military in prominent roles. Some festivals marked seminal moments in the history of the Revolution. In July 1793, for instance, they celebrated the arrival of the constitution in Alsace, on 10 August the overthrow of the monarchy, in Pluviôse the anniversary of Louis' execution, and in Messidor that of the taking of the Bastille. But not all marked anniversaries. Soldiers also participated in a number of clearly themed festivals during these months, celebrating, for instance, the destruction of the priesthood (on 21 Brumaire II), the commemoration of martyrs (in Frimaire), or the worship of the Supreme Being (on 20 Prairial). Only a few of the themes were specifically military. The army had an especially prominent role in ceremonies to mark the taking of Toulon from the federalists (10 Nivôse) and the honouring of Bara and Viala (which actually took place in Strasbourg on 10 Thermidor, the day after Robespierre was himself overthrown).[34]

Whereas the revolutionary image of the soldier had at its core the concept of citizenship, that could not continue to be the dominant theme under the Consulate and Empire. For if soldiers still had prestige and status, and if they could aspire to the highest honours of the state, that was rather different from the sort of civil liberties which so domi- nated Jacobin thinking. Now discipline and performance in the field were the qualities which were repeatedly emphasised, the qualities through which the soldier could distinguish himself and thus justify his standing in society. And for as long as victories and foreign glories

continued to flow, it was a heady message which the vast majority of
soldiers seemed ready to accept. After all, in Napoleon's own career they
could see evidence of the triumph of talent over seniority, and an
undiluted commitment to the military and to soldiering. His Corsican
origins were not undistinguished – his family belonged to the Corsican
nobility, owning three houses, a mill, a small estate and some vineyards,
but that in itself would not have sufficed to bring him to prominence
in the army of the Ancien Régime.[35] But he had captured the imagination
of the nation by his leadership and his military exploits in the service
of a succession of governments – from the capture of federalist Toulon
in the name of the Jacobin republic in 1793, through the famous 'Whiff
of Grapeshot' with which he scattered the Parisian popular movement
in 1795, to the military adventures of the Directory and the political
coup d'état that was Brumaire. And if Brumaire today is usually presented
as an act of political manipulation by Napoleon, who, though brought
in as the military wing of an insurrection masterminded by Sieyès, then
turned the tables on the politicians and seized power for himself, in his
proclamation to the French people he talked very differently about his
and the army's role. On his return to Paris, he declared, he had been
courted by politicians of all sides, united only by the belief that the
constitution was moribund and unable to save the people. He refused,
he said, to be the man of any party; but 'I believed it my duty to my
fellow-citizens, to the soldiers perishing in our armies, to the national
glory bought with their blood, to accept the command'. This was a
language which the army could appreciate, as was Napoleon's claim, in
the same proclamation, that he had acted with all the 'zeal' of a 'soldier
of liberty', a soldier, moreover, who was still dedicated to the ideals of
the French Republic.[36] At this point Napoleon might ostensibly have
been speaking to the civilian population; but he was also addressing the
army and doing what he so often did well, identifying with the soldiers
and with their routine, day-to-day sufferings.

Napoleon had, of course, an unparalleled gift for communication, and
he was at his best when communicating with soldiers. If he knew how
to praise and to flatter, to acknowledge publicly his debt to the armies
and his recognition of what they had achieved, he also knew how to
talk to his troops, to inspire their loyalty, to share their experiences and
identify with them on long marches or in the heat of battle. In return

they appreciated that recognition, the feeling that their Emperor understood their problems and shared their fatigues; and they continued to
regard him as one of their own, as a French soldier who had emerged
from the ranks and risen to the very highest position of state. In that
sense Bonaparte remained the 'little corporal', a commander who did
not follow so many others in distancing himself from those under
his command. The evidence is to be found in the speeches and proclamations he made to his armies, the morale-boosting words of their
Emperor on the eve of battle or on emerging from a particularly arduous
campaign. Through the pages of the *Bulletin de la Grande Armée*, in
particular, he maintained a steady communication with his armies,
always seeking to reinforce the impression, so beloved of Napoleonic
propaganda, that the Emperor was himself a *grognard*, eating the same
food, suffering the same deprivations, sleeping in the midst of their
camps. At daybreak on the morning of the Battle of Jena, for instance,
Napoleon paced from one unit to another, talking to the men, reassuring
them that the Prussians were no more formidable now than the
Austrians had been a year before, when the French had destroyed their
army at Ulm. The fifth issue of the *Bulletin*, dated 15 October 1806,
makes much of the Emperor's power to raise the spirits of his troops;
it notes that during the night he had 'bivouacked in the midst of his
braves'; and it points to his personal role in battle, galloping across from
one part of the battlefield to another to order fresh manoeuvres or to
change formations; at every turn, the paper adds appreciatively, he would
be interrupted by cheers from his own men and by shouts of '*Vive
l'Empereur!*' [37]

Often an issue of the *Bulletin* would take the form of an address to
the soldiers, the text an uplifting call to arms or a statement of the
Emperor's gratitude for their sufferings. 'Soldiers!', it would begin,
and Napoleon's own words would follow, words directed personally
and exclusively to the ranks of the army. They could not but be
impressed, affected and flattered by this personal mode of communication, so very different from that familiar to the armies of the Ancien
Régime or to those of their opponents. They were being asked to
understand that they had a leader who cared for them and who took
the time to address their hopes and their anxieties. Napoleon, according
to this carefully-nurtured conceit, remained one of their own, a soldier

like themselves, above all a man whose experience allowed him to understand their feelings. It was a powerful weapon, an inestimable propaganda benefit for the state, of which two examples may perhaps suffice. On 26 October 1806, from the imperial camp at Potsdam, Napoleon urged on his men in terms which emphasised their quality and hinted at their invulnerability:

> Soldiers! You have put up with shortages and fatigues as courageously as you have shown fearlessness and sang-froid in the midst of battle. You are the worthy defenders of the honour of my crown and of the glory of the French people. For as long as you are driven by that spirit nothing will be able to resist you.[38] *

Even in the depths of the Russian winter, Napoleon's skill in appealing to his troops did not desert him. From his encampment overlooking the Borodino he could still address them in stirring terms:

> Soldiers! This is the battle you have been longing for! Henceforth victory depends on you. It is a victory which we need to win. It will give us copious provisions, good winter quarters, and the prospect of getting home to France quickly. Conduct yourselves as you did at Austerlitz, at Friedland, at Vitebsk, at Smolensk, so that generations far into the future will tell with pride the story of your conduct on this day. May they be able to say of you that 'he was in that great battle fought beneath the walls of Moscow!'[39] †

Typically, Napoleon's words managed to stir their emotions and fuel their self-interest in the same breath: for he knew that the soldiers' thirst for glory was more than matched by their desire for peace and for immediate material comforts.

---

* Soldats! Vous avez supporté les privations et les fatigues avec autant de courage que vous avez montré d'intrépidité et de sang-froid au milieu des combats. Vous êtes les dignes défenseurs de l'honneur de ma couronne et de la gloire du grand peuple. Tant que vous serez animés de cet esprit, rien ne pourra vous résister.

† Soldats! Voici la bataille que vous avez tant désirée! Désormais la victoire dépend de vous: elle nous est nécessaire. Elle nous donnera l'abondance, de bons quartiers d'hiver et un prompt retour dans la patrie. Conduisez-vous comme à Austerlitz, à Friedland, à Vitebsk, à Smolensk, et que la postérité la plus reculée cite avec orgueil votre conduite dans cette journée; que l'on dise de vous, 'Il était à cette grande bataille sous les murs de Moscou!'.

One of the principal differences between the appeals made by the Emperor and those of the French Revolution lies precisely in this immediate and personal quality. For while the Revolution had to speak in the name of ideals, of abstract principles like the nation, or liberty, or the republic, Napoleon could speak directly to his men, appealing as one soldier to another and asking them for a personal commitment. The enemy might be the same – foreigners, princes, despots – but the nature of their own cause was very differently defined. Where once they had fought for their rights as citizens and for the liberties of the French people, honour was now far more openly emphasised, the honour of fighting men and of military units. And if they were still called upon to defend the regime, that regime was far more personal in nature, centred as it was around the person of the Emperor. Their cause, it was implied, was also his cause, their glory his glory. This identification with Napoleon's person grew over time, as the battles became more desperate and the sacrifices he was demanding ever more extreme. Increasingly he spoke as a king to his subjects – he even used the word *roi*, especially after 1809 – but as a king whose legitimacy came from the people, through a personal bond with his subjects that was not predicated on intervening institutions, whether electoral assemblies or parliaments. It reached its highest point at that moment of greatest desperation, during the Hundred Days, when Napoleon was singularly isolated and turned to his soldiers to support him and restore his legitimate authority. In his proclamation of 21 March 1815 he made no attempt to hide the fact that it is his hour of need:

> Soldiers! I came to France with six hundred men because I felt I could count on the love of the people and on the memory of those who had been soldiers. I have not been disappointed in my expectations. Soldiers, I offer you my thanks. The glory of what we have just done belongs entirely to the people and to yourselves; mine lies only in having known you and having appreciated your qualities.*

---

* Soldats! Je suis venu avec six cents hommes en France, parce que je comptais sur l'amour du peuple et sur le souvenir des vieux soldats. Je n'ai pas été trompé dans mon attente. Soldats, je vous en remercie. La gloire de ce que nous venons de faire est toute au peuple et à vous; la mienne se réduit à vous avoir connus et appréciés.

With these words he launched into another call to arms and to new military effort, assuring them that all his officers he counts as friends and making a clarion call to the army. Together, he promised, they would defeat the forces of the Bourbons and chase all the invading forces off French soil.

> The French people and I are counting on you. We do not wish to meddle in the affairs of foreign nations; but woe betide anyone who meddles in ours.[40] *

The soldiers listened because this was a language they wanted to hear, a discourse with which they could relate. But it was also the only language they were allowed to hear, such was the strict regime of censorship which Napoleon had instituted: neither in the ranks nor in civil society did the Emperor allow conflicting views to be expressed, particularly where the progress of the war was concerned. The result was predictable: the immediate decline of the press as a channel of debate or, indeed, of accurate news. Napoleon himself was known to dictate much of the content of the *Bulletin*, and the rest of the newspaper press was allowed to repeat only such information about the war as had appeared in its pages, thus removing at a stroke much of a newspaper's *raison d'être*. All papers were closely scrutinised for any deviation from the party line; they became blandly uncritical, rejoicing in a culture of victory and public happiness; some, indeed, were forcibly merged to make them easier to control. Civilians soon lost interest and treated the press with a guarded distrust, with the result that circulation dropped away and titles fell into extinction. Whereas in 1799 there were still seventy-nine papers published in Paris – and that after years of censorship from the Directory – by 1814 that figure had fallen to a miserly four. The troops who read in the papers about victories on other fronts or by other armies could, if they so chose, be cheered by the assurance of French successes; but the more cynical of them may have paused to ask themselves about the source of the intelligence they were reading, to contrast their own experience

---

* Le peuple français et moi nous comptons sur vous. Nous ne voulons pas nous mêler des affaires des nations étrangères; mais malheur à qui se mêlerait des nôtres.

on the ground with the constant air of celebration which seemed to prevail elsewhere. They could, but the temptation would always be to suspend their disbelief, to join in the celebration both of victory and of the Emperor. The *Bulletin* might be dismissed as the *Menteur*, its triumphalist tone the butt of jokes around the campfire, but that does not necessarily mean that its content was not read with hope and passion. Soldiers wanted to believe it when they were told that the enemy were in flight or that ultimate victory could be achieved with just one final push, one last collective effort. And they were encouraged to put their faith in Napoleon by a whole band of former political leaders who were now reborn as Napoleonic publicists – Roederer speaking to the 'Patriots of 89', Bertrand Barère to former Jacobins, Montlosier to those who had once been royalists. [41] If the *Bulletin* had its censors, it also had able salesmen devoted to promulgating the imperial cause.

Napoleon was not only a master of verbal propaganda and well-directed rhetoric. He was also keenly aware of the power of the visual, and he followed the initiative of the revolutionaries in commissioning artists to portray the splendour of his military achievement in both painting and statuary. His impact can be felt in the monumental legacy of his years in the streets and squares of Paris, from the Châtelet to the Pyramides and Concorde – and to the Louvre. Indeed, the French history rooms of the Louvre provide an object-lesson in the use of art in support of his regime, since nowhere is this message more clearly driven home than in the history painting of the period, the great canvases of Gros and David, Boilly and Géricault, which linger on those voluptuous images of military splendour that helped to cement Napoleon's role in France's *mission civilisatrice* and to create the lasting legend of the *Grande Armée*.[42] Artists were directed as to what themes to depict and were rewarded from the public purse, with large canvases commanding the very considerable sum of 12,000 francs. Indeed, Vivant Denon, as director of the museum, received an annual budget from Napoleon with the explicit brief to commission or purchase war paintings for the Louvre.[43] It comes as no surprise, therefore, that the themes of the paintings he acquired can seem remorselessly military, celebrating triumphs over the enemy, recording magnificent and exotic conquests, and, most especially, admiring the leadership of Napoleon himself, while underlining the strong personal ties that existed between the Emperor and his men.

The single year of 1806 saw a number of memorable works displayed at the Salon, each depicting the Emperor in one of his favoured military roles, leading his men, comforting them, inspiring them. They include some of the best-known historical canvases of the Napoleonic era – works like *Napoléon reçoit la reddition de la ville d'Ulm* (Berthon); *La mort du Général Desaix en présence du Général Bonaparte sur le champ de bataille de Marengo* (Jean Broc); *Le Général Bonaparte saluant les troupes lors du passage du col du Grand Saint-Bernard* (Thévenin); and *La bataille des Pyramides remportée par l'armée française sur les troupes de Mourad Bey* (Lejeune).[44] Elsewhere it was Napoleon's compassion that was portrayed, the image of an Emperor who personally shared the sufferings of his men. Perhaps the most famous illustration of this was Gros's painting of the Emperor visiting the plague victims at Jaffa, which shows a tender and caring figure surrounded by the sick and dying, reaching out his hands to them in a gesture of healing, administering to all alike regardless of rank or birth.[45] Napoleon, art historians seem agreed, had little artistic taste as such; but he was fascinated by the detail of a work, took a personal interest in judging the Paris *salons*, and rewarded artists in whom he saw especial merit. He understood the potential of art to project his imperial image and to win over public opinion; he followed the Bourbons in seeking to give artists work, and made sure that they worked for him. Napoleon used art to emphasise his greatness and to provide a visual record of his military triumphs. 'Bonapartist artists of the future might dwell on the retreat from Moscow or Napoleon's farewell to the Guard in the Cour des Adieux at Fontainebleau. His artists did no such thing – he was unmoved by pathos.' [46]

The most important question, of course, is whether such propaganda was effective. Did the young soldiers who manned the revolutionary and Napoleonic battalions respond to these appeals, and were they swayed by the stirring language used? Did the image peddled by Napoleon's artists of a kind, concerned Emperor sharing the hardships of his men cut any ice with the soldiers themselves? There was no necessary clash of interest here. After all, the young conscript had every reason to share in official optimism if he possibly could. He was young, generous of spirit, often fiercely patriotic, and, however apprehensive or fearful he might be, he was facing what on one level was the greatest adventure of a fairly predictable life. First letters home, when the young man had joined his unit and got to know something of his new comrades, were often particularly imbued with such optimism. And when they involve a discussion of actual fighting, they could present the progress of the war in almost surreal terms. Take this description, written by Pierre Robin, a young soldier from Riom in the Puy-de-Dôme, of his first taste of action near Collioure:

I've been with the Armée des Pyrénées-Orientales for no more than a fortnight, and the day after I got here we attacked the enemy and made him bite the dust with the result that he was forced to evacuate all the forts he held and had to leave his cannon behind; we took around two or three thousand prisoners.[47] *

It was a proud boast, the more easily made in that Napoleon's army commanders busied themselves spreading confidence and disinformation in equal measure, encouraging their men to believe in themselves and in the likelihood of imminent victory. It is clear, too, that many of the young soldiers desperately wanted to believe this propaganda, for, if true, it suggested that the war would soon be over and that they would once again be able to return to their homes and their families. With the passage of time, of course, this desire for peace would become one of the dominant themes of their letters, a desire for peace that was often more urgently expressed than any desire for glory. By Year V, for instance, in the Army of Italy, the signing of the peace was so ardently desired precisely because it was seen as leading to demobilisation. When that did not happen, when it became clear that the truce was to bring no release from soldiering, Alexandre Ladrix, a soldier since the Year II, made no secret of his own disillusionment. Any joy which the prospect of peace had conjured up had quickly evaporated. From Treviso he wrote with obvious bitterness:

* Il n'y a que quinze jours que je suis arrivé à l'armée des Pyrénées Orientales et le lendemain que j'arrivai nous avons attaqué l'ennemi et lui avons fait mordre la poussière d'une si belle manière qu'il a été obligé d'évacuer toutes ses redoutes et n'a pu emmener ses pièces de canon et en avons fait environ deux ou trois mille prisonniers.

Finally we are enjoying peace, but we enjoy it so little that we would prefer still to be at war. Then you only die once, instead of . . .[48] *

At that point his sentence trails away, poignantly incomplete.

* Nous jouissons enfin de la paix, mais nous en jouissons si mal que nous préférerions avoir la guerre, on n'y meurt qu'une fois, au lieu que . . .

4

The Voice of Patriotism

That the men who fought in the name of the Revolution and Empire did so with varying degrees of patriotism and political commitment is hardly cause for surprise. They were in a very real sense a cross-section of the youth of France. They had not been hand-picked for their patriotism or for their revolutionary zeal, except in as far as those who had volunteered back in 1791 or 1792 did select themselves, many after a period of apprenticeship in the National Guard. But they were exceptions, and they constituted a very small proportion of the men who were called upon to fight. The vast majority were conscripts who had taken no part in the decision to leave their family and their village, and who had little reason to see soldiering as an adventure to be savoured. A substantial number, indeed, served for money, as replacements for men who had been designated by ballot; they were in the main poor, without a trade or right to land, men who were rather isolated from their communities, and who could be lured or cajoled or bullied into accepting payment to leave for the armies. Before their call-up it may be safely assumed that those who became soldiers were no more patriotic or committed to republican ideals than the next man; they may merely have had insufficient savings to buy themselves out of service, or been less blessed with fortune when they went to draw their number in the ballot on the village green.

One might expect, therefore, that in their political opinions the soldiers would have ranged across the whole spectrum of political sensitivity, from extreme radicalism to entrenched royalism. And so it proved. The army did attract political radicals, especially during the months of the Jacobin Republic, when some generals, like Lavalette in the Armée du Nord, were chosen for their advanced *sans-culotte* views, and then proceeded to surround themselves with radical activists from the Paris sections. Lavalette knew these men well: he had himself been a sectional radical and had commanded the battalion of the Section des Lombards in the capital; and he was a close friend of Ronsin, the commander of the Parisian *armée révolutionnaire*.[1] In contrast, a few revolutionary generals dabbled in royalist and counter-revolutionary politics, most infamously, perhaps, Dumouriez in 1793 and Pichegru in 1796. And on that second occasion, despite frantic efforts by the republicans, we know that royalist propaganda made considerable inroads among the troops, especially in the Army of the Rhin-et-Moselle where it was blamed for a significant number of desertions.[2] But these were exceptions. In the writings of the mass of the troops there is little to suggest that they resisted the siren voices of political conformity, or showed any hostility to the endless stream of patriotic propaganda to which they were subjected. Seditious remarks and direct criticisms of the new political order were few and far between. As a body the army accepted its new place within the body politic. Army morale depended on it, and in turn the lives of the troops depended on the state of morale. In a sense, therefore, whatever their political views may have been back in civilian life, once men had been incorporated in their units, national duty and individual self-interest could be seen to correspond to a very high degree.

That is not to imply, of course, that the day-to-day letters of the troops were bulging with patriotic outpourings or ideological sermons. They were not, and for the very good reason that politics was not one of the staples of most family discussions, and political education was very far from the minds of most soldiers when they found time to write a few lines home. Even in the most politically aware families – and some soldiers were the sons of educated bourgeois active in their local political society – the moment was scarcely propitious. Occasional glimmers of patriotic pride in the cause for which they are fighting or expressions of contempt for shirkers or for *émigrés* are about as far as most men went in their personal correspondence from the front. To the historian these admissions are all the more significant in that they are so rare, buried in mounds of seemingly routine complaints about the deprivations they are suffering and the fatigues they have to endure. Statements of political loyalty were not casually or lightly made in routine correspondence. They represented a deliberate commitment, an expression of the extraordinary.

But not all the thoughts of the soldiers were consigned to private letters or personal diaries. For political opinions, in particular, it might have seemed more apposite to write to public authorities, to have their feelings recorded in the public sphere and participate actively where there was public debate. For much of the revolutionary period, indeed, soldiers' views were actively solicited as political leaders tried to impress on the troops that they enjoyed new status as citizens and that their views would be listened to with respect. And if in 1793 soldiers were encouraged to attend political societies and in this way contribute to policy-making, the process of consultation started much earlier. In 1789, for instance, officers and NCOs could express their ideas in memoirs and addresses to the King, the first time soldiers had been given the opportunity to convey their grievances and their ideas for military reform. It was a significant moment, especially for the non-commissioned officers, the *bas-officiers* of the old line army, who rushed to take advantage of the opportunity they had been given, suggesting a string of practical reforms which would improve morale and be consistent with the new principles of the Revolution.[3] Soldiers recognised, of course, that there must be differences between themselves and civilians, that once in the army men did not and could not continue to exercise the whole panoply of civil rights that had been granted to others. But that did not mean that they should be debarred from enjoying any of the fruits of the new political order, since, as the troops repeatedly insisted, citizenship was an ideal which had clear implications for the army as well. Nor did it imply that they should be content with some inferior status, subject to arbitrary or brutal punishments or left at the mercy of the whims of the officer class.

The *bas-officiers* emphasised their patriotism even as they explained the depth of their grievances. They were proud men, fiercely patriotic and convinced of the worth of their role as soldiers, resentful of poor pay and harsh discipline, but determined to go on serving France. As expressed by the Régiment d'Infanterie of Aunis, all that they were asking was that the country recognise the extent of its debt to the soldiers and grant them the rights with which their status as citizens endowed them.

Every French citizen is born free: he who sacrifices his individual liberty, and even his life, for the liberty of all, for the security of their lives and properties, and for the glory of his country, that man becomes a soldier. So recognise that his country has contracted certain obligations towards him. These obligations concern his personal existence and the respect which is due to him. These are vital matters which have been virtually ignored in the past; it is time to put that right and to give the soldier back his basic rights.[4] *

Though many of the addresses expressed the grievances of men unable to gain the promotion they felt their talents deserved, they did so in terms which expressed their faith in the army and in the new order which promised so much. They asked that pointless, repetitive chores and training routines should be abandoned, all those 'abusive and oppressive *corvées* which have no military value' (Normandy). They wanted the authorities to avoid harsh and arbitrary discipline in the armies, noting that in other countries when this has been tried 'they have by that odious discipline sapped gallantry, brought on despondency and destroyed the generous enthusiasm and sense of national honour which have been the characteristics of the French soldier' (Forez). And of course they sought an improvement in their own status. Non-commissioned officers should cease to be picked by officers, whose approach was marked by the bestowal of favours, but should be chosen by their peers, or by their immediate superiors, or on the basis of their years of service. Certain promotions in each branch of the army should be reserved for *bas-officiers*. They felt that they deserved to be given more responsibility, given that they had an intimate knowledge of the character and capacity of every man in their company. And if they needed more money in recognition of their fighting qualities, they also wanted access to honours on the same basis as their superiors. One memoir (from the Régiment du Limousin) even suggested that a special medal should be struck, distinct from those awarded to officers, which would honour the bravery and the originality of non-commissioned officers.

---

* Tout citoyen français naît libre. Celui qui fait le sacrifice de sa liberté individuelle, même de sa vie, pour la liberté de tous, pour la sûreté de leurs jours, de leurs propriétés, et pour la gloire de la patrie, devient soldat. Dis-lors la patrie contracté [sic] d'obligations envers lui. Ces obligations portent sur son existence personnelle, sur la considération qui lui est due. Ces deux points si essentiels ont été presque nuls jusqu'à ce jour. Il est temps d'y remédier, et de faire rentrer le soldat dans ses droits.

Addresses of this kind were mainly restricted to the opening months of the Revolution, when ideas of citizenship were still novel to soldiers and the Assembly was anxious to canvass military opinion. In later years a more suitable destination for patriotic or revolutionary outpourings was the municipal council or the Jacobin club of a man's home town, where his letter could be read out and applauded, and the soldier's qualities given public recognition. Some had little choice but to report back to their clubs, since they had been kitted out for war by the generosity of club members and owed it to them to report on the progress they had made. Others, however, wished to make a statement about their principles or to share with their fellow-revolutionaries some of their army experiences. These often dated from the first months of service, when the young men in uniform were, quite genuinely, volunteers who felt moved to communicate their enthusiasm to others back home. From their unit at Carvin, near Lens, a number of soldiers, including their captain and quartermaster, wrote a patriotic address in October 1791 to the Jacobins in Bar-sur-Aube, the club to which they had all belonged back home. The tone was deeply reassuring. They eagerly informed their friends that they were now on the Belgian frontier; they had not as yet seen real action, but they had picked up two Austrian deserters, which they had found rather exciting. The Austrian soldiers had, they recounted, abandoned 'the cause of the tyrants' to enrol in the French army 'beneath the banners of liberty'; they informed them that desertions were frequent in the Austrian army, that whole units had passed over to the French side. In this period of phoney war, before any actual fighting had started, the atmosphere was light-hearted, akin to that of a popular festival or feast day. The troops were received cordially wherever they went, feted and offered drink. A deputation of local Jacobins had come to greet them when they arrived, and generous toasts were drunk. Some, indeed, had joined political clubs in the towns where they were garrisoned, and all declared that they wanted to keep in regular contact with the popular society in Bar. For the moment soldiering contained at least an element of fun. 'We were all the worse for drink; it was then that we realised how true it is that it is a sweet and glorious thing to die for one's country.'[5]

Sometimes public correspondence of this kind had a rather harder edge to it, as their discourse assumed the customary tropes of Jacobin denunciation. In November 1793, for instance, Antoine Chatelain from Avallon (Yonne), a lieutenant with the first artillery battalion of Paris and a man of considerable political education, wrote to the municipal council of his home town in terms that were clearly intended to be savoured by a wider public. He swears that never will he dishonour his countrymen. If he should die in battle he commends his wife and his son to their care, asking particularly that they watch out lest aristocrats torment them or prey on them. Chatelain, it is clear, not only glowed with civic virtue; he also harboured deep hatred for all nobles and counter-revolutionaries, and his tone was much more redolent of a public address than of a personal letter. They have been warned that the war will be bloody: 'I promise you, he boasts, that I am no more frightened that I was when I went to sing mass at Saint-Lazare'. What led him to fight with greater determination was the fact that the nobles were supporting the hated Austrians, and that the local aristocrats from his region were to be counted among them. 'The notorious rascal of a Prince Louis is also with the army', he wrote; 'he had flattered himself that he would come to dine in his castle at Saverne because he was formerly seigneur there, but we taught him that he should never leave his guests out of his calculations.'[6] If the idea that a former noble could return freely to his family seat to dine struck Chatelain as an intolerable insult to the people, he was not alone. The sight of aristocrats and priests freely moving around in the regions to which they were posted surprised and disappointed many of the more radical recruits, and again their letters were quoted with favour by their local clubs, which fully understood their propaganda value among civilians.[7]

Public correspondence could impress by its heroism as much as by the political venom it conveyed. Thus when the Jacobin club of Agen read a letter from one of its members, a captain in the first battalion of the Lot-et-Garonne, describing the manner of their victory over the Austrians, it immediately ordered that two thousand copies be printed and distributed. For the letter not only told of the material contribution of local troops to the advance of the Army of the Sambre-et-Meuse and provided a vignette of interest to local people, though in itself that was a rare enough occurrence. It also provided an uplifting story of personal heroism to warm its readers' hearts. Faced with Austrian fire, the battle had been slipping away from the French and morale was low. The young drummer boys, in particular, became seized with panic to the point where their playing became wholly inaudible, when their drum-major, one Batifolie, turned his back on the enemy and ordered them to make their drums sound out. 'Don't abandon me', he told them; 'the first man to break rank will be punished; sound the charge; you will emerge victorious or you will die at my side. If you are afraid of bullets, then my body is here to ward them off.' His words, he believed, had an instant effect: they shook new life into the musicians who sounded the charge as they had been ordered, and the French attack resumed with more vigour than before. Before long the Austrians had been put to flight.[8]

It was not only to clubs and municipal authorities that soldiers were encouraged to write during the Revolution, since the spirit of openness and *franchise* demanded that the views of the humblest recruit should be heard and listened to. Soldiers could write to newspapers, which welcomed the opinions of ordinary infantrymen as much as those of their officers. But, once again, these letters were public documents, written to be read by a wide and often diffuse audience, and that inevitably determined their tone and content. Local papers in a man's home town would print accounts of patriotism and courage, or news of the army's exploits in faraway places, accounts that benefited from a sense of the exotic or picturesque or which served to reassure the relatives of other young men who craved news of their experiences in the military. Letters printed in the military press were often more interesting, since these were written with other soldiers in mind, providing their readers with a view of the army from below, a view that could be digested alongside the more official line followed by the editor. In the *Argus du Département du Nord*, for instance, the self-styled *Ami Jacques*, around 30 per cent of the material included in its pages took the form of news from below – addresses from the troops, letters from individual soldiers, accounts of individual experiences.[9] This was deemed to be popular with the men, since these texts were written in their imagery and their language, in stark contrast to the tone of official sources like communiqués from generals and addresses from deputies on mission sent out from the Convention. Inclusion of opinions expressed from below was typical of the new generation of papers which appeared after 1792, addressed to the literate infantryman with views of his own who wanted to be informed directly and succinctly and who was justifiably suspicious of news fed to him from those in authority.[10]

That does not mean, of course, that the opinions were printed randomly or that papers were giving over their pages to an open forum or a vigorous debate. Usually the press was concerned to maintain control and to back up discipline in the ranks; the soldiers' own voices were used to add potency to the editorial line. For an example of a military newspaper which regularly printed soldiers' views, one could do worse than turn to the *Journal de l'Armée des Côtes de Cherbourg*, published in Caen by Derché between August and December 1793, and limited in its distribution to the men of one single army. Here the purpose was clearly educative, since the soldiers cited were all enthusiastic republicans and most of their contributions had started life as speeches at the Caen Jacobins. The editor had no interest in stimulating genuine debate. He was a committed Jacobin, keen to denounce any sign of moderation and to encourage a strong Jacobin view of patriotism and virtue; and the soldiers he introduced to his readers all shared his opinions. Thus on 9 August great prominence was given to the words of a 'volunteer of the First Battalion of Paris', who had addressed the Jacobins in Caen in the uncompromising language of the Paris *sans-culotte* he undoubtedly was. 'He said that the greatest crime of the inhabitants of Caen was that they elected only the rich and powerful, former nobles and priests who, far from serving the common cause, did all that they could to destroy it. He accused the citizens of the town of rank cowardice.'[11] Elsewhere in Derché's columns volunteers who were quoted singing patriotic songs then saw the words of their songs printed in the paper so that others could emulate their fine example. The soldiers, in other words, were not independent actors here; they were part of a carefully prepared educative strategy. On 20 August, for instance, the editor published the words of a volunteer who had been on the frontier since the very start of the war, who explained to his readers that it was their duty to ensure that public opinion was soundly based since in wartime 'one patriot is worth ten aristocrats'. As on other occasions, the soldier's contribution was carefully gauged to offer support to the patriotic editorial line, to encourage obedience and boost morale among the troops.

If public correspondence from the armies could be depended upon to offer support and succour to the regime, it does not follow that the soldiers' private writings, whether diaries, memoirs, letters or *carnets de route*, necessarily adopt a conflicting tone. Many of the troops were fiercely devoted to the national cause, and that devotion comes across graphically in their writings. The idealised portrayal of the soldier which we find in both Jacobin and Napoleonic imagery cannot be dismissed as pure invention, for among their letters we find repeated declarations of faith by men deeply committed to the ideal for which they were fighting. The attitude of Joliclerc, a peasant boy from the Jura, is typical in this regard, his ardent patriotism underpinning his entire approach to fighting. He even pointed out to his parents that his life and faculties belonged not to him, nor yet to his family, but to the nation; and he urged them not to shed any tears for him, not to lament the day when he had left to join his regiment. Rather, he explained, they should rejoice, since 'either you will see me return bathed in glory or you will have a son who is a worthy citizen of France who knows how to die for the defence of his country'.[12] Underlying this bravado, of course, was also a fear of defeat and of the fate that awaited men at the hands of the enemy should they be taken prisoner. For the propaganda offensive that had assailed them not only created an idealised picture of the French soldier; it also portrayed the enemy as perfidious and ruthless, burning French villages and putting civilians to the sword. And woe betide any French soldier who fell into their hands. In 1792 Favier, from the town of Montluçon in the Allier, explained to his parents that the Austrians were trying to terrorise the soldiers as well as the civilian population in the east. 'Volunteers who are captured bearing arms are hanged. The monsters think they will frighten us by such means, but they are mistaken, we shall merely do our utmost to prevent them from taking us alive.'[13]

Many of the revolutionary and imperial soldiers did show in their writings a deep commitment to the cause or to the *patrie*: patriotism, after all, was one of the qualities with which they were increasingly imbued and educated. There were numerous expressions of pride in these letters, pride in the army, and pride in the country for which they were fighting. Patriotism could easily be created by service, by fighting alongside others in the name of France, and it could spread to those who were not born in France. Conscripts recruited in Belgium, in Holland and in Italy were not immune to the appeal of *la Grande Nation*.

Thus Jean-Joseph Pottier, a young peasant from Jalhay near Liège, could write in committed terms of his service in the Napoleonic armies: 'Don't worry about my fate. I shall perhaps live more happily and with greater satisfaction than the richest inhabitant of our commune. I have been in great danger, and I shall perhaps find myself there again. But if I die in service, I shall be dying for my glory and for my motherland.'[14] The most committedly Jacobin among the soldiers shared the outlook of the political leadership, underlining their commitment to the Revolution and seeking evidence of treason in high places to explain the unthinkable. French losses and defeats had to have a cause other than the failures of the soldiers or the inadequacy of their cause. Hence their preferred explanation was that their commanding officers had been bought or corrupted by the enemy, subverted by La Fayette or Rochambeau, or were in fact covert counter-revolutionaries, biding their time to undermine the Republic. When their lines were almost overwhelmed at Landau, for instance, one volunteer from the Indre explained that the traitors had been uncovered at the very last moment, that disaster had been averted only because 'the Supreme Being unmasked their crimes'.[15] For many republican soldiers, indeed, the Dumouriez Affair marked a real turning point, the moment when they realised the need for vigilance in the face of treason from both outside and inside the army. Hence the zeal with which club members pursued the peccadilloes of their commanders and exposed alleged incidents of treason for investigation and punishment. Indeed, the trial and punishment of officers was one of the characteristics of this period which left a deep impression on the men in the ranks. When, for instance, a cavalry officer was condemned to death at Perpignan for dereliction of duty in 1794 – he had allowed fifty of his men to be taken prisoner in Spain – he was guillotined in front of the entire army. Jean Massip, a young soldier from Saint-Ybars, was among those who witnessed his execution. 'We were', he told his father without any apparent emotion, 'assembled around the guillotine, some twelve thousand of us, to see him beheaded, but it was soon over, both the execution and our thoughts on the matter.'[16]

    With patriotism went a certain streak of optimism, as the young French soldiers – especially those who had volunteered to save the Revolution – convinced themselves that the cause in which they believed was inherently just and for that reason must necessarily emerge victorious.

Anything else would be inconceivable, an affront to all their dreams of bringing freedom to others and creating a better, freer society. They had, after all, rushed to volunteer back in 1791 or 1792, pressing their claims to be chosen to represent their department, demanding the honour of being incorporated in the first battalion chosen for active service. And once selected, then, in the words of one officer who had first joined as a volunteer in the Lot-et Garonne, 'it was even more flattering to our self-esteem to be persuaded to be among the very first to march against the enemy'.[17] Of course, such optimism was more likely to come from soldiers engaged in victorious campaigns who could look forward in hope to the moment when peace would be restored. Gabriel Bourguig-non wrote home to his parents in Châteauroux in 1794 flushed by recent successes and confident of more to come. 'The Republic is victorious and will continue to be victorious', he wrote; 'we would rather die a hundred deaths than cede an inch of ground to the enemy. Our cause is just; we shall defend it as we have always defended it, down to the last drop of our blood.'[18] Etienne Meunier, a barrel-maker's son from Grand-Charonnes near Paris, was sufficiently impressed by the scale of the republican victory over the Vendeans at Savenay that he convinced himself that the war would soon be over and that he would be returning home to his family. He had the smell of victory in his nostrils, and never seemed to doubt the outcome.

> I hope to be back with you in early spring, then we will be able to rejoice and to sing *Ça ira* together … You will not fail to go to see my little boy, you will give him a shotgun and send him out to join me, for he must be big enough now to come and observe the Republic in action.[19] *

Such enthusiasm was usually a product of political belief, but optimism was also aroused by a sudden change in military fortunes, by the capture of abundant booty, or by the desertion to their side of enemy soldiers. In the depths of the frozen winter of 1793, a young soldier from Auxerre, Barthélemy Lemain, told how every day deserters were crossing over to join their army. Their arrival sustained his own faith in the Revolution

---

* J'espère vous voir pour le commencement du printemps, là, nous nous réjouirons et nous chanterons, *Ça ira* … Vous ne manquerez pas d'aller voir mon fillot, vous lui donnerez un fusil et vous l'enverrez vers moi, car il doit être assez grand pour être très observateur de la République.

and gave him hope that the war might soon be over. As he wrote home
to his parents, with just a slight twist in the tail,

> They come across the river which is frozen over, because they no longer
> accept to be slaves, they want liberty; we are hoping that our troubles will
> end this year and that we shall emerge covered in the laurels of victory to
> share them with our father and mother, our brothers and sisters, and our
> mistresses ... [20] *

These were the sentiments of the true believer in the Revolution, of
a man whose confidence was bolstered by his belief. They were also
those of a young soldier in the early stages of the campaign, who could
still dream of his cause being triumphant, and whose idealism was not
yet dulled by war and disease, by the fear and nausea of battle, by the
inexorable marches and fatigues which made up daily life. When the war
was first declared many shared the eagerness to be off, to play their part
in a great national crusade. For some that eagerness had its roots in
ideology, for others in impatience, or in a simple desire to leave home
and see the world. 'How many times', exclaimed Sergeant Fricasse in his
youthful naivety,

> had I heard through the papers that our army had been beaten and was being
> pushed back on all sides! I burned with impatience to see things which I
> simply could not believe. You will say that it was innocence that made me
> think in that way, but ... it seemed to me that if I had been present, the
> damage would not have been so great. I would not have said that I was a
> better soldier than my fellow Frenchmen, but I did feel an upsurge of courage,
> and I thought that, with courage, I could achieve a great deal.[21] †

---

* Ils passent la rivière qui est prise par la gelée, ils viennent se rendre libres
et ne veulent plus être esclaves, ils veulent la liberté, et nous espérons que
notre mal finira cette année-là et que nous nous en retournerons couverts de
lauriers les partager avec nos père et mère, frères et soeurs, et nos maîtresses.
† Combien de fois j'avais entendu, par les papiers, la nouvelle que notre armée
française avait été repoussée et battue partout! Je brûlais d'impatience de voir
par moi-même des choses qu'il m'était impossible de croire. Vous direz que
c'était l'innocence qui me faisait penser ainsi ... Il me semblait que si j'avais
été présent, le mal n'aurait pas été si grand. Je ne me serais pas dit meilleur
soldat que mes compatriotes, mais je me sentais du courage, et je pensais que,
avec du courage, on vient à bout de bien des choses.

Another young soldier, François Vigo-Roussillon, took time in his diary to try to explain his eagerness to enlist, an eagerness, which, he acknowledges, might seem like naivety. He was only eighteen at the time, a young man from Montpellier who had never previously left home and who found leaving very difficult. And yet he felt drawn by a complex mixture of emotions, pride and shame, duty and comradeship.

> I was feeling a kind of shame not to be part of the contingent when one of my closest friends, a sergeant-major in the First Volunteer Battalion of the Hérault, suggested to me that I should join him in that unit, which was serving with the Army of Italy. I accepted his offer with pleasure, already enthused by the idea of going to war in such a famous country.[22] *

If he had difficulty persuading his mother to let him go, his problems may have been less than those experienced by others, for he came from a military family and his elder brother was already in uniform. Peer pressure was clearly difficult for young men like Vigo-Roussillon to resist, as is often the case when war is declared and patriotic rhetoric helps kindle youthful generosity of spirit. The same phenomenon was to be in evidence in the opening months of the American Civil War, when again men rushed to enlist, optimistic that their cause would prove victorious and that they would shortly return in triumph to their families, while youngsters left behind found their lot almost intolerable. Going to war in 1861 was seen as a community crusade, a cause for celebration, a 'rollicking experience'.[23] For many of the young volunteers of 1791 and 1792 war presented itself in a very similar light, as a glamorous adventure in which their generation had a duty to take part.

With the passage of time, that glamour inevitably wore thin as the realities of soldiering were better understood and the army began to assert its own values. For a minority, it is true, faith in revolutionary and republican principles remained strong, and more than compensated for the dangers they faced and the discomforts they endured. This was particularly true among that select band of volunteers who had started

---

* J'éprouvais une espèce de honte de ne pas en faire partie, quand un de mes amis intimes, sergent-major du 1er bataillon volontaire du département de l'Hérault, me proposa de servir dans ce corps qui était à l'Armée d'Italie. J'acceptai cette offre avec plaisir, enthousiasmé d'avance d'aller faire la guerre dans un pays si célèbre.

their military careers not in the army but with local units of the National Guard. Pierre Cohin, for example, was the son of a small merchant in the village of Bollême in the Orne, literate, ambitious and committed to revolutionary principles; he had rallied to the Revolution in 1789 and was rapidly incorporated into the Guard in his village. When war broke out he volunteered for active service with the Armée du Nord, and his early letters home reflect unwavering support for the revolutionary cause. The war, he proudly told his father in 1792, 'is not a war between king and king, nor yet between nation and nation. It is the war of liberty against despotism. There is no doubt that we shall triumph. A nation that is just and free is invincible.' 24 But even Cohin found his idealism sorely strained by long years of war. Like many committed Jacobin soldiers, he could not understand how a revolutionary army could suffer defeat, and rushed to ascribe reverses to treason or to incompetent generals. And as the war dragged on, he became impatient, ceasing to glory in soldiering and lamenting the fact that victory was so long in coming. In spite of his patriotic language, a larger and larger part of his correspondence was devoted to business matters and opportunities for bettering himself. In 1794 he was promoted away from the battlefield to a posting in charge of military supply, a much safer role than that of a volunteer in the ranks and one that brought the promise of rapid wealth. He harboured no regrets: although he remained a convinced republican, republicanism alone was no longer sufficient to provide the motivation for self-sacrifice.

Increasingly, indeed, the enthusiasm which was expressed by revolutionary soldiers was not ideological or to do with the success of the revolutionary regime. Victory was something to be relished for its own sake, for the encouragement it gave to the troops, the confidence they acquired before facing up to their next challenge. Embarking on a campaign which promised to deliver victory was therefore the cause of a special frisson of excitement, as soldiers dreamt of ending the war and with it their own calvary. In the process, many allowed their dreams to distort their sense of reality; in their optimism they would recite what they were told, without question or reservation.25 But there was also a strong sense of military pride in their accounts of the victories they had gained, a sense of relief that they had accomplished their mission as soldiers. This was often mingled with a rather different emotion as they gloried in the colour and bravura of their performance in the field. One soldier from the Indre, Georges-François Gaudrion, could not contain his joy when he described the French army of which he had been a part pushing the enemy back across the Rhine. As he reported the scene from Ingelsheim, 'it was superb to see the light artillery advancing, the artillery pieces in place, the cavalry, hussars, light horse and foot and all the regiments and battalions of infantry'.[26] Sometimes the joys of victory mingled comfortably with the pleasure of exacting retribution after a hard campaign, the rather more ambiguous pleasure of killing which is so often the illicit sub-text of soldiering in modern wars.[27] In their letters some men even admit to slaughtering prisoners in the aftermath of battle, and to doing so without emotion, almost as a matter of routine. Reporting home on the great battle with the English at Quiberon, a soldier with the Armée des Côtes-de-Brest not only took pleasure in the completeness of their victory, but went on to wallow in bloodshed, gloating over the numbers they had bayoneted on the battle-field or shot in prison.[28] Much later, during the Peninsular campaign, a conscript from the Vosges also admitted to enjoying the fruits of victory, though here he identifies the principal enemy they face as the clergy rather than the Spanish army. Monks, in particular, stirred up the local population and turned their hatred on the French; and, when he had the opportunity to exact vengeance, he did not hesitate. 'It was the monks who did most to make war against us', he wrote defiantly, 'we cornered fifty of them in a church, and massacred them all with the points of our bayonets.' This was written with passion and hatred; even in 1808, it might appear, he had lost little of the anticlericalism of the Jacobin republic.[29]

In the main, however, the political tone of soldiers' writings did change over time, losing much of its ideological edge and assuming a greater degree of professional pride, of commitment to the army and to their future within it. This was especially true of many of the officers and NCOs, who increasingly looked to the army for promotion, for provid-ing them with the status and position in society which they sought. In the army of honour which characterised the Directory, the Consulate and Empire, they looked for personal rewards, thirsting for active service as a route to glory and commissioned rank. Some longed for active service as a means of escape – from broken families, parents with whom they enjoyed no rapport, the constant quarrelling of adolescence. Joseph Vachin, for instance, had left his home in Mende in acrimonious circumstances; and had joined a corps of *vélites*, volunteers who were singled out for their promise and were given privileges as trainee-officers; many of them went on serve in the Imperial Guard, or passed into the line regiments as NCOs.[30] Vachin did not disappoint, since he subsequently secured promotion and enjoyed an honourable career in the military that would extend from 1802 until 1816. In the army, he explained to his uncle, he believed that he fitted in well and had a useful role to play; he saw soldiering as a way of making amends for his misspent youth.[31] Another young officer, who at eighteen also chose the *vélites* as a way of avoiding infantry service, explained the pride he felt when, in 1806, he passed out and was assigned to a regiment. He was an educated man, the son of a lawyer in Avignon, who felt honoured to be part of the army, honoured to wear the uniform of an elite regiment. For him honour and glory were not just the stuff of the battlefield. He was too sophisticated to believe all the propaganda which the army disbursed, too realistic not to recognise the reality of battle conditions. Honour, he wrote, was all about professional standing, about the pride he felt in his company and the prestige he enjoyed in the eyes of his fellow-soldiers.

> Pulling on an officer's dress coat, wearing an epaulette, buckling on a sword, these are such grand things when you are eighteen! We were soldiers; a minute later we had become officers! A single word had produced this happy trans-formation. Man always remains a child at heart; throughout his life he has need of baubles; and his self-esteem reflects the clothes he is wearing. Perhaps he is right here, since the people will judge him by his clothing.[32] *

The joys of preening himself, of being admired, of preparing for the formal elegance of the officers' mess – aspects of the Napoleonic officer corps that were immortalised in legend and in the popular prints of the

---

* Endosser un frac d'officier, porter l'épaulette, ceindre une épée, oh! les belles choses quand on a dix-huit ans! Nous étions soldats; un instant après nous devenions officiers! Un mot avait produit cette heureuse métamorphose. L'homme est toujours enfant: à tout âge il a besoin de hochets; il s'estime souvent selon l'habit qu'il porte: il a peut-être raison, puisque la foule juge d'après l'habit.

period – all found their place in his musings. Honour, elegance and gallantry were tightly interwoven.

The lure of promotion lay at the very heart of the soldier's professional pride, and few failed to express their delight at being rewarded with a higher rank. It was a sign of recognition for their military qualities, a symbol of the esteem in which they were held by others. Though some were more sophisticated than others in the ways they expressed their satisfaction, there is no doubting that all relished their moment of glory, regardless of whether they were high-ranking officers or humble infantrymen. The jubilant letter which Pascal Blazy sent to his wife in 1793 shows his excitement at being promoted to corporal. Indeed, he has no wish to discuss anything else, neither her health, nor the state of the crops, nor yet life in the army. For one glorious moment Blazy's whole world is encapsulated in his newly-acquired status. 'My dearest wife', he wrote, 'I was made a corporal five months back. Your good friend Pascal Blazy a corporal! When you write to me you should address the letter to Citizen Pascal Blazy, corporal in the Second Battalion of the Ariège, Captain Azéma's company, garrisoned at Chalange in the Department of Mont-Blanc.'[33] And that was all! Most officers probably described their emotions less naively, but their pleasure at being selected was little different. Promotion might bring with it significant expenses – honour demanded that appearances had to be maintained, in all arms but most especially in the cavalry – but it was the sign of recognition which soldiers all craved. When Alexandre Ladrix was promoted *sous-lieutenant* in Year XI he found it all the more flattering because he felt that his military merit had forced his promotion on reluctant superior officers, believing that his colonel had resisted it since he wanted to reserve the post for 'one of his creatures'.[34] Men might find inspiration in slightly different things, but all revelled in the added responsibility and public honour which promotion implied. When in 1811 a young man from Saint-Vallier (Drôme) learnt that he was to carry out the functions of *brigadier* in his regiment, he could scarcely conceal his joy. With the responsibility came higher pay: he would, he told his father, receive an indemnity of 14 *sols* per day, and – a fact which impressed him deeply – his horse would now be fed by the army.[35] There would doubtless be costs to be borne, and his pay might in the future fade into insignificance. But in savouring the pleasure of his promotion, it is this seemingly small detail that impresses him most deeply.

Besides the honour that came with promotion, and the public recognition of their efforts and qualities, men also aspired to the greater material comforts which officers enjoyed and which most clearly distinguished their lifestyle from that of men in the ranks. Some made no secret of this ambition, even welcoming the renewal of fighting after a truce since active service could open the door to advancement. By the time of the Directory, and particularly by the early years of the nineteenth century, many who had joined as volunteers or as conscripts had become career soldiers, seeking to make their name and their fortune in the military. A good instance is François Avril, who served, first as a lieutenant and then as a captain, in the 36th Line Regiment, from whom we have a virtually unbroken correspondence with his parents from February 1804 until September 1810. Avril comes across as a confident young man, who was generally satisfied with his career and with the benefits which it had bestowed on him, and who saw the army as a profession in which he wished to excel. In 1804 he had just joined his regiment after completing officer-training at the Ecole Militaire, and he was clearly bewitched by all he saw around him. He was not short of money: indeed, he had spent 800 francs on kitting himself out in dress uniform, while the Ecole itself had provided him with his sword, spurs and boots. At Boulogne, he reported, he had been very well received by his superior officers, who had treated him with politeness and respect; he had even visited the general and chatted informally to him, helped, he believed, by the fact that they were both from Normandy, he himself from Saint-Lô and his general from Avranches. As a young officer, he writes with commendable pride of his company and of his own role within it. The vast majority of the troops are old veterans: of the 1600 men in the two regiments to which he is attached, only two hundred are conscripts. And here he now stands, his sword in his hand, commanding twenty seasoned soldiers each with at least twelve years' service, who obey his orders with impressive alacrity. He was, he insisted, in no sense disconcerted by this responsibility; but he was proud, both of his company and of his position within it. And he took evident pleasure in the praises lavished upon him by his superiors.[36]

Careers like Avril's were legion in the armies that fought for the

Directory and for Bonaparte; and the professional pride which the soldiers took in those armies were a major element in military morale. Their fellow-soldiers became their close friends and comrades, sharing the same perils and moments of triumph; there was a warmth in the relationships forged in the regiments which men found difficult to communicate to outsiders, those who had not experienced the same intense emotions. Not all were as personally ambitious as Avril; some found, less dramatically, that an acceptance of a military lifestyle had crept up on them and consumed them, making them increasingly reluctant to contemplate a return to civilian life. What would they do back in their village? How would they settle down in a community where now they had no role? Would they be condemned to poverty and a marginal existence in a community where they had no land, no cottage, no children to support them? These questions worried the soldiers of the Consulate and Empire and many had no answers to offer. Others found that they had no desire to go back, to face the challenges of a civilian life from which they felt increasingly distanced. They had become professional soldiers almost in spite of themselves, spurred by the approval of their comrades, and responsive to the culture of honours and decorations which prevailed in the military. There was a part of them which felt that the army was their home, that their regiment had assumed the role of their family, exuding the warmth of comradeship and substituting for the real families they had left behind. 'I shan't conceal from you', Louis Godeau wrote to his parents in Year IX when he heard that he might soon be allowed to return home, 'that in some ways I should prefer to stay with my unit, where I have realistic ambitions for the future, coming back to see you from time to time.' [37] Godeau here reveals the career ambitions of an officer; but he is also acknowledging the fact that, as the wars dragged on, military and civilian society were slowly edging apart.

Men often spent long years in the military, and their outlook was shaped by these years. Those who ended up with commissions or rose to positions of authority under Napoleon had not always harboured military ambitions. Some, indeed, had been conscripted only reluctantly, but had been converted by the social ambience of the army, or by the taste of victory, or the sense of having found a vocation. Take the case of Jean-Michel Chevalier, born in Versailles in 1780, the son of a gamekeeper. After spending much of the Revolution in Paris, apprenticed to a chemist, he had joined the army as a cavalryman. If we judge his experience by the tone of his memoirs, his early campaigns were dominated by miseries and sufferings and he showed little taste for soldiering. But once in the army, he would make his career there, going on to serve Napoleon in over twenty campaigns. Promotion came, though at first slowly and relatively modestly. In 1808, he got his chance to serve in the elite Imperial Guard, and a series of rapid promotions followed – in 1810 to the rank of *brigadier*, in 1811 to *fourrier*, in 1813 to *maréchal des logis-chef*. After a long career he retired with the rank of lieutenant and ended his days in the Invalides in 1865. Looking back, he accepted that he was not a natural soldier and he recognised the value of his first promotion in inculcating a more responsible, professional attitude. Until then, for seven long years, he had remained in the ranks, and he admitted that

> I had no very pronounced taste for soldiering, on the contrary I had neglected terribly to involve myself in it, which is why I remained a *chasseur* for so long. But now that, almost in spite of myself, I had taken the first step on the ladder, I had to get a bit more involved. When a soldier is not on active duty, when he hasn't a sou to his name and is stationed abroad, it is hard to show any great passion for his trade!'.[38] *

What Chevalier is identifying in these lines is the process of professionalisation as he himself experienced it, the creation of an army whose members took pride in their craft and sought to acquit themselves well in battle, where training and discipline played at least as important a role as patriotism and ideological faith. It was a crucial stage in the development of morale, in the transition from the revolutionary battalions to the *Grande Armée*, from an army inspired by virtue to one imbued with honour.[39] That transition could only happen slowly, as the ideological fervour of the Jacobin Revolution gave way to greater

---

* Jusque-là, je l'avouerai, je n'avais pas pris un goût bien prononcé pour l'état militaire, j'avais au contraire terriblement négligé de m'en occuper, c'est pourquoi je restai si longtemps chasseur. Mais à présent que, presque malgré moi, le premier pas est fait, il faut s'occuper un peu plus du métier. Ma foi, quand un militaire n'est pas en campagne, et qu'il n'a pas le sou et est en pays étranger, il ne peut avoir une grande passion pour le métier.

pragmatism and army officers were chosen for their military capacity rather than for their political ideals. In its spirit as much as in its recruitment the *Grande Armée* that served Napoleon was a fascinating hybrid, the integration of successive attitudes as much as of successive generations, bound together by a culture born of war. It was not the creation of a single levy or a single year's conscription; and that, as one officer later reflected in his memoirs, was what explained its greatness and inspired such loyalty in those who served in it. For Pierre-Auguste Paris, then a sub-lieutenant fighting his first campaign, 1805 marked the high point in the quality of the Napoleonic armies. The secret of its strength, he believed, lay in the amalgamation of very different sorts of troops which composed the army at that formative moment, bringing four distinct types of mentality as well as of military experience. There were still amongst them a number of old soldiers, officers and *bas-officiers*, who had served during the Ancien Régime and who brought firm discipline and a certain technical precision in training. Beside them were volunteers from 1792 and 1793, men now aged between thirty and thirty-six, seasoned by years of service, 'solid, alert, retaining something of their republican enthusiasm'; and conscripts of Year VII, still in uniform years after they had undergone their baptism of fire at Hohen-linden or Marengo. Of the young men from subsequent conscriptions, 'good soldiers, even if they tend to play about and lie a little', Paris observed that they 'shared the same *esprit de corps*' as their elders and that they were well integrated in their units. They were, he added approvingly, 'capable of comporting themselves with honour during the long imperial campaigns'.[40]

Such pride, both in one's company and more generally in the glory of the army, was particularly characteristic of Napoleonic France. It was actively encouraged by a government that sought to promote a system of honours and military values throughout civil society. Officers, in particular, enjoyed new status. Generals were no longer treated with distrust, as had happened under the Jacobins, denounced for their moderate opinions or their noble lineage, or automatically suspected of disloyalty, treason and counter-revolutionary plotting. Their successors in the more professional army of the Consulate and Empire were judged by their tactical acumen rather than condemned for their political failings. They were decorated and honoured by the state in life, praised

and mourned in death. Public festivals and funeral processions were
organised in their honour. Commanders were heroes who would be
rewarded lavishly for their service, with lands and titles, with the ribbon
of the Legion of Honour or the title of marshal of France. And if they
were heroes in the official iconography of the state, so they were to the
soldiers who served under them. In their memoirs, in journals and even
in occasional letters men were wont to betray the pride and the confidence they felt in serving under a famous general or a prominent
Napoleonic marshal.

That pride was particularly strong when they served under Napoleon
himself. Few of his troops seemed to question the cause in which they
were fighting; few expressed any reservations about the proclamation of
the Empire in 1804; and there is no sense that they were tempted to
betray or even criticise their Emperor. It is true that few of their writings
indicate any deep ideological commitment to the principle of Empire,
but they do suggest – on the relatively few occasions when they make
any reference to him at all – an awe of the person of Napoleon. Officers
and men shared that awe: they often seemed to feel a real affection for
the Emperor, and they admitted to being dazzled by his style and his
presence. This affection had its roots in that feeling of proximity, of near
equality, which Napoleon had been keen to nurture. 'I have already told
you', wrote François Avril, 'that the Emperor, surrounded by several of
his marshals, came along the line of our army, and that he was escorted
by a large number of soldiers who had lit straw torches which produced
a magnificent illumination that could be seen from far away.' 41 The
respect which Napoleon inspired in his troops was not all, of course, the
result of torchlight and melodrama or his acute sense of the theatrical.
He understood what motivated soldiers and did not hesitate to play to
their self-interest, granting his men the honours they craved, including
the coveted Legion of Honour; appearing at the front to review his troops
in person; and never forgetting the material concerns that were so
dominant in the ranks. Avril, who was a dedicated Bonapartist, was
touched by Napoleon's evident concern for their welfare, by the extent
to which the Emperor himself became involved in matters of detail when
his soldiers' wellbeing was at stake. In March 1806 he noted how

> We have observed with the greatest interest the tender care taken by His
> Majesty to improve the lot of four or five thousand warriors charged with

the task of defending the integrity of French territory, providing them with bread for their soup and with a half ration of meat in peacetime, which has the effect of raising their pay by over a third, and which makes us hope that His Majesty will not forget the officer corps whom the Emperor of Russia appreciated so much at Austerlitz.[42] *

Above all, however, Napoleon was appreciated for his tactical prowess. He was perceived by his men as being a brilliant commander, a general who could lead them to victory and whose qualities in the field helped offset the army's own shortcomings. It was this, more than anything, that explains the apparent affection in which he was held and the pride and passion which his presence evoked. Vigo-Roussillon, like Avril a young officer setting out on a military career in which he rose to the rank of colonel, admits in his journal that, when they were first introduced to Bonaparte, the Army of Italy was scarcely overwhelmed by his physical presence, adding that some of the troops concluded from this that he was not as talented as the more imposing officers they were accustomed to see in command. But such reservations did not last long as the quality of Napoleon's generalship rapidly won over the army. As a battle commenced, Bonaparte would ride up and plunge immediately into action, stimulating heroic efforts from the troops and helping through his vision on the battlefield to offset what Vigo-Roussillon admits to have been a lack of tactical sophistication on the part of the French army.[43] Officers and soldiers alike were filled with admiration; Napoleon's stock with his army had been established and would follow him from campaign to campaign.

It is perhaps significant that praise for the Emperor was not confined to the writings of his officers. Ordinary soldiers sometimes paused to express admiration for him or to remark on the pride they had felt when in his presence. Being inspected by the Emperor would be commented on; while even being on the same battlefield might be deemed worthy of mention. Of course the troops were encouraged to indulge

* Nous avons vu avec le plus vif intérêt la tendre sollicitude de Sa Majesté pour améliorer le sort de 4 à 500,000 Braves chargés du soin de faire respecter l'intégrité du sol français en les gratifiant du pain de soupe et d'une demi-ration de viande en temps de paix, ce qui revient à plus d'un tiers en sus de solde, ce qui nous fait espérer que Sa Majesté n'oubliera point le corps d'officiers que l'Empereur de Russie a si bien apprécié à Austerlitz.

in this identification, which was both good for army morale and useful
in building up the mystique of Napoleonic power. Under the Empire
many soldiers bought sheets of headed notepaper, sold to them in their
regiments, for the express purpose of writing home. Designs varied,
though all carried a version of the official insignia – some a crown and
an imperial capital 'N', others a picture of a frigate or a citadel, many
the emblem of the imperial eagle. To the left and right of the emblem
were printed the words 'Empire français', a firm reminder of France's
constitutional status since 1804, while down the left-hand side of the
letter were printed the details of the soldier's unit – his company,
battalion and regiment, the numbers filled in by the soldier himself.[44]
As time passed these designs became more complex, the identification
with the regime and with the imperial family more intense. In the wake
of Napoleon's remarriage in 1810 to the Archduchess Marie-Louise, for
instance, regiments were issued with a letterhead which depicted an
ordinary soldier, a conscript like the writer himself, in characteristic
pose, leaning on his musket or standing to attention, flanked by portraits
of Napoleon and his new Empress. The picture of the soldier took the
form of a line drawing, often quite naively portrayed, which cried out
to be coloured in, or painted, by the young man in his bivouac, eager
to show his parents how he himself looked in his smart bright uniform.
Many of the troops, we know, did buy their regimental notepaper and
took great trouble to add the right colours.[45] In doing so, they conveyed
more effectively than any official text the message that ordinary soldiers
were proud to serve in the French army, and proud, too, to be identified
with the Napoleonic regime.

André Dupont-Ferrier was just such a man. Born in the village of
Crolles in the Dauphiné, and the fifteenth of sixteen children, he had
joined the army as a simple *grenadier* in 1791. By 1797, when we encounter
him writing a barely literate letter home, he had been promoted to
the rank of corporal. What had impressed him most was Bonaparte's
incisiveness on the battlefield and the effect of his arrival on the troops.
'By good luck the general-in-chief arrived. The other generals did not
know what to say, whereas he began to sing: "Everything you can see
is ours. I have called up twelve thousand men as reinforcements".'[46] It
was Napoleon's bravura, his confidence with his men, which he recalled
as the key factor in restoring army morale. Another soldier, a peasant

boy from the plains around Beauvais, described to his uncle in 1807 the kind of excitement which Napoleon's arrival had created in the Army of Italy, an excitement that had been shared by officers and ranks alike. True, he was there to reward his troops with promotions and medals, but their joy and their identification ran deeper. 'At last', he wrote,

> we have enjoyed the presence of our Sovereign, which we had been promised for a long time; he inspected our Division at Palma-Nuova in the midst of rain, mud, and snow; I don't think I have ever been as cold as I was that day, and I don't know how the Emperor could bear it, since the soldiers were scarcely able to handle their weapons; but it seemed that his very presence warmed us, and repeated shouts of '*Vive l'Empereur!*' must have convinced him how much he is cherished. Time did not allow him to go through all the ranks; he spoke only to the officers, but those soldiers who wanted to say something to him could do approach him with confidence, certain of a warm welcome.[47] *

Because it was Bonaparte, it would appear that the men did not resent the fact that he conferred only with officers; rather it is the informality of the occasion and the opportunity offered to them to have their say which left a permanent mark. If they held him in awe, they also seemed to regard him with a certain affection, and did not hesitate to draw favourable comparisons with other commanders under whom they had served. Of course, the jottings of two random soldiers cannot be regarded as in any sense representative; most do not mention the Emperor, or where they do talk of their pride and admiration, it is when they have been reviewed by him or have accepted a medal from his hand. But they are not without significance, for here, in the words of two ordinary soldiers, words straddling a decade of war, we are presented

---

* Enfin nous avons joui de la présence de notre Souverain que depuis long-temps on nous annonçait; il a passé en revue notre Division à Palma-Nuova au milieu de la pluie, de la boue, de la neige; je crois que je n'ai jamais eu aussi froid que ce jour-là, et je ne sais comment l'Empereur pouvait y tenir; les soldats ne pouvaient à peine manier leurs armes; mais il semblait que sa présence nous rechauffait; les cris multipliés de 'Vive l'Empereur' lui devoient faire voir combien il est chéri! Le temps ne lui permettoit pas d'aller dans tous les rangs; il parlait seulement aux officiers; et ceux des soldats qui voulaient lui dire quelque chose pouvaient s'approcher de lui avec confiance, surs d'être bien accueillis.

with the Napoleon of legend – Bonaparte as an inspiring presence, a trusted commander, a man of the people whom the lowliest recruit could confidently approach, a glorious leader whose very presence among his troops gave them a glow of pride and appreciation. It is an instance where the new professionalism of the army led to a transfer of loyalty to the person of Napoleon, whether as revolutionary general, First Consul or Emperor – and where the spontaneous insights of the serving soldier reinforced the image which Bonaparte had created for himself and which was so carefully fostered, in painting, in theatre and in print, by the imperial propaganda machine.

5

From Valmy to Moscow

The twin calls of patriotism and ideology played a significant part in motivating France's soldiers for war. There were many among them who shared the revolutionary leaders' anger at the tyranny of foreign kings and who rallied under Bonaparte to the appeal of national sentiment. Young Frenchmen were often intensely enthusiastic and patriotic, and this helps to explain their courage in battle, those qualities of *bravoure* and *élan* which, if we are to believe contemporary reports, were their most salient characteristics. Having joined the army, they were often raring for action, convinced that the war would be swiftly won, and impatient to get the job done.[1] This enthusiasm was particularly important in the early stages of their military careers, in those weeks just following their incorporation into the ranks, when the novelty of army life was still capable of dazzling them, when military uniforms and badges could still leave a deep impression, and when speeches from officers and political commissars still had a challenging and refreshing tone. And it was especially prominent during the early period of the Revolution, before cynicism and fatalism had had a chance to set in. But we should not allow ourselves to be carried away by government propaganda here: patriotic enthusiasm could not last indefinitely, nor could it serve as an explanation for every French success. It would figure less prominently during the later phases of the war, when battle-weary troops had become familiar with the realities of soldiering and the idealistic volunteer of 1792 had turned into the *grognard* of Moscow and the Peninsular campaign.

Nor should it be assumed that patriotism alone provides an adequate explanation for the performance of the French in the field. Troop motivation is far more complex than that, and it is different at different times and in different contexts. The most telling analysis for the Revolutionary and Napoleonic Wars is that of the American historian John

Lynn, who, in his dissection of morale in the Armée du Nord, follows military training manuals and divides the issue of troop motivation into three distinct elements. 'Motivation' he defines as 'the set of reasons, both rational and emotional, which leads a person to decide to act or to do nothing'. And these change with the circumstances in which he finds himself. 'Initial motivation' concerns the decision to enlist, to volunteer or accept the draft, and here patriotism and ideology play a major part. It arises, necessarily, from the young man's experience as a civilian, from what he hears from his parents and friends, from the state of opinion in his town or village; this helps explain the wide regional divergences in responses to the various levies and conscriptions of the period. Once he is in the army, other influences will come to bear, though the propaganda offensive launched by both the Revolution and the Empire is proof of a political determination to build upon and strengthen that initial motivation to fight. 'Sustaining motivation', Lynn's second category, derives from life in the army itself, from training and activity to offset boredom, from the growth of harmonious relations between the young men of a company, a unit, a peer group. Cultivating a sense of companionship among the soldiers, providing a new family to which each member will feel both loyalty and obligation, is crucial to strengthening sustaining motivation of this kind. It is also crucial to how well or how badly a unit will perform in combat. And that leads to Lynn's third category of motivation, 'combat motivation', that which pertains in the heat of battle when fear and death and injury are to be seen on all sides. Here self-interest combines with the interest of the group, since the fate of each individual is dependent on group performance. This is a context where the will to survive is paramount. 'Such elevated concerns as patriotism and ideology cannot be entirely read out of the combat picture for all armies in all circumstances; however, for most soldiers ... it seems that patriotism and the like are far from their minds. The effects of combat motivation cover a spectrum from abject surrender, to the non-use of weapons, to aggressive initiative.'[2]

It is certainly true that declarations of patriotic commitment do seem to be more forceful from soldiers who had recently joined their regiment, on whom the colour and comradeship of army life could make a deep impression. Or they might have heard a patriotic address from their commanding officer or from a deputy on mission and be indicating their agreement. Thus Joseph Ladrix reported on the patriotic fervour of the soldiers he encountered in 1794 near Hendaye: 'The ardour of our brothers in arms is unbelievable; they are impatient for action, and if they have some anxieties, it is because the order to attack does not come quickly enough.'[3] Auguste, a committed revolutionary and volunteer of 1792, is another who remained loyal to the principles of the Revolution, and who, in his despatches from the Armée des Vosges, both declared his total commitment to the ideals of liberty and equality, and expressed his disgust at the conduct of the nobility, whether in the armies or in civil society. Indeed, he also endorsed Jacobin ideas about military tactics, insisting that the army should commit itself to outright attack to drive back the enemy, and dismissing counsels of prudence as cowardice and treachery.[4] But ardour such as his was relatively rare, and it was to be found less and less frequently as time passed. Indeed, men's initial impressions of the army were not always so rosy. Marquant, a patriotic revolutionary who volunteered as a dragoon in 1792, was disconcerted when he was attached not to a volunteer regiment from his own department, the Meuse, but to a former royal regiment of the line, the oldest in the French army. His first days in uniform seemed to justify his unease, as he was struck by the disorder all around him.

> There were no more than a few tents spread out across the plain and on the hillsides, although there were large numbers of men. We were astonished at the degree of negligence we encountered, whether it was in distributing tents and utensils or in providing food and fodder. We went three days without either tents or cooking pots.[5] *

And why? Because, he noted with disgust, the person responsible for distributing these things had deserted to the enemy, as had many of the officers. The young man who had left home full of hope and patriotic ambition admitted to anger and disillusionment.

The first days could also be a time of confusion and perplexity as the young soldier adjusted to a very unfamiliar environment; indeed, the process of adjustment, of acclimatising to the values and norms of army

---

* Il n'y avait alors que quelques tentes éparses dans la plaine et sur les collines, quoiqu'il y eût déjà beaucoup d'hommes. Nous fûmes étonnés de la négligence répandue tant sur la distribution des tentes et ustensiles de guerre que sur les vivres et fourrages. Nous passâmes trois jours sans tentes et sans marmites.

life, was crucial to building up morale. Instilling discipline was not only a way of ensuring that orders were obeyed and natural fears overridden; it was also designed to provide a comprehensible framework in which daily life could be conducted, a means of replacing the familiar routines of village life with an alternative structure that would give daily life shape and meaning. For doing nothing, hanging listlessly around in camps and barracks, was one of the commonest forms of demoralisation in eighteenth-century armies. So was the feeling that neither they nor their young and necessarily inexperienced officers really had the authority to provide leadership or offer security. After the first days of a march, as one of them explained, the overwhelming impression was of being lost, rudderless and confused, and at the end of the day what he most dreaded was the moment when he left the others to return to his lodgings and was abandoned to his thoughts and anxieties.[6]

Loneliness was well-known as a destroyer of morale; hence the importance which all soldiers attached to companionship. This was true at all levels of the army, but it was most obvious in the ranks, when new recruits arrived, fresh from the familiar world of family and farm. Friends and comrades were not just a luxury or a distraction from the ardours of war; they served a more serious function, in that they could cheer a man up even in the darkest moments of despair. As Chanal, a shoemaker from the Vosges who was newly incorporated into his unit, wrote thankfully in a letter to his parents, he was saved from gloom by the presence in the same regiment of friends and acquaintances, boys from his own region who welcomed him the evening he arrived, settled him into his quarters, and helped to provide diversion. Among friends his perspective changed. 'Military service is not as dreadful as I'd been given to believe', he wrote, 'I could even get to like it.'[7] Recruits often commented that they found the army a curiously unfamiliar society, but that served to make familiarity all the more precious. Drinking and noisy masculine sociability could not only help them forget the dangers they had to run; they also went some way to creating the sense of belonging for which they so desperately craved.

Friends, comrades, fellow sufferers with whom stories could be exchanged and experiences discussed, these were important elements in helping create the 'sustaining motivation' of John Lynn's analysis. So was the daily routine in the camps which gave shape to their existence

1. Napoleon Bonaparte, crossing the Alps in 1800. Engraving by Tassaert.

2. Volunteers enrolling.

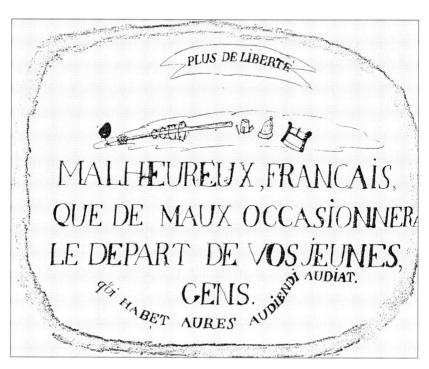

3. Placard from Le Mans protesting against the demands of recruitment.

LE DÉPART DU CONSCRIT.

Je suis t'un pauvre conscrit,
De l'an mille huit cent dit;   *(bis)*
Faut quitter le Languedo,
    Le Languedo, le Languedo
        Oh !
Faut quitter le Languedo,
    Avec le sac sur le dos.

Le Maire, et aussi le Préfet,
N'en sont deux jolis cadets;   *(bis)*
Ils nous font tiré r'au sort,
    Tiré r'au sort, tiré r'au sort,
        Ort;
Ils nous font tiré r'au sort,
    Pour nous conduir' r'à la mort.

Adieu donc chers parents,
N'oubliez pas votre enfant,   *(bis)*
Crivés li de temps en temps,
    De temps en temps, de temps en temps,
        En;
Crivés li de temps en temps,
    Pour lui envoyer de l'argent.

Adieu donc chères beautés,
Dont nos cœurs son't'enchantés;   *(bis)*
Ne pleurés point not' départ,
    Not' départ, not' départ
        Art;
Ne pleurés point not' départ,
    Nous reviendrons to't'ou tard.

Adieu donc mon tendre cœur,
Vous consolerés ma sœur;   *(bis)*
Vous y dirés que fanfan,
    Que fanfan, que fanfan
        An;
Vous y dirés que fanfan
    Il est mort r'en combattant.

Qui qu'a fait cette chanson,
N'en sont trois jolis garçons;   *(bis)*
Ils étiont faiseux de bas,
    Faiseux de bas, faiseux de bas,
        Ah;
Ils étiont faiseux de bas,
    Et à c' t' heure ils sont soldats.

Propriété des Éditeurs (Déposé)   P. V.

Imp. Lith. Pellerin et Cie à Epinal.

4. The conscript's departure. Below is the song 'Conscrit de 1810'. An *image d'Epinal* of *c.* 1840.

5. Crossing the Rhine, at its confluence with the Ille. Rivers were both frontiers and obstacles.

6. French troops on board ship on their way to Egypt, as General Bonaparte lands to take possession of Malta, 13 June 1798.

7. A column on the move, with wagons and camp-followers. Dutch engraving after Langendyk.

8. French troops enter Rome, February 1798. Engraving by Bertaut after Girardet.

9. Payment of suppliers was a key issue for French soldiers – and for the citizens of occupied cities.

10. The attractions and availability – or not – of local women was of perennial interest to the soldiers, and frequently a cause of tension with the local population.

11. The capture of cities and then garrisoning them was a constant theme in French campaigning. Here Bonaparte accepts the surrender of Mantua, 2 February 1797. Engraving by Motte after Adam.

12. The battle of Eylau, 7–8 February 1807, painting by Antoine-Jean Gros. Napoleon surrounded by the dead and dying. (*Louvre/Bridgeman Art Library*)

13. The crossing of the Berezina, 27–28 November 1812. Of the 600,000 soldiers of *la Grande Armée* only around 30,000 returned home safely.

14. The battle of Waterloo, 18 June 1815. Fighting around the south gate of Hogoumont farm. (*National Army Museum*)

– training sessions, mounting guard, firing practice at one level; at another the familiar rituals of singing songs, listening to stories, or gathering round the *marmite* at meal times. Yet none of these, important as they were, could quite prepare the young man for his first experience of battle. For battles seldom lived up to the heroic descriptions provided by the military press or the propagandist statistics they were given by their commanders. Some did copy these accounts into their own letters, describing the majesty of an advancing army or thrilling to the scent of victory. But many betrayed a contrasting emotion, the anxiety which men inevitably felt on the eve of action. Again, they might try to conceal it, pretending that they were in little real danger and rebuking over-anxious parents for their fears. They were young boys in the main, dutiful sons who saw it as their responsibility to reassure their families, to minimise the risks they faced. Jean Mullier, for instance, a Parisian serving with the *Grande Armée* in 1813, did what he could to reassure his alarmed mother:

> I can't think why you go on tormenting yourself about my lot without good reason. My life has been marked by thousands of more or less unsettling events, but have I not always managed to master the capricious turns of fortune, and – besides a few debts which I shall not put off repaying – what do I have to reproach myself with? Nothing, absolutely nothing. *

He pointed to the experience he had gained in the army and hints that, returning with all his faculties intact, he will be excellently placed to make a good living once the war is over.[8]

But between the brave sentiments and words of reassurance, men often betrayed the uncertainty they so naturally felt. This could take many different forms, since not all were prepared to confess to their parents that they felt afraid or believed they would never return. Some talked about their outstanding debts and the ways in which they might repay them – debts entered into during long weeks of marching eastwards when pay was no more than a pittance, or the larger debts

---

* Je ne sais pourquoi vous ne cessez de vous tourmenter sans motif sur mon sort. Mon existence a été marquée par mille et mille évènemens plus ou moins inquiétans mais ne m'a-t-on pas toujours vu maîtriser les caprices de la fortune et, à quelques dettes près, car je n'en manque point en ce moment, et qu'au surplus je ne tarderai point à acquitter, qu'a-t-on à me rapprocher?

contracted through illness, during periods of hospitalisation. How, worried a young corporal from Vimy in the Pas-de-Calais, could he be sure that he would be able to repay his benefactors, especially as he faced interminable campaigns in Italy and Spain?[9] Others talked of the uncertainty which they faced in a career which could send them to the ends of the earth at a few days' notice, an uncertainty that was only made worse by the fear that they would forever be cut off from their families. A young soldier with the Armée de l'Ouest in Brest admitted that it was this which was depressing him most. He feared that he would be sent to fight in the Americas, but knows that there will be so little warning that he may not even be able to alert his parents. If they do not receive another letter from him within a fortnight, he concluded, they should assume that he is on a ship to the New World, and his desolation was only increased by the thought that he may be quite alone, cut off from his home and from his friends.[10] Others again, while making the point that they were enjoying army life and were well integrated in their regiment, words of reassurance which every parent longed to hear, rather spoilt the effect by seeming over-anxious about the fate of their younger brothers or their friends in the village. Their interest in the details of the conscription process was itself telling. Had they had to take part in this year's ballot? What sort of number had they drawn? In part, of course, this was a symptom of homesickness, of the desire to remain part of village and family life. But it was also a sign of deep unease. Whatever the case they made – and their interventions on behalf of others could take many different forms – they were all saying essentially the same thing, that if at all possible those near and dear to them should be protected from the brutality of military life and should be spared the unhappy experience to which they themselves had been subjected.[11]

Anxiety showed in other ways, too. Men with religious faith did not hesitate to pray for divine intercession to protect them and to safeguard their return home; and, though rare during the dechristianising years of the 1790s, expressions of Catholic piety became more common under the Directory and Napoleon, when they were no longer confused by associations with royalism or counter-revolution. Men expressed the hope that 'with God's help' they might be spared injury or find their way back to their families; they referred to saints' days and the nativity of the Virgin; and even in 1794 a substantial number of letters make formulaic invocations of God, in phrases like '*Dieu merci*' or '*grâce à Dieu*'.[12] Some regretted that churches remained closed or that they did not have the opportunity to attend mass, while a young man from the Vaucluse could quite naturally thank the *abbé* back in his village for the prayers he had said during his recent illness.[13] Others seemed to accept that it was God's desire that they should be fighting this war, and took comfort from the fact that they were fulfilling His divine wishes. 'It's God who has willed it that I should be here', wrote Pierre-Antoine Pellicier, a Savoyard, 'He will always defend me from danger.'[14] Soldiers from Liège figured among the more devout in the Napoleonic armies. As Jean-Philip Lecloux wrote home in 1809: 'Keep praying for me, for we are not able to pray. When we can do so, we do. I always manage to pray a little each day.'[15] Another soldier was disturbed to find himself among non-believers during his tour of duty in Germany. 'Since leaving Frankfurt I have not found any true Christians', he wrote. 'In Saxony there are only Protestants. As I can't go to mass, I beg those who may have time to go and listen to mass for me from time to time, so that God may spread his holy blessing upon me.'[16] He had not been to confession since he had left home, and it troubled him deeply at a time when he was more than averagely in need of solace and reassurance.

The issue at the very heart of their fears was, of course, death itself, the very real fear of dying and dying in a painful, even gruesome manner. Once the army was in the field, death was omnipresent, and it was difficult to excise it from their memoirs and personal correspondence. What differed was the directness with which men would talk about it. In their letters home some soldiers were tempted to skirt around the question, playing down the risks and hiding behind bland generalisations. They had no wish to cause gloom and consternation at home or in their village, and understood the impact which continual accounts of carnage would ensure. Others seemed much more cavalier about death, such was its role in the everyday experience of the army in the field, and accepted that life in the ranks was necessarily fragile. Jean Douciet, from Saint-Ybars in the Ariège, wrote, even before his unit had left for the front, telling his father that he had now received his uniform and equipment, and instructing him where his things could be found in the event that he did not return.[17] He may have been doing little more than organising his affairs as an act of simple prudence, but others raised the subject with more than a tinge of foreboding. Another man, whose health was already failing, wrote to his home in the Mayenne in 1809 on the eve of his departure for the *Grande Armée*. He was desperate for news before he left on what he feared would be his last campaign, and finished his letter with a poignant, fatalistic postscript, asking that his father give his jacket and trousers to his younger brother 'since I believe that I shall not have the pleasure of wearing them'.[18] Fear of imminent death was well nigh universal, a part of that common culture which bound comrades together, and references to it could be curiously casual. Thus, after a generally chatty letter to his father, André Desbruères wrote that he would discuss his travels at length on a future occasion, adding, as though it were to be expected, 'if I am not killed first'. His mother would perhaps have expected this, since we learn that she in turn has been drawing cards in order to tell his fortune.[19] More generally, many soldiers acknowledged that on the eve of a battle they usually drank – and spent – lavishly, not just to anaesthetise their fears, but from a realisation that there was little point in saving their money since the next day might be their last.[20]

Some men, of course, talked more bluntly about the realities of war and gave graphic, searing descriptions of what they had encountered on the battlefield. It is then that the bravura and insouciance gave way to greater realism, and that the initial exuberance was often tempered. On the previous day soldiers had been raring for action, writing how much they looked forward to the battle, to charging the enemy and ending the tedium of waiting. Some seemed able to maintain that enthusiasm after the battle, describing their part in the action in graphic and heroic detail. But they were relatively few, and boasting may have been their way of coping with horror. For many of the young soldiers their first battle was also their first experience of dying and mutilation, and they were clearly deeply affected by what they had lived through. Rémy Thirion offered his father this description of his first engagement: he had been an infantryman and had seen bullets at close quarters. He had, he said, watched good men fall alongside him and had seen soldiers flee into narrow village streets that were not wide enough to carry them. He had, he admits, known fear. 'When we saw the first men fall, then we were afraid; our sergeant gave us brandy, saying "Be brave, don't be afraid", but when then I saw him fall I was not singing, I was just waiting my turn, and I saw the shell and the bullets coming straight for us.'[21] Excitement gave way easily to panic in the heat of the battle. Some emerged with horrifying vignettes permanently etched on their memory. The young musician Philippe-René Girault was one who could not banish the physical image of death from his mind, recalling seeing a soldier carrying a wounded comrade on his shoulders. As they staggered forward, the victim 'had his head blown away by a bullet, and the man who was carrying him marched forward another ten paces before he became aware of it'.[22] Images like this, fresh and terrifying for the soldier exposed to his first battle, became sadly commonplace as raw conscripts were rapidly turned into seasoned campaigners.

Recreating a verbal picture of the battlefield and of the harrowing scenes they had witnessed always seemed easier than translating their fears and emotions into writing – something which soldiers who had lived through the horrors of a battle were almost universally reluctant to do. Few tried to conjure up the atmosphere of battle or to analyse their own frame of mind during the fight; and those who did were mainly officers, often reflecting on their experience years later. Jean-Michel Chevalier, who made his career in the army and rose to be a *sous-lieutenant* in the Imperial Guard, was one who attempted through his memoirs to recall his first impressions of battle, and if his account is full of ambivalence and apparent contradiction, it is all the more credible for that. He set out to trace the first impressions made by the sight of the battlefield on the young soldier who has not previously been exposed to conflict. 'When I first stepped out onto a field of carnage', he wrote, choosing his words with care,

> it is difficult to say what I felt seeing my comrades, horses and men knocked head over heels. The number of the wounded emerging from the battle, mutilated, dishevelled, carried on stretchers, their faces pale, their bodies covered with dust and blood, the shouts of the dying, the frenzy of fighting men, the collective image of it all troubled my senses in a way that is difficult to define. When I found myself exposed to the enemy artillery batteries, vomiting terror and death into our ranks, I was struck by trembling, but was it was it fright or dread? ... I felt ready to faint ... But we hurled ourselves at the enemy, and then I no longer felt fear ... The blood of a Frenchman was coursing through my veins ... I still quivered in every limb, but it was

a trembling caused by rage ... I wanted to knock them all down, to avenge my brothers in arms, and I charged my horse into the midst of the enemy. That was the moment when, under attack from all sides, I felt my courage grow. Not only did I parry all the blows that were directed at me, but those I struck were terrible in their force; my anger and rage guided them, and they went straight to their target. Old soldiers and raw recruits, all sought to outdo one another in the blows they struck and the courage they showed, and soon everything was swept from their path.[23] *

In this way, he argued, fear turned to desperation and desperation to patriotic anger; all, he suggested, contributed to the power of the French army and to their ultimate victory.

Death was ever-present in the French battalions, and it would take a peculiar sort of foolhardiness for a man to claim that it did not affect him. Once he had lived through a battle, had seen friends and comrades slaughtered, had smelt the stench of death that lingered in the nostrils for days afterwards, he could not be stirred by the patriotic language of his officers in quite the same way again. Even glory became tinged with sadness and regret. Many became so hardened by the sight of the dead and dying that they were prepared to describe what they had seen, often in the most harrowing terms. Louis-François Cointin was a lieutenant in 1812 when he wrote back to his mother in Caen describing the carnage he had witnessed in Russia.

---

* En paraissant pour la première fois sur un champ de carnage, il est difficile de dire ce que j'éprouvai en voyant tomber mes camarades, les chevaux et les hommes se culbuter. Le nombre des blessés revenant du combat, mutilés, portés, pâles, défaits, couverts de poussière et de sang, les cris des mourants, la rage des combattants, tout cela portait dans mes sens un trouble indéfinissable. Exposé devant des batteries d'artillerie ennemie, qui vomissaient la terreur et la mort dans nos rangs, un tremblement me prit, était-ce effroi ou peur? ... J'étais prêt à défaillir ... Mais nous sommes lancés sur l'ennemi, alors ce n'est plus de l'effroi ... le sang français circule dans mes veines ... J'éprouve encore un frémissement, mais c'est celui de la rage ... Je voudrais tout culbuter, venger mes frères et je lance mon cheval au milieu de l'ennemi. C'est alors que, me voyant assailli de toute part, mon courage s'en accroît. Non seulement, je pare tous les coups qui me sont portés, mais ceux que je porte sont terribles, la colère et la rage les guident, et ils tombent d'aplomb. Vieux et jeunes soldats, tous rivalisent d'action, de courage, et tout fut bientôt culbuté.

If you had seen the dead, the ground was carpeted with them. There were at least eight Russian dead for every Frenchman. The regiment suffered huge losses. I just missed having both legs amputated by a shell. It knocked me over, but in the end I was able to pick myself up.[24] *

He realised that he had been lucky, and that in the next engagement it could easily be his turn. The same was true of Captain Coignet, describing his part in the battle of Aspern-Essling in 1809, the battle in which Jean Lannes became the first of Napoleon's marshals to be killed in combat. Coignet survived, but the experience he describes was indelibly etched on his memory.

A cannon-ball ripped through a whole line of men very close to me. I received a violent shock, my rifle fell to the ground; I no longer had any feeling in my right arm. Looking down, I saw a bloody shred of uniform clinging to me just where my arm was bleeding, as though my arm had been shattered. It was not; it was just some remains of my poor comrades which had been thrown up against me.[25] †

In such conditions even Napoleon's presence on the battlefield proved inadequate to prevent panic and nausea spreading amongst the troops.

In truth, battlefields were desolate places, destructive of men and their horses, but also of every other living organism. Those who had lived through battles forever associated them with death, both the sight of mutilated bodies and the piercing cries of the dying. It scarcely mattered whether the cries were those of Frenchmen or of the enemy; the horror of the dying was inescapable, and the sounds of carnage did not stop when the battle was over. Even when the majority of the losses were of Prussians, one young revolutionary soldier could not conceal his concern and fellow-feeling. 'It was heart-rending, during the rest of the night',

---

* Si vous aviez vu les morts, la terre en était couverte. Il y avait au moins huit Russes morts pour un Français. Le régiment a beaucoup souffert. J'ai manqué à avoir les deux jambes coupées d'un boulet. Il m'a renversé, mais enfin j'en ai été quitte pour me ramasser.

† Un boulet emporta de nouveau toute une file voisine de moi. Je reçus un choc violent, mon fusil tomba; je ne sentais plus mon bras droit. En regardant, je vis un lambeau sanglant attaché à la hauteur de la saignée, comme si j'avais eu le bras fracassé. Ce n'était qu'un débris de mes pauvres camarades qui avait été lancé contre moi.

he wrote, 'to hear those poor wounded men crying out for mercy without being able to offer them any help. At daybreak there was a suspension of hostilities for two hours so that we could remove the wounded and bury the dead.'[26] The morning after a battle was always a moment for reflection and for a certain sadness. Even the satisfaction of victory could not erase the essential bleakness of the scene, while defeat made it seem tragically worse, a fact which was as true in the revolutionary battalions of 1792 as it would be under Napoleon on the wide plains of Poland or Russia. Marquant was one soldier who appreciated the landscape he passed through and left behind some excellent descriptions of the local countryside in bloom. How much more harrowing, therefore, is this description of the fields of Flanders in the days after a bloody confrontation, a scene which he recorded as one of utter desolation. Like other French soldiers he had been forced to retreat in disarray.

> On our road we came across the wounded and the bloodstained remains of the dead who had been taken back to Maubeuge. Arriving at Grisuelle, we saw, in the muddy ditches that ran along the road (for it was raining), the corpses and the remains of soldiers, both ours and the enemy's, with the bodies of a few horses scattered across the plain. The sight of great trees and strong walls felled by cannon fire, of deserted houses, sacked and pillaged, one of them still smouldering from the fire which had consumed it, filled us with anger.[27] *

Some admitted to feeling sickened by what they have seen. Young Girault, who as a musician had lost his vocation with the closure of the cathedral chapter in his native city of Poitiers, had volunteered for the army as one of the few places where he could continue to make music. He was clearly repelled by the carnage which he had to witness, and his account includes this description of the village of Ebersberg after a

---

* Sur notre chemin nous rencontrions les blessés et les dépouilles sanglantes des morts qu'on rapportait à Maubeuge. En arrivant à Grisuelle, nous vîmes, le long des fossés bourbeux de la route (car il pleuvait), les cadavres et les dépouilles des nôtres et des ennemis, avec quelques chevaux tués épars dans la plaine. L'aspect des grands arbres et des murs abattus par le canon, des maisons désertes, saccagées, dont une fumait encore du feu qui l'avait consumée, nous gonflait de colère.

particularly bloody battle. 'As the fighting the previous day had been very murderous', he wrote,

> the houses, the streets, the banks of the river were piled high with the dead and wounded who had been overcome by the fire, and when we were able to make our way into the village, all we found were heaps of partly-burned corpses. The sight was so horrible that they wanted to spare the army from seeing it; they made the troops pass to the right of the village along a path which they built for the purpose. Curiosity drove me to visit this scene of carnage. Never have I seen anything so frightful as these grilled carcases which no longer bore any resemblance to human beings. Near the farthest point of the village a heap of them barred entry to a street; it was a pile of arms and legs, of shapeless bodies that had been half incinerated. On seeing them my heart failed me, my legs gave way under me, and I was unable to move either forward or backward, remaining quite motionless, contemplating that fearful spectacle.[28] *

Military manuals and political addresses might continue to spur men on with dreams of glory, or to suggest that dying for one's country was a sweet and satisfying thing, but these were not sentiments that were often expressed by those who had lived through the wars. They knew better, because they had been there, because they had experienced shelling and knew what death in battle really meant. In the thick of a battle comrades counted more than patriotism, brandy more than glory. By 1813 men were clearly demoralised by the perpetual presence of death and by the sheer scale of human destruction. They knew that their chances of survival were not good, just as they knew that there was now

---

* Comme le combat de la veille avait été très meurtrier, les maisons, les rues, les bords de la rivière étaient encombrés de morts et de blessés qui furent atteints par l'incendie, et lorsque l'on put pénétrer dans le village, on n'y trouva plus que des monceaux de cadavres à demi brûlés. Le spectacle était si horrible, qu'on voulut en épargner la vue à l'armée; on la fit défiler à droite du village, sur un chemin que l'on fit exprès. La curiosité me poussa à aller visiter cette scène de carnage. Jamais je n'ai rien vu de plus effrayant que ces cadavres grillés n'ayant plus aucune ressemblance humaine. Près de l'extrémité du village, il y en avait un tas qui bouchait l'entrée d'une rue: c'était un amoncellement de bras et de jambes, de corps informes à moitié carbonisés. A cette vue, le coeur me manqua, les jambes se dérobaient sous moi et je ne pouvais plus ni avancer ni reculer, restant malgré moi immobile à contempler cet affreux spectacle.

no reserve, that virtually all the young men from their communities were now being scooped into the army. They asked more and more about the fate of their younger brothers and sent certificates back from the front, but without any real hope that an exemption would follow. And they talked increasingly of the men they had lost, the staggering numbers of deaths which their units had suffered. One soldier lamented the fact that his unit had left France 800 strong, but was now reduced to fewer than 200; while of the young recruits who had marched out of Liège in the conscription of 1813 the gravediggers of Luxembourg buried 110 during two short months of the following winter.[29] It saddened soldiers like the Belgian Nicolas-Joseph Halleux, lying sick in a hospital bed, to think that the countryside around his home had been stripped of its young, leaving it bleak and ageing and desolate, inadequately farmed, denied the fun and laughter of youth.[30] It saddened them, too, because increasingly it was their friends they saw dying, the boys of their *classe* who had set forth from the village together in more optimistic days, their companions through the vicissitudes of war.

If they were saddened, they were not, in the main, diverted from the job in hand. Indeed, it is striking how much soldiers accepted that fighting was their job, and that it was to be preferred to boredom and inaction. However much they may have feared the battlefield, those who survived generally threw themselves into the next conflict, responding to the call for extra effort to ensure victory. Combat motivation was a complex of ambitions and feeling – the desire for victory, the emulation of others, the fear of disgracing oneself or of letting down one's comrades, noise, tumult, expectation and adrenalin, all were mixed into a surging cauldron of emotion. If men feared death in battle, they were well aware that there were other, less honourable and more lingering ways to die – of fever in a hospital bed, of gangrenous wounds and botched amputations, of treachery and exhaustion. Men slumped to the ground out of sheer exhaustion after days on the march or without sleep on the battlefield, victims of cold and fatigue and poor diet rather than of enemy action. Others died groaning in agony in primitive field hospitals, denied any but the most primitive medication. 'He died', René Jendry wrote of a friend who died of fever in just such misery, 'the most terrible death you can imagine, for he suffered dreadfully; for more than a week he could neither see nor talk, and he was unable to recognise anyone.'[31] The fear of defeat in a war where the opposing armies often took no prisoners could be greater than the fear of combat. Victory could bring a shot of short-term exhilaration, whereas defeat was almost bound to leave a sense of hollowness and failure. In Ernouf's words, 'to die fighting is to accomplish one's mission; but the ultimate misfortune is to die without honour, miserably stifled on the approaches to a bridge or drowned while trying to swim away. That was the fate of far too many of my comrades.'[32]

When friends were lost, in battle or after a lingering illness in hospital, news of their deaths had somehow to be broken to their families back in France. Sometimes it fell to their friends to perform this service, one which few found easy or reassuring. Just how should such news be communicated? How much detail was it appropriate to give? Were all deaths to be described in heroic formulae, or was it better to tell the truth, even when the truth had a harsh and unwelcome ring? Often, when the dreaded letter came from a man's commander or from a fellow-officer, it was couched in the language of military glory, expressing sorrow at their loss but offering consolation in the circumstances which surrounded it. Thus when Guidon, a captain in the 36th Regiment, had to inform the parents of François Avril that he had been killed in a battle against the British in 1811, he duly commented on the dead man's bravery and the affection which he had inspired in his men. Other niceties were also carefully observed. He introduced himself to them as a fellow-Norman, one of themselves, a man in whose humanity they could have confidence. He emphasised the importance of the action in which their son had given his life, since 'before he was wounded, he had had the satisfaction of seeing the British pushed back from their formidable position and giving ground shamefully before our bayonet charge'. And he conjured up an image of a peaceful death, in the arms of his commander, surrounded by those who admired him. 'It grieves me', he wrote, 'to have to inform you of such sad news. But I owe this sacrifice to the spirit of a friend, who with his dying breath gave me the most touching evidence of his love for his parents.'[33] It was nicely expressed, emphasising the nobility of spirit of a Napoleonic officer who had served, first as a lieutenant, then as a captain, since Year XII. And it may have done a little to assuage his parents' grief.

Not all the letters of condolence were quite as delicately turned.

Ordinary soldiers might share the feelings of their officers, but their expression was generally simpler, more factual, and certainly less contrived. And quite frequently it was left to fellow-soldiers to communicate the news – either men from the same village who already knew the parents of the dead man and could write as neighbours and friends, or else the *camarades de lit* with whom they had shared so many experiences during their years in the regiment. These letters could be both personable and rather touching, as the writer, himself barely literate and struggling to find appropriate words, related the circumstances of their son's death and urged them not to grieve. Their own sadness and sense of bereavement was often quite transparent, as they tried to hide their feelings of loss and to suppress their fears for the future. Or else they asked their own parents to assume the responsibility of passing on the fateful news, adding something of what they knew of the circumstances of their friend's death. They seldom hid behind formulae, and were less interested than their officers in empty expressions of military glory which they knew could have little meaning for those left behind. Sometimes, indeed, there was little honourable to tell:

> You must tell old Martin, at Grands-Moulins, that there were four of us out skirmishing – me, Linard, Chaumard and his son. When we came back from taking shots at the enemy, we went for a drink in the village near Chreutznach, after which his son didn't want to leave with us as he had got drunk. The next day we learned that peasants had attacked him with an axe and that he had died immediately.[34] *

If there was little consolation here, at least the parents had received a personal message from someone who knew their son, who had been a friend and companion in his leisure hours, and, unlike many, the comfort of knowing what had really happened.

For many soldiers, of course, that reality was less than glorious, a lingering and agonising death in a fever hospital being far more frequent

---

* Vous n'avez qu'à dire au père Martin, des Grands-Moulins, que nous étions quatre en tirailleurs, moi, Linard, Chaumard at son fils. En nous en revenant de tirailler devant l'ennemi, nous sommes revenus boire dans le village proche Chreutznach: son garçon n'a pas voulu s'en revenir, il s'est trouvé pris de boisson. Le lendemain nous avons appris que les paysans l'avaient haché, qu'il est mort sur-le-champ.

than a heroic one on the battlefield. Though the revolutionaries did take some steps to improve the standard of care in military hospitals and to provide better training for their doctors and surgeons, their efforts were soon reduced to insignificance by the scale of the demands made on them. And Napoleon's much-vaunted efforts to portray himself as a caring friend to the sick and wounded stood in stark contrast to the primitive, overcrowded conditions which his troops encountered to the rear of the battlefield, where the only treatment was often amputation, the major killer fever and disease. Soldiers might long for a period of rest away from the front, but the hospitals and ambulances enjoyed such a fearful reputation as *mouroirs* that many approached them with ill-concealed dread. In hospital, it was known that men lost contact with home just when they had the most urgent need of consolation and emergency funding. One soldier from the Haute-Loire complained in 1809 that a letter from his parents had remained in his sergeant-major's hands for two months while he had lain in hospital, unaware of their efforts to get in touch with him. Another, writing from hospital to his father in the suburbs of Le Puy, explained his fear of dying without having heard a word from his family. 'I remained very dangerously ill for two months without having any real hope of being cured; during this time I would cry day and night without being able to see my father and mother, brother and sister.'[35] When he did get round to writing it seems that the worst was over, and that he was safely on the road to recovery. But during his long illness he had lost all hope of getting better, and had suffered weeks of demoralisation and desolation.

Demoralisation was clearly lessened by action, by the flow of adrenalin and sense of danger. But few, after their first experience of battle, could rush into action without expressing some fears or snatching a surreptitious prayer. French soldiers were noticeably reluctant to express any spirit of vengeance against the armies they fought or the peoples whose lands they occupied. The *grognards*, in particular, were never wholly consumed by their own propaganda, while republican soldiers who came into personal contact with their English or Austrian counterparts soon saw them as human beings rather than as the 'slaves of tyrants'. Increasingly, indeed, the men against whom they fought came to be portrayed as ordinary lads like themselves, caught up through no fault of their own in a dreadful and bloody war from which there was no easy escape.

Battles might be savage affairs, fought with tenacity by both sides, but there was little systematic antagonism towards the men against whom they were pitted. They were simply soldiers like themselves, men who with whose fate they could sympathise, whose wounds and suffering they could understand. A conscript from the Mayenne, Jean Cosnard, described to his brother how he had been assigned to accompany an English prisoner-of-war on town leave in Quimper. Though he headed his letter in the most bellicose revolutionary terms – 'Liberty, equality, fraternity: war to the *chouans*' – he revealed that the two men had chatted and eaten together most amicably, concluding that the English 'are just like us, they would all like to have peace'.[36] Another noted the apparent bonhomie that was established between enemy soldiers during these grim moments when the fighting stopped to allow the dead and dying to be removed. 'At these moments', he recalled, 'we fraternised together, shaking one another's hands like real friends; but, as soon as the truce was over, we split up again, promising that soon we would be greeting one another with artillery fire.'[37] And even when insults were exchanged, they do not seem to have been particularly malicious. One convinced Jacobin in the summer of 1793, writing to his cousin, the mayor of Paris, recalled a moment when the French were surprised by German soldiers as they were bathing in the Rhine. 'When they mounted their guard posts to observe us, we showed them our backsides and sang the *carmagnole*.'[38] There were, of course, periodic denunciations of enemy outrages and alleged atrocities – of the pillage committed in the Nord, or the 'brigands' they encountered in Spain and Russia – but for the most part the private writings of the soldiers remained surprisingly non-judgemental, showing little of the moral superiority that oozed from official discourse.

But in French eyes the different enemies against whom they were ranged were not all equally fair-minded, and not all earned the same right to courtesy and respect. From soldiers' accounts it is clear that certain frontier areas and theatres of war were regarded with more fear and disfavour than others, and not simply because physical conditions were hard or the climate cruel, as in the ravines of Switzerland or the snow-blocked passes into Italy. Battle-hardened troops could adjust to difficult terrain and to the vagaries of mountain weather. And if they often complained of fatigue and exhaustion after protracted marches or sleepless nights on look-out, they seem to have accepted the propriety of pitched battles in which both sides respected military courtesies and where the outcome depended on tactical brilliance and physical courage. What they found much more difficult was having to fight in countries where they came under constant attack from an enemy who goaded and ambushed them, where they encountered the hatred of civilians, or where they could not count on their opponents to respect the customary rules of warfare. It was in circumstances such as these that their opponents were denounced as bandits and brigands, and that villagers were suspected of feeding and harbouring enemy terrorists. It was here, too, that French discipline was most likely to break and atrocities to take place.

The Italian front was one that was regarded with some trepidation by French conscripts, especially those from the northern departments who found it all too easy to paint an exaggerated image of the Mediterranean character: they were notoriously prone to suspect local people of stealth and treachery. In Italy, too, they might expect their first taste of guerrilla warfare, adding new fears to the more familiar rigours of cold and fatigue. Savoyard soldiers sent into the Italian Alps complained that for the first time they were fighting brigands rather than soldiers, outlaws who held local villagers to ransom, who burst into villages and demanded money and provisions before slinking back into a highly protective countryside. The French were undermined both by a local population that was always prone to rise in revolt and by a brigand army whom they could not repress; each day villagers joined with escaped prisoners-of-war to attack the French; each day, as one soldier expressed it, 'we hunt down these villains who are set on murdering us, and when we do take prisoners, we have no choice but to have them shot on the spot'.[39] By 1809, as Claude Lavit wrote home to his father, the ravages committed by brigands and the scale of French retaliation had effectively turned his regiment against the local population. 'In the little town where I am stationed the troops have their work cut out. The brigands are causing us a lot of trouble, for we are shooting large numbers of them, and we are the only ones to hunt them down, day and night.'[40] While this may have seemed an effective form of policing to an increasingly desperate army, it can hardly have made them loved, especially as the so-called brigands were also the brothers and sons of the local inhabitants.

If service in Italy seemed threatening, Spain was even worse. The war in the Peninsula enjoyed a particularly fearsome reputation, in part – but only in part – as a consequence of the army's intensive propaganda against the Spaniards. Napoleonic soldiers seem to have shared a horror of fighting there, especially after experience of other theatres of war, notably Germany and Central Europe. Spain was widely believed to be a savage and inhospitable country where French soldiers were left to die by callous villagers set on vengeance, where local people refused to sell them foodstuffs, and where they were virtually prisoners in their camps because of the activity of local 'brigands'.[41] Even in hospital beds they were not safe, since in Spain public morals were such that no form of brutality or deception could be ruled out: Joseph Vachin, a soldier from Mende, complained that during his spell in hospital he had been reduced to penury, since the orderlies stole from their patients while they were weak or delirious.[42] And the course of the war was so unpredictable that they had no idea where the danger would appear from next. Letters spoke of troops being stoned and ambushed by civilians, of prisoners being brutally massacred, even of soldiers being burned alive. In the words of Marnier, here French troops faced a quite different sort of war from that to which they had become accustomed elsewhere in Europe,

> one of constant ambushes, murders and extermination. There were not any battles to compare with Eylau or Friedland, but fighting on a daily basis against invisible assailants, spread out in their thousands behind bushes, at the bottom of ravines, hidden at the corner of every wall; we never enjoyed a truce or any rest, and treason was a constant risk, day and night, whether at the other side of the road or at the head of one's bed. Everyone was to be feared, even those seemingly hospitable people who took you in to their homes.[43] *

Spain was to French soldiers a country of brigands, where the rules of civilised warfare were not respected, and where, as a consequence, any form of reprisals seemed justified. The Convention itself had set

---

* Un autre genre de guerre allait commencer pour nous, une guerre d'embûches incessantes, d'assassinats, d'extermination. Plus de batailles comparables à celles d'Eylau et de Friedland, mais des combats tous les jours: partout des assaillants invisibles, semés par milliers derrière les buissons, au fond des ravins, embusqués à l'angle de chaque mur, jamais de trêve ni de repos, la trahison toujours et partout, le jour comme la nuit, au revers de la route aussi bien qu'au chevet du lit. Tout était à redouter, même l'hôte qui vous prêtait son toit.

the tone back in 1794 when it had insisted that in Spain the troops should fight to the death and refuse to take prisoners. At the time, as Amblard makes clear in his memoirs, they had been fighting against regular soldiers and the instruction had occasioned deep disquiet. He relates how, when his regiment took the city of Bergara, they captured not just Spaniards but other troops, including men from the *Gardes Wallons*. They sacked the city without compunction, but baulked at the order to shoot all their prisoners.

> So as to avoid being forced to have them shot, we pretended that they were deserters. The policy of war to the death was not carried out; the French soldiers said openly that if that was what the Convention wanted, they should come and carry it out themselves. The Spanish troops said the same of their government, with the consequence that we treated one another with all the respect due to prisoners in accordance with the laws of war.[44] *

But by the time of the Peninsular War attitudes had hardened: if they were dealing with bandits, they argued, they could not afford to treat the enemy or the civilian population with the respect which the rules of war demanded. Any reprisals, however brutal, came to be justified as guerrilla warfare disintegrated into tit-for-tat killings, with the French forced to accept the tactics and the methods of the guerrillas. Let Lieutenant Avril take up the story in 1809.

> Our light infantry picked up all those who had taken to flight and had hidden in the rocks. Not a single prisoner was taken. As thirty-five dragoons had been murdered by the inhabitants of this area, all the villages were burned and their inhabitants put to the sword. On the following day the same routine was repeated. †

---

* Pour n'être pas obligés de les faire fusiller, on les fit passer pour des déserteurs. La guerre à mort n'eut pas des suites, les soldats français dirent ouvertement que si la Convention voulait la guerre à mort, qu'ils vinssent le faire eux-mêmes. Les soldats espagnols en dirent autant de leur gouvernement, de manière qu'on se porta de part et d'autre tout le respect dû aux prisonniers d'après les lois de la guerre.

† Nos voltigeurs ramassèrent dans les rochers tous ceux qui cherchaient leur salut dans la fuite. Il n'y eut pas un prisonnier de fait ... Comme il y avait eu trente-cinq dragons d'assassinés par les habitants de cette contrée, le feu fut mis dans tous les villages et les habitants passés au fil de l'épée. Le lendemain la répétition de la veille.

All this might sound barbaric in any context other than Spain, where torture and massacre had become commonplace. The French had torched the Spanish town of Amarantes, he added, after a number of men of the 17th Regiment had been seized and thrown onto a fire of live coals. The fire had been lit for the purpose, with an almost sadistic deliberation, and the soldiers had been left to burn painfully to death.[45]

For many soldiers the issue at stake was the nature of the war itself. They were prepared to treat other armies with decency because they shared the same conception of war, exposing themselves to the same dangers, admiring the same qualities of courage and military science. But guerrillas were different, respecting no known rules of war and reducing the troops to the tactics of irregulars and bandits. They knew all about guerrillas, of course; indeed, the irregulars who served France in the mountain areas of their frontiers – whether they were known as *barbets* in the Alpine valleys or *miquelets* in the Pyrenean foothills – were guerrilla fighters in all but name. But they detested fighting against them, or responding to tactics which only too often were intended to goad regular troops into anger and outrages that would, in turn, help to unite local people against them. For the troops found it very hard to resist turning their fury on the local population; they were tired, constrained by military discipline, and revolted by what they saw; often their tolerance had been pushed beyond endurance. Chevalier cites this lurid but very typical instance from the war in Calabria, but it could just as easily have taken place in Spain. The French had reached a little town called Lauria, perched on a rock over the plain, and their general had sent an officer to negotiate with its citizens and to ask for food to provision the army. Their response was abrupt.

> As soon as the officer entered the town, he was murdered by the inhabitants, who brutally cut his body into pieces, put them in a basket and got French prisoners to return them to us with the message: 'This is the ration of food which the inhabitants of Lauria send to the French, the only one that can suit them.' Then our enraged soldiers scrambled up the rocks and, despite the desperate defence mounted by the inhabitants and a hail of bullets fired against them, they stormed the village. Everything was then sacrificed to pitiless vengeance. The old men, women and children fired on us from their windows or threw stones at us; it was just like Saragossa. We were forced to set fire to every quarter of the town. A horrible scene then unfolded, as

women, children and old men rushed from their blazing houses and threw themselves at the feet of the victors, only to be massacred by the enraged and furious troops.[46] *

If any enemy was more hated or more liberally denounced for its barbarity than the guerrillas of Spain and southern Italy, it was the peasant soldiers of the Vendée, who engaged the French republic in a bloody civil war in 1793–94, ostensibly in the name of the monarchy and of the Catholic religion. Against them an even more forceful propaganda offensive was mounted, since, unlike the other armies against whom the revolutionaries fought, this was an army composed of Frenchmen who, the republicans believed, had followed their priests and their nobles to destroy every last vestige of liberty. Many of the republican soldiers had served in the National Guard of nearby towns, where they had already learned to regard the countrymen of their immediate hinterland with a somewhat patronising contempt. Others who had been moved to the west or who had had military experience on other fronts saw the war as a simple police operation, one which should be over after a few months, against counter-revolutionaries and traitors. In the west republican soldiers talked with more than average ideological passion, for here the war was far more demonstrably political than elsewhere. Many of the men shared the contempt of their Jacobin officers and of the military *commissaires* sent to accompany the army, agreeing that Vendean peasants were putty in the hands of their priests and demanding exemplary

---

* Notre général envoya un officier français en parlementaire à la ville, pour demander des vivres pour l'armée, mais l'officier fut, aussitôt son entrée, massacré par les habitants, ils eurent la cruauté de couper son corps par morceaux, de les mettre dans un panier, et de nous le renvoyer par des prisonniers français, avec ces mots: 'Voilà la ration de vivres que les habitants de Lauria envoient aux Français, la seule capable de leur convenir …' Alors, nos soldats en fureur gravirent partout les rochers, et, malgré la défense désespérée des habitants, malgré une grêle de balles, nous pénétrâmes au centre de la place. Tout fut alors sacrifié à l'implacable vengeance. Les vieillards, les femmes et les enfants tiraient sur nous par des fenêtres ou nous assommaient à coups de pierre, c'était une nouvelle Saragosse. Nous fûmes alors obligés de mettre le feu aux quatre coins de la ville. Alors se déroule sous les yeux un tableau horrible: les femmes, les vieillards, les enfants sortent précipitamment des maisons embrasées, viennent se jeter aux pieds des vainqueurs … Mais les soldats exaspérés et furieux les immolent.

punishment for any refractory clergy who might fall into their hands. They agreed with General Turreau when he wrote, six months after returning from the Vendée, that the war had its roots in the mentality and the age-old beliefs of the peasantry, beliefs which had already helped stoke up other conflicts, most notably the Wars of Religion. Those who wished to find an explanation for the insurrection should, he added, read the history of the region, for there they will find 'in the very nature of the country, and in the ignorance, customs and superstition of its people, the cause of its present troubles and the origin of the Wars of Religion of which Poitou had always been both the theatre and the cradle'.[47] The Vendean, in other words, was not as other men; he was more ignorant and more primitive, was incapable of understanding patriotism, and, it was implied, must be treated accordingly.

Soldiers fighting in the west expected the worst from an enemy known to take no prisoners and to recognise none of the rules that governed war. They were continually frustrated by the Vendean refusal to engage in open battle, by a preference for guerrilla fighting and for laying ambushes in the *bocage*, the dense thickets and hedgerows which so characterised the landscape of southern Brittany and the Loire. For Aubuy, a cavalryman from Coutras (Gironde), therein lay the secret of their military success, for 'if they had not acted like wild beasts and sought refuge in the woods', they would surely have been destroyed'.[48] Another soldier, an infantryman in the First Battalion of the Deux-Sèvres, described to his sisters in Parthenay the kinds of dangers which faced the army in the west. 'The brigands', he said,

> are not the sort of men to fight a war as we do. What do they do? They form groups of ten or twelve and slip along the side of the main road, protected by a few trees. When they stumble upon three or four poor volunteers, unarmed, perhaps making their way to or from hospital ... then they appear and try to kill them in order to strip them of their belongings; that is the extent of their military prowess.[49] *

---

* Les brigands ne sont pas les hommes à faire la guerre actuellement comme nous, que font-ils, ils se rassemblent au nombre de dix ou douze et suivent une grande route à l'abri de quelques arbres. Voyent-ils trois ou quatre pauvres volontaires qui ne sont point armés allant ou venant à l'hôpital ... ils se montrent et tâchent de les tuer pour avoir ce qu'ils ont, voilà leur beau chef-d'oeuvre qu'ils font maintenant.

In such accounts contempt mingled easily with fear, since most republicans identified the rebels with murder, savagery and crimes against humanity. They knew comrades who had been butchered, in some cases before their very eyes. Nicolas Poincenet, a peasant boy from the Champagne who kept a journal of his experiences, witnessed a massacre by Vendean cavalry which left a dozen of his comrades dead by the roadside. 'Their handiwork consisted of shooting and running through my unfortunate brothers in arms who had stayed on the road. I turned round to see this horrible sight and then continued to flee across country, through the woods.' 50 On the following morning he was able to rejoin his company, but he was unable to forget the massacre, or the thorn-bush where he had been hiding.

Soldiers fighting in the Vendée quickly learned that danger lurked on all sides, that neither enemy soldiers nor the civilian population could be trusted, since villagers were widely suspected of harbouring guerrillas and furthering terrorist attacks. That in turn meant that no quarter was given, as is so often the case in civil war. Here compromise was impossible, and the dominant discourse was that of rooting out counter-revolution and destroying the cancer of fanaticism. The troops may even have shared the enthusiasm of their political masters for killing and destruction, contributing willingly enough to Turreau's scorched earth policy across the departments of the west. 'We shall go in', wrote Joliclerc, 'with a rifle in one hand and a torch in the other; men and women, all will be put to the sword.' 51 Civil war was as brutalising for the soldiers as its language was for the politicians, and some revelled in the slaughter. Writing back to the Club National in Bordeaux, Boissé gloated that it was unthinkable to pardon the traitors they encountered in the Vendean armies. 'Forty thousand brigands have drawn their last breath', he wrote; 'if some off these cowardly slaves thought they might save their lives by declaring themselves to be prisoners, they soon realised their mistake, for as soon as they fell into our hands they were dead and buried.' 52 The experience could be especially harrowing for those assigned to the firing squads and ordered to shoot tens, even hundreds, of fellow-soldiers whose only crime had been to lose a battle and fall into their hands. When they took Noirmoutier, for instance, the French republican army executed thousands of prisoners and, since the Vendeans did the same when they had the chance, it was easy to convince themselves that this was the right thing to do. The lesson was soon learned that in the Vendée human life was cheap. As one soldier told his father, executions became part of their daily routine. 'We shoot them daily', he wrote, 'in batches of fifteen hundred.'[53] Not all carried out these functions willingly, or without some expression of regret. Amongst their correspondence we find admissions that they found it distasteful and rather sad when they had to shoot their prisoners, the more so when they had come to know them a little, to sympathise with them as peasants, as fathers of families, as fellow human beings. But shooting grown men was not the most distasteful task that fell to them. Girardeau, a sergeant with the First Battalion of the Gironde, was one who expressed reservations about the methods which they had to use. 'The battalion is in the Vendée, he wrote from hospital in Nantes, 'and we have beaten the brigands well. Burned and killed them, men, women and children, indeed anyone who got in the way of the army, but what was saddest of all was the sight of those poor little children.'[54] The harrowing memory of their butchered corpses would live with him for the rest of his days.

For the volunteers of 1792 and the young men of the first revolutionary levies the Vendée came to represent the very nadir of soldiering, the kind of fighting which they treated with the greatest disdain. By 1808 and 1809 that role had been passed to Spain and the horrors of war in the Peninsula; and for the conscripts of 1811 and 1812 it was encapsulated in the unending miseries of the Moscow campaign. The tone of their writings as they marched relentlessly across Europe turned increasingly sour and pessimistic, in stark contrast to the rather curious mixture of optimism and sadness with which they had left to join the *Grande Armée*. At first many had greeted the news of the campaign with relief after months of uncertainty and tedium in the barracks towns of the east; but soon that relief gave way to despair and a certain fatalism. They had seen so much suffering, so much needless death, and fearful images had become etched on their consciousness as a result of their experiences. Letter after letter described the horrors which the soldiers witnessed, the piles of corpses, the miles of burned out houses. The sight of Moscow in flames saddened one French officer all the more in that he could not get Paris out of his mind. 'It's a very hideous thing, a great city in flames. Just think of Paris if it were burned, all the houses without roofs or doors or windows, filled with smoking remains, with only a few houses conserved and apparently intact, like the Cité or the Ile Saint-Louis.'[55] Many talked of the misery they saw on all sides, the shortage of supplies, the cold which froze them in every artery. It was just so much worse than any of them had imagined. 'One thing which they will scarcely believe back in Paris', wrote an adjutant to his brother-in-law, 'is that all those men who had already been with the army in Spain now look back on that country with a certain nostalgia when they compare it to this.'[56] But then back in Paris they had no experience of what the armies were suffering on that terrible campaign, from the snows on the Russian steppes to the sight of Moscow in flames, from the crossing of the Niemen or the Berezina, from the gruelling, murderous battles like Smolensk or Borodino. In a touching letter, written at Doubrowna in November 1812, the director of provisioning for the army, François-Louis Réau, bade his wife a tender adieu, making the fatalistic assumption that he would never see her again. He asked her to be patient and not to get anxious if letters took months to get through, and to 'calm herself in her purgatory, which certainly is less terrible than our hell'. Behind a facade of gaiety or a certain bravura, there were many like Réau who could no longer conceal their sufferings. Their masks finally cracked and they admitted to despair, to a presentiment of death, to an awful acceptance that they would never see their loved ones again. That, far more than the battlefield, was what they feared in Russia, and what they meant by those terse references to 'our hell'.[57]

6

Everyday Life in the Armies

It may seem rather perverse, with such memories of the horror of battle etched on their minds, that those soldiers who survived the wars so frequently looked back on the army with a degree of affection, continuing to revere the Revolution or the Emperor in whose name they had fought, and joining veterans' associations in order to meet up with old comrades and relive their years of army service. That they did so, just like the veterans of other wars in modern times, suggests that their military experience was not one which they entirely wished to forget, even if many chose to brush out from their memory moments of particular brutality or overarching fear. The fact that they found it so difficult to communicate with civilians, with those who had not shared their arcane rituals and absurdities, made the need for veterans' associations all the greater, helping in the process of healing in which they were all involved, of searching for a meaningful narrative of their lost years. Often that narrative was not dominated by battles. Combat might constitute the basic purpose of armies, with death an unavoidable concomitant, but active fighting was never more than sporadic, moments of extreme violence which punctuated their years of service. They were certainly the most vivid moments, and in retrospect most soldiers felt proud to have been involved in war, proud to have served their country and its Emperor, aware of the sacrifice which they had made. But there was more to it than that: they knew that they had something in common with other soldiers that civilians could never fully understand, the experience of a shared culture of fear and comradeship, of mutual dependency and masculine sociability, which marked them out from others. For a key period of their lives they had entered another world and had sublimated their individual wishes for the good of all. It made little difference whether they had enjoyed it or loathed it: soldiering had been a curiously intense and at times exciting experience, made more intense by the long years in uniform, by relentless campaigning, by that sense, shared by the soldiers of 1914–18, that the war would go on for ever, that the suffering would never end.[1]

The men they sought out after the return of peace were those on whom they had been so dependent in the thick of battle, friends and comrades with whom, in the very abnormal world of the army, they had formed a cohesion and closeness without parallel in civilian life. Their shared memories would linger long after their retirement from the military and their return to their town or village; at the time their companionship was one of the more pleasurable aspects of a hard military routine, which helped them to endure forced marches and fight off homesickness. Men recalled the joys of eating and drinking together, of singing around the campfire, of long conversations into the night. These were occasions to escape from more immediate dangers and fatigues, for smoking and playing cards, flirting with the *cantinière*, boasting about their conquests in love. Drink could both enliven conversation and wash away the sour taste of the battlefield, and much of the sociability men treasured took place in cafés and wayside inns, bars and country taverns. Like wine, a pipe of tobacco became a regular routine once the evening meal was cleared away, a companionable moment to relax after the tensions of the day, to chat with friends or fellow-officers. Indeed, smoking or chewing tobacco became one of the hallmarks of the French soldier at this time, the young following the more battle-hardened troops in their taste for tobacco. Writing home, young Noël noted this with interest and a degree of repugnance that showed him to be unaccustomed to smoking and unappreciative of it charms. 'Here are our smokers smoking their pipes', he wrote with a disdain worthy of the anti-smoking lobby today.

> They do nothing else. It is an infection. What pleasure can be gained from filling one's mouth and throat with stinking smoke? Others have a strange taste for chewing tobacco. But whether they have tobacco in their nose or in their mouth or in smoke, it is an ugly drug! There is scarcely a young volunteer who does not smoke like the oldest veteran, though your son hopes that he is one who will never take up this bad habit.[2] *

Companionship provided warmth and reassurance in what for many young men remained a forbidding environment. Most were bachelors aged between eighteen and twenty-five, at exactly the time of their lives when they most appreciated freedom and most needed the companionship of their peers. Theirs was necessarily a communal existence, since they ate, drank, talked and slept in the company of others, and privacy was always a scarce commodity. In a world where men slept two to a bed they could not but get to know the *camarade de lit* with whom they were condemned to spend so much time, while the average bivouac held seven or eight men, again pushed unquestioningly into one another's company. Of course they could get on one another's nerves, and reports of quarrels and even violence breaking out between soldiers were not unknown. More commonly, however, these attachments became deep and enduring, so that it was to his *camarades* that a man turned in times of trouble, to borrow small sums to tide over a financial crisis, to visit the sick in hospital, to bear a letter home to anxious parents. In a world where they found themselves suddenly cut off from their families, friends played a vital role in sustaining morale and providing a sense of belonging. 'Melot and I', one young man wrote home to his father in 1808, 'see each other every day and for three-quarters of the time we live together.'[3] The closeness of their friendship seems to have reassured both the young soldier encamped on the Spanish border and his father back in the Charente. Officers, too, took pleasure in friendships that had their origins in the mess, or where men were thrown together by circumstance. In his memoirs Pierre-Auguste Paris remembers the warmth and camaraderie of the Napoleonic armies, a camaraderie which sometimes straddled differences of rank. And he recalls an instance where it was a man's thirst for literacy that led to a lifelong friendship. 'Sergeant Fayet did not know how to read or write. I taught him to sign his name, and in 1811 I obtained for him his marshal's

---

* Voilà nos fumeurs qui fument leurs pipes. Ils ne font que cela. C'est une infection. Quel plaisir peut-on donc avoir à s'emplir la bouche et le gosier d'une fumée puante? D'autres ont le goût singulier de mâcher du tabac. En vérité tabac dans le nez, tabac dans la bouche, tabac en fumée, c'est toujours une vilaine drogue! Il n'y a presque pas de jeune volontaire qui ne fume comme les vieux soldats; mais le vôtre espère ne jamais prendre cette mauvaise habitude.

baton and sub-lieutenant's épaulette. He was very happy about it, and
so was I.'[4]

Very often the bond between close friends in the regiments was
strengthened by shared origins and upbringing. Many of the comrades
who are mentioned in their correspondence are specifically noted as
coming from the same province or *pays*, from the same town or from
a neighbouring parish. Indeed, once the revolutionaries had given up
their somewhat idealistic goal of blending boys from all over France
into their battalions – a scheme devised in the hope that they could
emphasise their national character and dilute any vestiges of provinci-
alism – the army consciously played on local loyalties and identities,
encouraging lads from the same area to socialise together and use their
local patois in a bid to avoid the problems of depression and desertion.
The evidence of their correspondence suggests strongly that this policy
worked, and that a regional recruitment base gave units greater cohesion
and improved men's motivation. Sometimes, of course, they were in
the same battalion as their brothers and cousins, and then the bond
could be especially close. 'Let me tell you of the goodheartedness of my
brother Valmur', wrote Mignard *dit l'Enfant* to his mother in 1793 as
he lay encamped on the plain before Valmy; 'He had two silver watches,
and he made a present of one of them to me. That's a real brother for
you, and brothers like that are exceptionally rare.'[5] Others expressed
their reassurance on finding a cousin, or a neighbour from the village,
or just someone speaking the same familiar dialect, serving alongside
them in their unit.

The presence of other young men form the *pays* provided a vital
psychological link between their temporary life in the regiment and the
society to which most felt they still belonged. Often soldiers seem to
have chosen to serve in the same regiments as boys from their home
villages, and even after long months of service their closest friends would
still be from their own localities, men who spoke the same dialect, knew
the same places, understood the same inflections and gestures. They felt
that they could count on such men, whose communities they knew and
whose values they shared, in moments of adversity, sickness or injury;
they were the sort of men who would try to help, who would inform
their relatives and visit them in hospital. Their presence in the regiments
was itself a source of reassurance, and, when they were separated,

whether by injury or by a simple change-over of regiments, this would be remarked upon with a particular sadness. Shortly after arriving with his unit in Troyes, Louis Godeau wrote with evident regret that, though they had travelled together so far, the boys from his area could not hope to stay together for much longer. 'We have been told', he wrote, 'that we shall be split up into different corps in accordance with our height, and so we shall almost all be separated.'[6] Louis Ruzé, a peasant boy from the countryside west of Paris, echoed this sentiment in 1813 when he regretted the loss of many of his friends since his unit had left Courbevoie; but he still had his closest friend, 'who is my *camarade de lit* and in whose company I have been constantly since the moment we left home'.[7] Commanders often recognised the value of such friendships in cementing a certain cohesion within their units, and they might be reluctant to sacrifice the benefits it conferred. As one young man from the Ariège noted in the Year II, they were imbued with a real sense of solidarity, that which comes from being pals together in difficult and often dangerous circumstances. 'They have left all of us', he wrote, 'our whole company, together, and it is only the officers and captains who are out of place.'[8] That he was mightily relieved is abundantly clear, since it made his life both more bearable and more familiar. Again and again soldiers' letters bear witness to the importance of such friendships, to the joy of rediscovering each other and the fear of being separated. Even on the blackest of days when he learned that he and his unit would be leaving for Moscow, François Bourbier found time to explain that things could be worse, and that he was consoled by the company of his friends from the Oise. They had, he told his father, been issued with backpacks, and they knew that soon they would have to join the troops heading east. But there were four of them marching together, all boys from the Ile-de-France, from villages around Beauvais. 'And the four of us, we are all good friends together.'[9] Being with them brought a guarantee of wellbeing and good cheer.

When they rediscovered lost friends, or when regiments passed each other as they criss-crossed Europe, it was, of course, an opportunity for a quiet celebration or for more raucous drunkenness. Chance meetings brought outpourings of joy, usually mingled with a sense of relief that their brother, cousin, or childhood friend had also managed to survive the vicissitudes of war. Meals were consumed in local inns, beer and wine were quaffed, and these moments were recorded as memorable landmarks in their usually routine lives. Or else their meeting served to remind them of how little they had, how little security for the future, how little material comfort, how little freedom to enjoy themselves. When Martin-Louis Pottier ran into another young man from the Oise in distant Cremona in 1807, they got to gossiping and catching up on news from home; but, he complained, 'we were so poor that we couldn't afford to drink a bottle of wine together'.[10] Jean-Baptiste Depoulis was another whose thoughts were tinged with regret. A somewhat reluctant conscript in 1806 who had been arrested at home in Nice and dragged from prison to prison to get him to the Pyrenean frontier, he noted simply that meeting old friends provided a welcome element of familiarity in which he found solace 'amongst all the miseries' he had suffered.[11]

Food and drink were among the few pleasures of a soldier's life, especially when consumed in company. Joliclerc was one who took to drinking heavily in the armies, a habit which he justified on the grounds that it relieved stress and tension, and that in any case he had earned it. As he explained to his anxious and somewhat outraged mother back in the Jura, this did not make him a wastrel; it was his right to drink if it gave him pleasure, and he believed that it was wine that gave him the courage to fight and to be a good soldier. Besides, he assured her, he was not drinking away his inheritance: 'If we were both to die, to whom would our property then pass? To people who would laugh at us for having taken such good care of it.'[12] He was not alone. The young soldiers were notoriously spendthrift, seeing little reason to save up for a rainy day that might never come. As Jacques Collette confessed from Spain in 1810, when he and his friend had three *sous* between them, they headed for the nearest bar. 'We are afraid to hold on to them till the following day lest we die a sudden death during the night. So we spend them on drink the day we receive them.'[13] It was both a source of instant gratification and a route to thankful amnesia.

Meals, too, would be avidly and companionably consumed by the soldiers, whether those they ate while billeted on civilians or those they had taken in inns and hostelries on the rare occasions when they could afford to celebrate and escape the awful monotony of army cooking. In their letters soldiers would describe both the food they had eaten and the creature comforts they had enjoyed when they had been billeted on local families. The pleasure here could be in seeing how well other people ate when compared to their own peasant experience, or it could come from being back in civilian society, sharing a meal and a roof with families, being surrounded once again by women and children. One young man from the Oise, Jean-Pierre Laine, wrote ecstatically that in Bavaria they had been so well fed that 'I thought we had all become seigneurs'. He recalled that, although they were billeted on a peasant family, they had been treated to all the meat they could eat – stews, roast meat and hams – and had been offered some brandy in the morning before they set off.[14] Not all, of course, were as lucky – or as appreciative. Describing the time when he had been billeted on a German household in Augsburg, Sébastien Mevel placed all the emphasis on obligation, on the fact that his hosts had been compelled to feed him according to army regulations. Nonetheless, he seems to have eaten rather well. They were, he said, 'obliged to feed us soup in the morning; at midday, soup again, ten ounces of meat and a ration of bread, with half a pot of beer; and in the evening half a pot of beer and vegetables'. It was not that Mevel was accustomed to a life of luxury, for he was a peasant boy from Plougastel in rural Brittany who could neither read nor write; his letter was penned for him by one of his friends, who signed himself, rather touchingly, as 'Pouliquen, soldier in the same regiment, a Breton'.[15]

If soldiers talked relatively frequently about eating and drinking, they were rather more coy in discussing their relations with local girls. This may, of course, reflect the social convention of the times – there are things that were better left unsaid; there are things, too, that a young man would have found it hard or inappropriate to express in a letter to his family. But, like any army, the men serving the Revolution and the Empire dreamt of female company and suffered pangs of sexual desire. The fact that theirs was a mass army, and that conscription specifically targeted the young and single, those without wives and dependants, only made the problem more widespread. The military authorities met the men's needs, at least in part, by turning a blind eye to the noisy, often rather disreputable crowds of women who accompanied each regiment, whether as army wives or as camp followers and common prostitutes. Some men, it is true, were lucky enough to see their wives or girlfriends follow them to the regiment, though these were relatively few and the object of understandable envy. A Belgian conscript, Jean-Denis Lejeune, from Mortroux, was one such man: we find him writing home in 1812 to announce that he and his wife have been happily reunited in Berlin, where his wife has found work as a laundress for the army. His main concern was for his young son, who remained at home in his mother's care until such time as he might return.[16] Amidst the confusion of advancing and retreating armies Lejeune could count himself fortunate to have found the woman he loved. Others had little choice but to adopt a more predatory approach at village fairs and in the garrison towns through which they passed.

Their opinions of the girls they met locally ranged between the chivalrous and the ribald, depending on their mood, their audience, and possibly the degree of success they had in winning local affections. French soldiers had always been associated with a certain swagger and gallantry where women were concerned, or such was the image they sought to convey, the image that had entered military legend. Those who served the Revolution and Empire liked to portray themselves as having inherited this honourable mantle, claiming in their writings to have used their charms to good effect among the womenfolk of half a continent. Girault, for one, boasted shamelessly of his success with women, doubtless embroidering the truth in the process and leaving us with the most delicate cameos of his prowess in seduction. He did not hesitate to resort to guile to entrap the young ladies on whom he had intentions. In Germany in 1795, for instance, he directed a theatre group which attracted audiences from miles around. 'As I was the one who handed out the tickets, I was able to shower attentions on the young girls, and to that I owed a number of adventures which have left me with delicious memories.' Five years later, near Salzburg, he tells how the French troops celebrated carnival in an Austrian town.

> We seized hold of all the girls and made them dance, to the great displeasure of the priest who went into the pulpit to forbid them to share in our amusements. A few of them obeyed, but for the most part they stayed with us. So, once we had gone, the priest had the job of baptising lots of little Frenchmen. That was all that we left in the area, for we had ruined it with taxes and requisitions.[17] *

Not all, of course, found it so easy to find the girls or to mix in local society. François Lavaux, who had been a carpenter before becoming a soldier in the 103rd Line Regiment, was unrestrained in his description of the local women he encountered in the Tyrol, where he found customs and fashions less than appealing. The girls who made themselves available to the troops all had venereal diseases, he claimed. They 'wear bonnets that resemble beehives. They also wear skirts that do not cover their knees, and when they bend down their private parts are all revealed.' [18] It was hardly the most flattering of descriptions, but then neither were the views of local people when faced with the morality of the French themselves. Village morals were easily outraged by the easy virtue of many of the soldiers, while women were too often the victims of sexual violence and assault. But at least Lavaux was right to warn of the dangers of disease, as the admission records of frontier hospitals very often confirm. As Chevalier noted in Italy in 1802, Italian girls were 'so ardent in love-making that the most robust of men ends up succumbing ... The hospitals, piled high with the victims of a depraved love, close their eyes to all other sufferers, till it seems as though man is nothing more than an unthinking animal, following his brutal natural instinct like any other animal. There are, of course, a lot of women who are not to be feared, but they are not the ones with whom the poor soldier can associate.' [19] As with soldiers from time immemorial, their rough and violent reputation deterred respectable women from seeking their company, while their own desperate search for sexual pleasure made them obvious targets for local prostitutes.

Some soldiers wanted more than occasional female company or fleeting sexual gratification. As in any war – and especially in a war stretching over two decades and across half of Europe – there were those who sought and found love in far-flung corners of the continent, or who elected to forget their former sweethearts in France and settle down

---

* Nous avions accaparé toutes les filles que nous faisions danser, au grand déplaisir du curé qui monta en chaire pour leur défendre de partager nos divertissements. Quelques-unes obéirent, mais le plus grand nombre nous restèrent. Aussi, après notre départ, le curé eut-il à baptiser beaucoup de petits Français. C'est tout ce que nous laissâmes dans le pays, que nous avions ruiné par les réquisitions et les contributions.

with a bride from Germany, or Austria, or Poland. If they were to marry they needed the permission of a superior officer, which may rather have limited its incidence. But on occasions permission was granted, and letters would bring unsuspecting parents surprising and, for many, somewhat shocking news. Sons knew that in these circumstances their main task was to offer reassurance that parents would not be losing them forever: this was especially true in rural regions where people had no experience of travel and where Belgium or Holland could seem desperately far away. In 1793, for instance, Marie-Joseph Duport broke the news to his family, near Saint-Ybars in the Ariège, that he had taken a Swiss girl for his wife. 'Be reassured', he wrote, 'that if your son has got married far from home, he has taken a good woman for his wife who will give you as much cause for satisfaction as your son himself. She is not rich, but that is her only shortcoming.' [20] Sometimes the news went down rather better than the soldier was entitled to expect. One conscript from a village near Crépy-en-Valois in the Ile-de-France, on receiving a letter with the news that his sister had married, was able to reply that she was not alone. He asked his mother to 'tell my sister that on the day after her marriage I went through the same nuptial ceremony' in Antwerp, where he was stationed. He enclosed a portrait of the daughter-in-law, adding that he hoped the coincidence of two weddings on consecutive days would bring good luck to them and to their children.[21]

Along with food, drink and sociability, travel was cited as a source of pleasure and wonderment by men who would not normally have had the opportunity to visit the towns of their province but who were now marched with their battalion from country to country across Europe, from capital to capital. Many barely noticed the changes around them, but for others travel was a source of pleasure and enrichment, and their writings reflected a certain wonderment at what they have seen. Joining the army was also an adventure which had opened up a new world of experience and colour, and, like so many before them, they loved talking about the exotic sights they had seen. 'I am very happy to have seen the countryside', wrote one Liégeois with a disarming simplicity, 'because if I was still in Metz I should have had nothing to tell you about.' [22] Another soldier, on his way to join the *Grande Armée* for the Russian campaign, wrote excitedly back from

Warsaw, pointing out that, if Paris were included, he had now passed through three European capitals on his march. Though the idea of joining the fighting did not appeal to him, the army had at least given him the opportunity to see other countries and to learn something of the people who lived there.[23] The result could be a rude culture shock, as men from Languedoc were confronted with the Germanic lands of the east, while those from the north and Belgium found themselves introduced to the diet and lifestyle of the Mediterranean. Sometimes, of course, this led to the unharnessing of dislike and prejudice: men from Savoy found that Rome was uncomfortably hot, Poland a land given over to stark misery, and the lower Po valley an unhealthy country infested with brigands and a prey to malarial swamps and fevers.[24] But not all voiced criticism when they came in contact with the unfamiliar. When Pierre Dupin wrote to his brother from Genoa in 1812 he could not hide the sense of wonder he had experienced on seeing the sea. As a country lad from the land-locked centre of France – the canton of Cayres in the Haute-Loire – he had never set eyes on the ocean, and the sight entranced him. 'I tell you, my dear brother, that we can see the sea from our beds, and lots of ships pass every day and in every direction, and that is something I find very curious, for never in my life had I seen such things.'[25]

Some men did little beyond describing the countryside and the dress of the inhabitants. Others offered critical vignettes of the people whose towns and cities they visited. Alexandre Ladrix, a volunteer from the Gers, was one who offered a telling commentary on the attitudes and mores of local people. In Germany he depicted the inhabitants as mean, demanding payment up front before they would part with even the most essential foodstuffs; in Rome he noted slyly that 'even as they profess the principles of religion, they murder Frenchmen for the love of God'; whereas in Lille, which must have seemed to the young southerner to be a very foreign city indeed, the inhabitants 'behaved like gods; they watch their own houses being knocked down and burned and yet still they cry 'Vive la Nation!'[26] Others, drawn particularly from among the officers, commented on the local architecture where they were, or offered perceptive descriptions of foreign cities like Rome and Venice, Berlin and Basle, comparing them with Paris and the cities they knew in France. So in the countryside, they commented on the passing of the seasons, the neatness of foreign farmyards, or the tools used to till the soil or bring in the harvest. They described the passing of the agricultural year in knowledgeable detail when they themselves were of farming stock and were writing to peasant families well able to assess the techniques used in Poland or the Palatinate against their own day-to-day practice. Take, for instance, this lyrical description of the land in Calabria, culled from the memoirs of Pierre-Auguste Paris. 'The countryside', he wrote,

> is magnificent and extraordinarily fertile. The low-lying areas which bordered on the sea were covered with cotton fields or with plantations of oranges and olives. The hillsides that lay immediately behind them produced great quantities of cereals mingling with mulberry bushes; higher still, vast areas of pasture irrigated by mountain streams supported large flocks of animals. The sides of these mountains were carpeted with huge forests of chestnut trees. *

But, he goes on, 'it could be said that this beautiful country is a paradise inhabited by devils. And, indeed, the people of Calabria were always armed to the teeth and ready to use their weapons. That peaceable ploughman whom you saw ploughing his field had hidden his shotgun in a nearby furrow and a huge sheath-knife in the right-hand pocket of his breeches'.[27]

In large parts of Europe it was not just the agriculture that was different or the methods used to cultivate the fields. French soldiers might also encounter for the first time people of other beliefs and religious practices, and occasionally they consigned their thoughts on these to paper. Gabriel Noël, who had joined up as a volunteer in 1791 and strongly supported the Revolution's stance on religious tolerance, was struck in Metz both by the extent of speculation by Jewish money-lenders against the paper currency – in the Jewish quarter of the city he had been hustled and pestered by them as they sought to exchange

---

* Le pays est d'ailleurs magnifique et d'une fertilité extraordinaire. Les parties basses que borde la mer étaient couvertes de champs de coton ou de plantations d'orangers et d'oliviers. Les collines qui viennent ensuite produisaient en abondance des céréales entremêlées de mûriers; plus haut, de vastes pâturages arrosés par les eaux dérivées des montagnes nourrissaient de nombreux troupeaux. Les flancs de ces montagnes étaient tapissés d'immenses forêts de châtaigniers.

coin for *assignats* and *assignats* for coin – and by the degree of hatred shown towards them by the local population. And he was rather shocked by the levels of intolerance he witnessed: 'The windows of their homes are smashed and their furniture broken. The prejudices against their race still persist among ordinary people.'[28] More thoughtful were the reflections of Louis Godeau, the former high-school teacher from Pontlevoy, when his unit was billeted on Lutheran families in Germany. Godeau was unfamiliar with Lutheran ways, and was eager to discuss them with his parents back in the Catholic west of France, especially as he was himself lodging with the pastor and had every opportunity to learn about their faith. In a letter from Hochelheim in Year VII he concluded that the Lutheran community are 'good people', even if they do things very differently from Catholics. The pastor, he explains, is a married man with a wife and a large family. Lutherans do not say the mass, nor are their churches filled with images and statues; rather they are austere buildings 'where you see little more than the four walls and a pulpit for the preacher'. Their ministers wear no special vestments for church services, which are conducted in their own language, not in Latin; the faithful do not confess to a priest, but only to God; and, he noted meaningfully, their priests do not take money to pray for the souls of the departed. Overall, Godeau seemed favourably impressed by their simplicity and by what he had learned of their theology, which he summed up with admirable objectivity: 'They believe, as we do, in the divinity of Jesus Christ; they take communion in both kinds, but they do not believe that Christ is actually present in the communion; nor do they believe in the virginity of the Mother of God, nor yet in the infallibility of the Pope.'[29] Clearly, he had found much food for thought in what he has heard and witnessed, and was eager to discuss it with his family.

Few of the troops who served the Revolution and Empire were as well educated as Godeau or had his intellectual aspirations; and few were able to discuss the cultures they encountered in anything like this degree of depth. Most saw the peoples over whose lands they tramped merely as another source of plunder and pillage, to be exploited at will. It was not just a question of reprisals or of military necessity: they plundered what they could find, to the extent that many soldiers regarded booty as their right, a source of profit and even of entertainment which led inevitably to conflict with the local population. Writing in 1793, one young volunteer from the Yonne talked of his role in the pillage of Deux-Ponts with barely concealed excitement. The town had resisted their siege; so, he explained, when they finally captured it, they had killed some four hundred people, townsmen as well as soldiers. Then they had imposed a tax on the inhabitants of two million francs, and had laid waste three castles belonging to the local prince, taking more than three hundred cartloads of booty back to France.

> We rounded up all their oxen, cows and sheep: where a peasant had three cows, we would take two, so that the enemy would not be able to profit from them. After that, we waited until all the corn had been brought in, before taking all the carts belonging to the peasants and transporting their grain to French granaries, with the result that this town is now deserted, abandoned by French and Prussians alike.[30] *

The young man was excited by what he had seen and would seem to have thought little more about it. Besides, they knew from what their generals had told them that, when the Austrians or Prussians entered French villages, the enemy did the same or even worse. With this comforting thought they set any scruples aside. Still in 1793, a *caporal-fourier* from the Nord boasted of the plentiful supplies of meat which they enjoyed in Germany and the lavish quantities of cheap wine. He tells how they had stolen leather to the value of 2700 livres and had sold it for the profit of the battalion. And for entertainment there was always pillage and rape. 'We took their horses, chickens, cows, sheep, pigs, indeed all the livestock we found, and after these expeditions we went into the peasants' houses, and when we had eaten and drunk well, we bedded their wives and daughters.'[31] He showed little compunction at ill-treating the subjects of the Austrian Emperor; but he could hardly have been outraged if people from the Germanic countries continued to view the French with resentment and hatred.

---

* Nous leur avons ramassé tous leurs boeufs, leurs vaches, et leurs moutons; où il y avait trois vaches chez un paysan, nous en prenions deux, de peur que l'ennemi n'en profitât. Après cela, l'on a attendu que tous les blés aient été ramassés; l'on a pris toutes les voitures des paysans pour conduire leurs blés dans les magasins de France, de sorte que cette ville est déserte et délaissée par les Français et par les Prussiens.

If most of the soldiers joined in these marauding expeditions without chagrin, some did show a degree of remorse and expressed regret for the brutality with which they had treated local people. Most often such qualms find expression in memoirs and autobiographies written after the event, when the writer has had time to assess and reflect; they seldom found their way into letters scribbled at the time. They indicate an unease with the army's acceptance of pillage as a necessary part of warfare, with the assumption that it was simply an aspect of an age-old tradition. Girault, for example, felt unhappy that villagers who had previously helped the French soldiers and offered them shelter not infrequently found themselves victims to the greed of these same soldiers some months later. 'The entire country that we trudged across had already been devastated by the enemy troops; we carried on the devastation, respecting nothing: men were beaten, women ill-treated, houses sacked and sometimes burned.' He felt rather shocked by such a breach of the basic laws of hospitality and unable to justify what he termed the 'sad rules of war'.[32] In his journal Marquant is even more savage: he had joined up as a committed revolutionary and could not believe that the principles for which he was fighting were being so flagrantly betrayed by the armies themselves. Is it surprising, he asked rhetorically, if, after seeing the conduct of the French troops, the rest of Europe decided to engage them in battle? 'Is it so astonishing that they should take us for hordes of barbarians and brigands, that they should prefer their masters to our laws and take every opportunity to defeat us?' To Marquant the lesson is obvious, that they must practise what they preach if the call of liberty is to be heard across Europe. 'If we are the defenders of humanity and of property, let us not violate them on the soil of others whom we are seeking to convert to the status of free men.'[33] Pillage, in other words, was potentially counter-productive, in that it undermined the most basic ideals of the Revolution and alienated those with whom the armies had contact.

The majority of the troops, however, were far too concerned with the miseries of their own lives in the battalions to worry about those they were inflicting on others. Both in the 1790s and under the Empire the soldiers were noted for their grumbling, their constant complaints about the dullness and deprivation which characterised their daily existence, and such grumbles were the very stuff of much of their correspondence.

They were forever impoverished: their pay had failed to come through, was inadequate to the basic needs of survival, or was diminished by the spiralling rate of inflation, itself often exacerbated by the presence of the army in a local community. French insistence during the revolutionary years that the men be paid in *assignats* rather than in coin merely magnified the problem. In Year II we find Jean Cartaut writing back to his parents in Auxerre that even in eastern France local peasants declined to accept payment in paper currency. 'It is not that the farmers are short of wheat', he wrote, 'but they are no longer prepared to take *assignats*; they all say that if we have hard currency then we can have some grain, but they go so far as to say that they have no use for *assignats* other than to make bedding for their cows.' [34] For this reason the majority of the soldiers' letters home contain some element of begging, whether for food, for articles of clothing, or, most frequently, for small sums of money which would allow them to eat adequately or to repay debts to their friends. These debts were often sizable, sometimes to more fortunate comrades, at others to officers who sympathised with their lot. Of course, there were parents whose own poverty was such that they could not answer these pleas, and others who suspected their sons of simply wanting money for drink. But their need was real enough. Parents had to be told of the depths to which their boys had sunk, and they had to be discouraged from sending them parcels containing irrelevancies, like pairs of stockings, or handkerchiefs, or presents of cake.[35] Only cash, as many of the soldiers knew, could repay the debts they had incurred in the daily struggle to keep themselves alive. Without financial help from home, as they repeatedly emphasised, they would be reduced to the basest forms of human degradation.

Misery and discomfort took many forms, especially during the long months between campaigns, when they were dug in in the Alps or the Pyrenees or on the plains of central Europe. The soldiers complained bitterly of the ravages of the weather, whether the torrid heat of the plains of central Spain or the mountain snows of a northern Italian winter. Heat sapped their energy and, when combined with the long forced marches of the Peninsular campaign, went far to explain the exhaustion and lassitude suffered by French troops south of the Pyrenees. But the Alpine and central European winters were feared even more. Snow, in particular, could pose a mortal threat to young troops who often had little experience of the mountains and who were inadequately clad against the cold. 'On 22 December', reminisced Vigo-Roussillon of his time in Piedmont in Year IV,

> such a huge quantity of snow fell that we had to run for our lives. We abandoned our camp and everything contained in it – artillery and munitions, horses, everything – happy to be able to take our rifles. The wind was violent. It drove iced snow into our faces which left us covered in blood. We lost a lot of soldiers who either died from the cold or were buried under the snow (an artillery company disappeared beneath the snow while scrambling down from the keep to our camp).[36] *

Snow, in other words, could be a killer. It left men exhausted and enervated, at a time when the army demanded of them yet more physical exertions. And though the Italian experience was sobering, it could not fully prepare them for the icy wastes they would encounter on the road to Moscow.

By 1813, indeed, one soldier could claim that it was no longer the enemy that posed the greatest threat to their welfare, but sheer exhaustion after months of fighting in extreme conditions. They were 'on their feet day and night', since they could not relax and the enemy continued to harass them and to wear them down.[37] Weariness presented a constant threat to the health of the troops; back in 1793 a republican soldier complained that he was worn down by tiredness, that he had gone forty nights without proper sleep or without getting out of the clothes in which he stood; they got to sleep, he said, on those days when there had been fighting, after a battle.[38] Men craved for sleep, for relaxation, for the chance to forget and obliterate the reality they saw around them. When Pierre Girardon wrote to his brother in Year II from the Army of the Rhine, he wrote with all the mangled logic of the soldier, at the same time immensely patriotic and committed to his cause and so ill

---

* Il tombe une si grande quantité de neige que nous fûmes contraints de nous sauver. Nous abandonnâmes notre camp et ce qu'il renfermait: l'artillerie et ses munitions, les chevaux, etc., trop heureux pour pouvoir emporter nos fusils. Le vent était violent. Il nous poussait au visage de la neige glacée qui nous mettait tout en sang. Nous perdîmes beaucoup de soldats qui moururent de froid ou restèrent ensevelis (une compagnie d'artillerie disparut sous la neige en descendant du donjon au camp où nous étions).

and demoralised that despair was taking over. 'I am in a really critical
state', he wrote:

> What can you do, you can either march or lie down and die. No discussion
> is allowed. I have a sickness which I would gladly pay a hundred louis to get
> rid of; a fortnight's rest would see me better, yet I would not abandon my
> post for all the treasure in the world. I'm suffering the most dreadful of
> miseries. A cannon-ball or a bullet would be welcome to finish me off; and
> I would have no cause to reproach myself, I would have worked as a true
> republican and I should die gladly with my arms in my hand.[39] *

Though his response was extreme, there were many who in their
letters home betrayed signs of despair and depression because of the
appalling condition of the armies, the lack of proper clothing and
protection against the elements which, they felt, was exposing them still
further to danger. They bivouacked where they could, but there were
times when the lie of the land was unsuitable and even pitching camp
proved impossible. Rains and melting snow served to exacerbate these
conditions till the soldiers were having to sleep in fields that were turning
into swamps. Gilbert Favier described one night as quite desperately
uncomfortable. 'We were sleeping on a ploughed field', he explained,
'which incessant rains had made as soft and clawing as the mud in a
pit.'[40] Some talked of having to sleep in the open air, or in unheated
barns on mattresses of straw, sleeping conditions which encouraged
disease and skin ailments, with lice and other vermin adding to their
discomfort. Besides, they had very little decent clothing, and almost no
fresh linen, with the result that they were forced to sleep in the same
damp and frayed uniforms in which they had laboured and fought. The
men's health almost unavoidably suffered. In part this was due to
shortages in supply – most of the armies were seriously short of the
jackets, trousers, shirts and boots which they needed to equip the troops

---

* Je suis dans un état bien critique. Que veux-tu, il faut marcher ou crever,
il n'y a pas à dire. J'ai une maladie que je ne voudrais pas avoir pour cent
louis; quinze jours de repos feraient bien mon affaire, mais je ne quitterais
pas mon poste pour tous les trésors de l'univers. Je souffre comme un mal-
heureux, je suis bien à plaindre! Une balle ou un boulet ferait bien mon affaire;
je n'aurais rien à me reprocher, j'aurais travaillé en bon républicain et je
mourrais avec plaisir les armes à la main.

– but in part, too, it was a side-effect of the exigencies of war. For six weeks, Jean Cordelier told his daughter, he had slept fully clad, with his knapsack still on his back, present at his guard post lest the enemy should attack.[41]

If a lack of warmth and hygiene exposed the men to fevers and disease, they were even more debilitated by shortages of food in the army, the subject which without question caused the greatest incidence of complaint. Nothing was more likely to cause unrest or mutiny than the fear of starvation, especially since in their daily manoeuvres they were being forced to expend so much energy. The troops quickly grew hungry, and that hunger sapped their strength, as all too often familiar foodstuffs proved impossible to find or quite impossibly expensive given their meagre resources. Bread, meat, wine and beer were for most soldiers the staples of their existence, the bare essentials without which they could not function and whose absence would lead to outrage. But often these proved unobtainable, especially in the countries across which they passed, and the men were prone to suspect that local people were cheating them, with farmers and shopkeepers preferring to hold on to their stocks or attempting to exploit their uninvited guests by charging inflated prices. As a result the men were forced to go short, or even to starve. In the mountains, in particular, they often found themselves reduced to a single meal each day because rations had run short, whether through supply failures or, more frustratingly, because it proved impossible to get through to the army on isolated mountain cols. Alexandre Ladrix, stationed with his unit in the Alps north of Nice, explained that the real problem was a shortage not of bread, but of mules. That in turn had logistical consequences: 'We are obliged to fast some days; the shortage of mules means that we can only get bread in the late afternoon around four or five o'clock, with the consequence that we can only have one meal per day.'[42] This might seem harsh, but it was not unusual at a time when troops were constantly on the move and the supply network was at the mercy of so many intermediaries.

As a result, French soldiers did find themselves threatened with starvation, and their morale suffered accordingly. From Metz in 1813 Sébastien Marie contrasted the misery of the soldier with the relative wellbeing of the average agricultural labourer. For three days, he explained, they had marched on empty stomachs with nothing to eat except potatoes which they had pulled up themselves from the fields they had passed; they had not seen a loaf of bread for over a fortnight. Disillusioned with his treatment, he asked, rhetorically, why the soldier could be left without rations in this way at a time when anyone taking even the most menial job in agriculture seemed to find enough to eat.[43] Others agreed. 'We don't live; we struggle to stay alive', wrote one soldier stationed near Mannheim. 'We are reduced to a daily ration of two pounds of potatoes which have completely rotted and three ounces of dried peas which have been gnawed by weevils.'[44] Survival was a constant struggle, in which the soldiers ate what they could find, kept going by the support of their comrades and by a primitive urge to stay alive. To satisfy that urge any form of sustenance would do, and if there was no bread that did not necessarily mean that they would starve. From Smolensk in 1812, deep in the Russian winter, one French officer explained to his mother just how they managed to keep themselves alive in the appalling landscape in which they found themselves.

> The army has been without bread on its march, but it did have large numbers of horses which had died from exhaustion, and I can assure you that a slab of horsemeat, sliced and cooked in a pan with a little fat or butter makes a very reasonable meal. At Wiazma we enjoyed a very good cat stew; five of us consumed three fine cats, and they were excellent.[45] *

In extreme conditions it took a little ingenuity to stave off starvation.

Cold, damp, poor clothing and near-starvation, these were the conditions which soldiers most resented and grumbled about, sometimes letting slip an admission that they felt the Nation or the Emperor owed them rather better. The majority of the young conscripts did little more than announce that basic foodstuffs were unobtainable or were too costly to afford, or complain about the monotony and poor quality of what they were offered round the *marmite*. Occasionally, however, they would give up all attempt to conceal their sufferings from their families

---

* L'armée a manqué de pain sur la route, mais elle avait en abondance des chevaux morts de fatigue, et je t'assure qu'un morceau de cheval coupé par tranches minces et passé dans une poële avec un peu de beurre ou de graisse n'est pas un mauvais manger. A Wiazma nous nous sommes régalés d'une fort bonne fricassée de chats; à cinq nous avons mangé trois beaux chats qui étaient excellents.

and provided harrowing descriptions of the conditions they had faced. Joseph Vachin, who started out as a private soldier but rose rapidly through the ranks, wrote a series of letters between Year XI and 1816 to his uncle, a public notary in Mende. In one of these letters, written in the winter of Year XIV, he gave a graphic account of the realities of army life. He was not particularly given to moaning about his lot: earlier in the same year he had explained that they were off to join the *Grande Armée* to the east, mentioning that that would, of course, involve hardships but adding that food was still plentiful and the weather fine. How different things would become by midwinter! Then Vachin explains that he has had more misery to sustain in this campaign than he believes he can tolerate.

> It will suffice that I tell you, my dear uncle, that on one occasion I spent six days with only half a pound of biscuit and some potatoes, that for around two months I have only taken off my breeches to wash them, otherwise I have always slept on a bale of straw or under the stars. Sometimes I have wakened covered in snow, with nothing in my belly and nothing to put into it.[46] *

Hunger, fatigue and cold conspired to undermine his spirits.

So, very often, did boredom, that feeling of utter stagnation and demoralisation which overcame large numbers of soldiers in the long months between campaigns, and which, however great the dangers, made men long to see active service. Their longing for company, for diversion and conversation, concealed the deep-seated boredom which many of them felt. For – and is a truism with which men who have served in other wars rush to concur – life in the regiments during the long periods between campaigns could be quite stiflingly dull, mindless hours spent on patrol or guard duty or in menial tasks around the camp, life a seemingly endless succession of marches, exercises and routine fatigues. The march did, of course, have its dangers, particularly when the army had to cross a river and there was a risk of drowning, but the hundreds

---

* Il suffira de vous dire, cher oncle, que j'ai passé une fois six jours avec une demi-livre de biscuit et quelques pommes de terre, que depuis environ deux mois je n'ai quitté ma culotte que pour la blanchir, autrement toujours couché sur une botte de paille ou sur la terre à la belle étoile, quelquefois se lever couvert de neige et rien dans le ventre ni rien pour y mettre.

of miles across central Europe were remembered less for the few moments of drama than for the inexorable, grinding tedium. As for training
and exercise, which the army regarded as essential to instil a sense of
discipline and to maintain physical fitness, they were dismissed by the
men as cruel and largely pointless impositions on their lives, endlessly
repetitive, and destructive of any enthusiasm they might have had for
the cause. Training lasted eight hours a day, complained Léonard Peigne
from the barracks at Rueil in 1812; it was the only thing a trooper knew
from one day's end to another.[47] Those who had known other trades in
civilian life lamented their fate in being reduced to such dull, mind-
numbing routine. They complained of its tedium, and some questioned
its usefulness as well. Bonnel, writing from Parma to his father in Savoy,
cursed the endless chore of training and declared that he would rather
be back home on the farm, hacking at the most unyielding earth and
weeds and 'breaking up the soil from morning till sunset', rather than
be condemned to mindless exercises.[48] Nor were things much better in
the cavalry, at least for the young until such time as they were promoted.
For there, too, between campaigns novice soldiers found their dreams
of glory shattered by long hours of drill or of mucking out the stables.
'When we are on campaign,' wrote Chevalier, 'it is another matter, but
when we are on garrison duty we die of boredom.'[49]

The army believed that regular exercises of this kind, though they
might be dull and monotonous, were necessary to maintain morale in
the units; like most modern armies, the French feared the atrophy
caused by inactivity and empty tedium and believed that drill helped
maintain alert minds as well as supple bodies. Many of the soldiers
clearly saw it differently, as a physically and mentally numbing regime
imposed by a harsh and often inflexible disciplinary code. They felt
worn out by the hours of tedious and repetitious exercise ordered by
drill-sergeants for whom many had scant respect, among them men of
limited ability and vision who gloried in the tyranny they could impose
in an army where acts of insubordination were not tolerated. But if
the soldiers at times resented the harshness of the military code, they
also feared it, and were wont to comment on some of the more savage
sentences handed down by courts-martial and military councils established in the armies. Military justice had an inexorable quality, and the
courts were empowered to pass death sentences for a wide range of

offences. Some of these the men were prone to approve, in particular in cases of treason by high-ranking officers which, they were asked to believe, explained defeats in the field or the failure to press home their strategic advantage; cases involving royalists and *émigrés*; and those of men who had sought to profiteer from the soldiers' misery by speculating in *assignats* or in supplies. Others seemed to them to be over-harsh, out of proportion to the seriousness of the crime, especially the executions of ordinary soldiers for minor acts of pillage or for showing cowardice in the face of enemy fire, situations in which many soldiers found it easy to imagine themselves and where they could sympathise with the failings of their comrades. Here they would sometimes write with a mixture of awe, fear and a subdued sympathy for their condemned comrades.

Instances of capital sentences being carried out in the camps loomed large in the soldiers' memories, especially during the Jacobin years when the law was particularly severe. In Year III a soldier from the Nord described an incident in his battalion in which seven men, three sergeants and four fusiliers, had gone off into the surrounding countryside and had terrorised local peasants, going so far as to wound one farmer with two sabre blows. The deputies on mission in Holland saw no reason to show mercy, insisting that the letter of the law must be observed and that all seven must be shot.[50] Such incidents made a deep impression on others, and the sentences helped restore temporary order to the ranks: they were a crude method of control. Bricard, for one, was impressed by the brutality of military sentences rather than by their justice, particularly since the executions took place publicly, in the midst of the regiment. The intended message was obvious, that in no circumstances would plunder and theft be tolerated. But his tone suggests a hint of sympathy, a note of regret that useful lives were being thrown away. 'In the evening at eight o'clock, and surrounded by our brigade, they shot a soldier from the 13th Horse who had been convicted of having exchanged his old hat for a new one with a man from the countryside around.' A short while later six drummer-boys were convicted of having robbed an old woman, who had denounced them to their general. Again little mercy was shown. The council of war ruled that the two eldest boys should be shot, while the other four, too young to suffer the death penalty themselves, were condemned to watch the execution of their friends.[51] Bricard found it hard not to register regret and compassion, especially since across the period of the wars the military code was applied very unevenly. At those moments when the army needed to restore internal order – as it did to control outbreaks of pillage in Austria in 1805 when some of the French were committing unacceptable outrages against local people – exemplary punishments were imposed to maintain a discipline that was necessary to achieve military success.[52] At such times fear of retribution merely added to the miseries and anxieties of the men in the ranks.

Those who fell sick or were victims of the innumerable fevers which swept the regiments were more miserable than most, since they had little choice but to drag their weary bodies along with the rest of their unit or face the desperate insecurity and loneliness of a military hospital. In some parts of Europe fevers were endemic, with the men forbidden to drink local water and with dysentery and diarrhoea sweeping through their camps. And though, for some troops weary of the endless marches or shell-shocked in battle, hospital could seem to offer a welcome rest from soldiering, the reality of a military ward or a field ambulance could be grim indeed. The reputation of these hospitals was poor and, as the wars dragged on and everyone knew others who had died there, rumours spread rapidly through the ranks. They were widely believed to be *mouroirs* where the sick went to die, and where damp, insanitary conditions created fertile breeding-grounds for fevers and lice. From the descriptions left by those men unfortunate enough to spend long weeks in hospital it is not difficult to see why. They felt desperate and abandoned, fearing a lingering death at the end of the world, cut off from those they love. As one young man wrote home in 1809 to his father in Le Puy, 'I've been in bed for two months now, dangerously ill, without any real hope of getting better, and I've been crying day and night that I haven't seen my father and mother or brother or sister'. When he wrote the worst was behind him and the fever had passed, but during his illness he had hit the depths of depression and had felt utterly alone.[53]

Despite Napoleon's eagerness to identify with his sick and wounded troops, and the work of surgeons like Larrey in helping the wounded on the battlefield, the standard of care offered in French field hospitals in this period remained poor. Men were piled into cramped and insalubrious conditions where fevers could rage and epidemics strike as readily as in the camps, and often with more deadly effect. Jean Lalle-mant, a soldier in the 4th Line Regiment, described in 1813 the pitiful conditions of the dead and dying when pestilence struck his regiment. He was lucky, in that he recovered sufficiently to avoid being taken to hospital; but there soldiers were dying like flies: 'the hospital was already crammed with the wounded when fever struck, and they buried sixty bodies in a communal grave of those who had died in the previous twenty-four hours'.[54] Of course, the figures may be inflated, or the story may all have been hearsay; but it does illustrate the deep fear with which the troops viewed military hospitals, a fear which also explains the widespread hostility among local people when a hospital was mooted for their area. Soldiers admitted that they feared a spell in a hospital bed more than death itself, and certainly more than death on the battlefield. For one thing, the chances of survival seemed slimmer: as one young Jacobin serving in the Army of the Vosges in May 1793 presciently put it, with fifteen to twenty men dying every day in hospital in Metz, he would rather take his chances on the *champ d'honneur*.[55] Even more dramatic was the testimony of a young Savoyard deserter who had survived a catalogue of adventures in the mountains while fleeing the authorities – he had been attacked by thieves and had nearly been swept away by a torrent – but who believed that these dangers were as nothing compared to the threat to his health which was posed by the periods he had spent in fetid prisons and in military hospitals.[56]

Many of those suffering from fevers would do anything they could to avoid being sent to hospital, consigning themselves to the care of their comrades or – if they were lucky – of their wives. In 1795 young Chertier, a drummer with the Army of the Sambre-et-Meuse, had suffered spasmodic fevers that had lasted a week; but, he reports with some relief, he had avoided the need to go to hospital since he had been cared for by the wife of his drum-major. It was a much more reassuring situation, and Chertier felt that he was already well on the way to recovery.[57] But, of course, there were many who could not avoid hos-pitalisation, whether as a result of battle wounds or fevers, gangrene or simple fatigue, and the letters they wrote from their hospital beds bear witness to their distress. Hospitals were cramped and overcrowded to the point where the patients had scarcely any rations, such was the constant drain on food. Jean-Henri Levieux, in hospital in Perpignan, asked his family for a little money to help him survive. If he did not get something, he warned, 'I shall be like so many other miserable wretches who die on their feet. Just think of it: a hospital with more than three thousand patients! The rations are so tiny that men die here of neglect.'[58] Others died from the surgery they received, whether from the frighteningly poor hygiene in the wards, often infested with lice and bed-bugs, or from the lack of any form of antiseptic or anaesthetic treatment to assuage their pain. Or they were made to suffer because the hospitals had insufficient stocks of drugs, or because to save money they systematically cut down on the medicines prescribed to their patients.[59] In such circumstances it is hardly to be wondered at if the troops had little confidence in doctors and preferred to stay as far away from their clutches as possible.

In the eyes of many soldiers hospitals were places of doom and disease, to be discussed in the same breath as prisons or prisoner-of-war camps, with which they had much in common. For in both a young soldier felt helpless and cut off from his friends, his fate in the hands of others over whom he could have no control. And in both the physical conditions were so bad that they could be life-threatening. One conscript of 1799, François Lavaux, was taken prisoner almost immediately and served nine months in various gaols and prisoner-of-war camps across Carpathia, before he was released, 'sick and gnawed by vermin', in a negotiated exchange of prisoners. In a letter to his father after his release, he described the acute shortages and overcrowding that had characterised the camps where he had been held. In one, close to the Turkish border,

> we were put in army quarters, forty men to a room. For walks we had only a small exercise yard which had no fresh air. We were not allowed to leave the building. For food we were given a loaf of bad bread and, every day, nothing other than beans cooked in mutton fat. We slept on a handful of rotting straw which had been half-eaten by vermin. *

---

* On nous a mis dans les quartiers, quarante hommes par chambrée. Nous n'avions pour promenade qu'une petite cour qui n'avait point d'air. Nous ne pouvions aucunement sortir. Nous avions pour nourriture un mauvais pain, et tous les jours rien que des haricots accommodés avec du suif de mouton. Nous étions couchés sur une poignée de mauvaise paille, mangés par la vermine.

Unsurprisingly, men fell ill and died. To make matters worse, they had to put up with abuse from the local population, who spat in their faces and insulted them. 'At the festival of Corpus Christi in 1799', he adds, 'the peasants had gathered together to form the procession. They would leave their places to hit us with the butts of their rifles or to punch us in the nose, without our being able to retaliate in any way.' [60] Like those sick in hospital, they felt alienated and terribly alone. They did not know if they could hope to be exchanged, or even which country they would end up in. Alexandre Goffart was just one of many Belgian conscripts who were taken prisoner while fighting in the Peninsula and found themselves embarked on British naval vessels and consigned to gaols in England, a country of which he knew nothing.[61] Everything seemed strangely unfamiliar and their future terribly uncertain, with the consequence that the prisoners often seem to have been in even greater need of psychological reassurance, of news, of human contact with their families. It was at such times that the feeling of weakness and vulnerability were at their greatest and a man's thoughts turned most naturally to home.

7

The Lure of Family and Farm

The young men who fought for the Revolution and Empire, regardless of whether they were genuine volunteers or the product of revolutionary levies or those conscripted in the inexorable series of annual *classes* that punctuated the Empire, remained citizens as well as soldiers. They continued to identify with the villages which they had left behind and to dream of the day when they, too, would be able once more to bring in the cattle or turn a lathe in the local workshop. The numbers who had left home in anger or who had been thrown out by resentful parents were always small, and even those who had left willingly, seeing the army as a source of adventure or an opportunity to kick over the traces, soon felt the call of home. For most leaving had been a wrench: they had dragged themselves away from civilian life with great reluctance, separating from wives and girlfriends, brothers and boyhood friends, and leaving behind the warm familiarity of their village for the first time in their lives. It is not surprising that they were eager to keep contact alive. That was why letters from parents were so precious, and why men took such painstaking care in communicating the most mundane details of their daily routine, anxious to share with their families the strange new world into which they had been plunged. This did not change over time: the tone of letters home remains remarkably constant, the regrets and homesickness thinly concealed. This is, indeed, a common feature of citizen armies, for whom the idea of devoting the rest of their lives to soldiering proved less than appealing. It would be equally true of the men who formed the Confederate armies in the American Civil War, who rushed to make contact almost as soon as they had left for their units. Indeed, one of the first actions of the young soldier on joining his regiment was to acquire pen, ink and paper, so that he could write home as often as time and capacity allowed. 'Thereafter till death or war's end, he continued to write of things that he observed and experienced in camp, on the march, under fire and in prison. At the same time he received missives – though not so often as he sent them – telling of crops, dogs, parties, gossip, health of the family and countless other details of life at home.'[1]

These were the things that seemed to guarantee continuity in a vacillating and uncertain world, and the young Frenchmen grasped at them eagerly. They wanted to be reminded of home, to feel that they were still part of a family and a community. As they marched across Europe they were exposed to different landscapes and contrasting cultures, which both opened their eyes to the comforts of civilian life and provided them with constant reminders of the farms and villages they had left behind. Very occasionally, it is true, they commented on the unfamiliar, responding as countrymen, as interested tourists, to the strange landscapes through which they passed. More commonly, though, their interest was tinged with a certain nostalgia, with the need to inform themselves of the state of things back home. Soldiers asked repeatedly about the health of the family smallholding or the condition of the crops, their memories suddenly jolted by the sight of peasants toiling in the fields of Alsace or Piedmont. Or they were reminded by the sight of vineyards along the Rhine or the Moselle of the charms of the *vendange* back home. The immediate trigger to their concern varied widely, of course, with the landscapes through which they marched and with their mood of the moment. Daniel Griveau, from Courveille in the Mayenne, saw the wild flowers in bloom in the Belgian countryside and was at once reminded of all the little pleasures of home.[2] Near Hamburg in the summer of 1813 Jean-Baptiste Dourlens watched the wheat standing in the fields and instantly his thoughts turned to his home in Songeons. 'Do tell me, he wrote, if the work of the farm is going well and if the harvest is good. I think it will be fine in France for in this region it is quite superb.'[3] So many of the soldiers were country boys who had little desire to escape from their roots; their interest was awakened by the sight and smells of the countryside, by the crops and farming practices they observed in the fields, and by the regular cycles of the rural calendar.

For some there was something deeply nostalgic about the villages they passed through in other countries, especially in Catholic lands which had not undergone the revolutionary process of dechristianisation and where the church remained the natural centre of the community. It reminded them of their childhood, of another world – often a simple, rural world – where they had felt secure and which had about it a reassuring sense of permanency, of timelessness. Or they found themselves overwhelmed by the rich colours and smells of Christian pageantry, and lamented its almost total absence in contemporary France. In June 1809 a young Savoyard remarked on the impression which the Corpus Christi procession in Parma had made on him and his comrades-in-arms. There had been two hundred soldiers present that day, and, he said, 'never have I seen such a magnificent procession; it's not in our parish that you can see things like that, nor yet in Saint-Jean-de-Maurienne'. Experiencing it had turned his thoughts to God and to prayer.[4] He was not alone. Soldiers from Catholic areas missed their *curé* and the solace of the mass; they sometimes refer rather sorrowfully to having seen a priest standing in front of the church door or going about his daily business in the villages they pass through. Here the young soldiers were not just missing France; they were missing the France of earlier days and quietly lamenting a world they had lost. François Dumey was one who expressed his commitment to the pre-constitutional church when, in Year III, he found that the old religion had been widely restored in the countryside around Lille. He did not hide his pleasure, telling his parents the glad news that

> the holy religion professed by our fathers for so many centuries is beginning to rebuild its altars, shattered by the impiety and the wickedness of the monsters who subjugated humanity beneath their iron yokes. Already a large number of villages have dismissed those lying priests who deceived them and have shown confidence in more worthy ministers of Almighty God. Our commune is among them. The former religion has been restored and, in response to general demand from the people, a priest has been brought from Tournai.[5] *

---

* J'allais oublier de t'apprendre que la sainte religion que nos pères ont professée durant tant de siècles commence à relever ses autels abattus par l'impiété et la scélératesse des monstres qui accablaient l'humanité sous leur joug de fer. Déjà grand nombre de communes ont congédié leurs prêtres menteurs qui les ont trompées, pour accorder leur confiance à de plus dignes ministres du Très-Haut. Notre commune est de ce nombre; le culte ancien y est rétabli; d'après la demande générale un prêtre est venu de Tournai.

Such thoughts might betray Dumey's antipathy to sectarian Jacobinism, but they did not in any way undermine his quality as a soldier. In the regular letters he sent home from the armies, indeed, he showed considerable military professionalism, and he was proud to have been promoted to sergeant-major under the Directory.

The troops thirsted for family and village news: no detail was too insignificant, since they knew only too well that their family's wellbeing depended on it. A few days after Valmy, one cavalry officer from the Ardèche seemed more concerned by the state of farming back home than he was by the outcome of the battle. He had heard nothing for over five months and bombarded his mother with questions. What was the harvest like? Was the wine as good as he had been given to believe? And had they had lots of cocoons, an abundance of the silk-worms on which the Ardéchois economy relied?[6] These matters were, of course, vitally important to him, as he, like most of these troops, had every intention of returning to share in his family's modest prosperity. Only the detail varied from region to region, from culture to culture. Men from Liège asked anxiously about the health of their cattle, the fruit yields and the quality of the fodder; one wanted to know about his bees; another thought of the tobacco harvest while smoking locally-grown tobacco.[7] In the Yonne they were more concerned with sheep, asking about the health of the flocks and enquiring how the lambing had gone, or hoping that some of the new-born lambs would be put aside for them on their return.[8] Everywhere they felt obliged to keep in touch, to ensure that they were not forgotten when beasts were shared out or inheritances allocated. Their correspondence provides a constant reminder that they remained peasant boys at heart, reluctantly drawn into a military lifestyle which meant little to them. Like Nicolas Bognier, a notably reluctant soldier from Savoy, they made continual references to their rural origins, asking incessantly about the farming life they had left behind. Bognier repeatedly commented on the state of the crops he saw around him, offering advice to his parents even as he voiced concern for his family's welfare. He enquired about the harvests, the sales of cheese, the cutting of wood: 'I wrote to Joseph, I don't know if he has sold the gruyères'; on the health of the animals: 'we won't make much profit this year if the cows fall sick'; and he worried continually about the upkeep of the property and of the house: 'keep a check on whether brother Joseph is looking after our land as he does his own'.[9] He might be temporarily in the army, but he still clung to his role on the farm.

Soldiers waited eagerly for the mail to be distributed, and they found it hard to hide their disappointment if the longed-for letter failed to arrive. It was a lifeline to many, a vital form of reassurance that in a violent and volatile world some things were guaranteed, some values eternal. It was also a means of remembering happier times, when the family had all been together and when their greatest worries, as Dominique Vergès recalled, had stemmed from the 'innocent pleasures' of child-hood. Receiving letters from his home in the Béarn was, he told his father, 'the only consolation that remains for a son who finds himself so very far from the family he loves'.[10] Men regularly complained of mail being ripped open, of letters being lost and money stolen, and of a callous disregard for their feelings by the military authorities. The mail service to and from the armies was unpredictable at best, and with the troops criss-crossing Europe for much of the period, receiving orders to leave camp at only a few hours' notice, it was perhaps inevitable that precious letters should sometimes get mislaid. That unpredictability caused understandable anguish. In a series of letters in 1796 Alexandre Ladrix expresses the sense of grievance which many of the troops felt when their communications remained unanswered. Taking up the cause of his friend, Bourbon, he wrote that he was deeply anxious about the fate of his family, from whom he had received no reply. 'That is scarcely surprising', he adds, 'because of the negligence in the postal service; whereas I have received your last letter in less than four days, the previous one took more than a month to get here.'[11]

But there was more to it than that. Silence implied loss, abandonment, perhaps disapproval by those to whom they felt most close, and it came at the very time when their need was greatest. Men felt hurt and confused when they received no reply to their communications, when their parents had seemingly lost all interest in their hardships. When Michaud, out in Russia with his regiment in 1812, sent several letters home without ever getting a reply, he knew that the mails were still coming through and could only surmise why his letters went unanswered. But he also grew worried in case there was a major crisis back home, something of which he was being kept in ignorance. 'Perhaps my letters have been lost on the way', he mused, 'but I hardly think so, since I don't believe that you would have left me in a state of anxiety for as long as you have.'[12] Another soldier, while rebuking his parents for a painful silence, explained why he could not sublimate his alarm. He was with the army in the West Indies, thousands of miles from his native Vosges, and their silence seemed all the more ominous. For, he explained after learning from a friend that his father was still alive, 'I presumed that the cruel weather this Easter had cut short your days'.[13] It was not only in the army that life could be short and brutish, and the young man could not be blamed for fearing the worst. Indeed, parents and loved ones had to take care in deciding what to write and what to omit when sending news to their sons in the regiments. The silence of omission could in some circumstances seem every bit as ominous as the failure to communicate at all. 'My dearest mother,' wrote Jean Lassalle from Saint-Florent in Corsica,

> I was very surprised to read the letter which you have just sent me, and to note that you wrote for yourself only and made no mention of my father, for it made me very sad to hear no news of him. My first thought was that he must be dead, but then I was surprised that you had said nothing of that either.[14] *

Parents did not always realise how carefully their sons scrutinised their letters, or how much time they had to brood and worry in the long intervals between battles or in the empty hours of the night.

The thirst of the troops for news of their own communities is one of the most persistent themes of their correspondence. This was partly, of course, a matter of filial piety and evidence of genuine concern for those closest to them; they were well aware that with every year that passed their parents were getting older, less able to cope on their own, and they were genuinely concerned about their health and welfare. It was inevitable, in over twenty years of war, that some of the soldiers would find themselves away from home at critical moments when their families squabbled over money or tore themselves apart over some

---

* Ma très chère mère, je suis bien surpris de la présente lettre que je viens de recevoir le premier may, que vous m'avez écrit en votre faveur sans rien parler de mon père, car cela m'a mis dans le chagrin de ne pas entendre de ses nouvelles. Vous pouvez croire que d'abord j'ai eu la pensée qu'il étoit mort et je suis bien surpris que vous ne mais l'écrittes pas.

long-festering dispute. They would be absent when domestic crises broke, when uncles died, fathers were arrested, or mothers were abandoned by the rest of the family. Absent, they felt shunned and irrelevant; but they could not pretend they were unaffected. For some the breakdown in communication was more permanent as parents failed to write or dismissed their urgent pleas for money; in such cases the veneer of respect and affection could be replaced by seething resentment. They complained of their parents' insouciance in leaving them to their fate, or implied that the relationship had broken down completely as a consequence of their military service. Joseph Vachin, for instance, had left home to join the army without his father's permission; he had since risen to be an officer and was working hard at his military career, seeking to 'make up for the time he had wasted previously'. But Vachin's father proved unforgiving, to the extent that he never replied to his son's letters and effectively cut him off from the family he had left behind; the young man therefore communicated through his uncle, a public notary in Mende, to whom he wrote a stream of letters across the period from Year XI to 1816, in which he just occasionally allowed his bitterness to show.[15] Even more harrowing is the tale of a young conscript from the Vosges, whose pleas for a little money had fallen on deaf ears and whose letters had again been left unanswered. Yet in the meantime he could feel that had suffered appallingly without receiving even a morsel of comfort from home. At Narbonne he had been court-martialled and sentenced to death; and though his death sentence had been commuted, he had almost immediately been sent back to the front at Sarragossa, where he had been wounded by a bullet through his thigh. By February 1811 he could write that he was better and ready for active service once more. But he was still in desperate need of financial help, and he was keenly aware that during his entire sorry plight he had been cruelly neglected by parents for whom he still felt able to express a degree of affection.[16] It was hard for the young to stop their thoughts turning to home.

Where family relationships did become so strained that all contact was broken, money was often the underlying cause of tension. The dreadful deprivations suffered by the troops meant that, inevitably, their letters home were often thinly-disguised cries for help, for small sums that would enable them to buy some food, to have a drink with friends, to repay debts or to replace the rags on their backs. These pleas were not always answered, whether through poverty or greed or lack of sympathy with a son from whom the parents had long been estranged. When Coignet wrote home asking for money, for instance, he met with a blank refusal to help, his father telling him that had he been closer to home he would have sent him something, and his uncle adding that he needed to keep his money to buy *biens nationaux* – cold comfort indeed for a soldier who had to put his life at risk doing extra guard duties in no man's land in order to pay off his debts. He was so outraged that from that moment he never wrote another line to his parents, cutting them off completely from his thoughts.[17] In the same vein, soldiers whose parents had the money to buy them out of service but who chose not to do so could incur their undying wrath. Basile Costery had just emerged after two weeks in a fever ward when he learned that his father had hired a labourer to help him with the work of the farm. He reacted angrily, hurt that his father could find the money to pay someone else when he had refused to buy his own son out of the military, angry that some stranger was doing agricultural work which he could so easily be doing himself.[18] Where such anger festered, real rancour could seep into relations between father and son, a rancour that was born of their experiences in the armies and of their family's apparent lack of concern or understanding. Occasionally their bitterness was allowed to shine through. 'The God who lights up our lives should punish my father', wrote one young Savoyard in 1810. 'I have always been a bastard in his eyes ever since I could first walk, and he has never recognised me as his son; of all the family he thinks only of his eldest son, but I hope I'll be able to pay him back for that very soon when I get home leave at the next inspection.'[19]

More commonly soldiers feared the death of a parent or relative almost as much as they feared their own. They felt helpless to do anything, especially as they often heard the news months afterwards and in a faraway land. Nor were their reactions purely emotional, since often there were other questions to be considered, the animals to be cared for, the inheritance to be assured. Sometimes their words can seem strangely cold and single-mindedly practical. When Aimé Chaboud learned of his father's death in 1812, he got over the emotional niceties pretty sharply before turning to what was really on his mind, asking his mother to check, if she did not already know, whether his father had come to an arrangement with his cousin before he died over the working of the land. This did not indicate any lack of human feeling on his part, though many found sentiment difficult to express; it merely underlined the harsh realities of daily life in rural Savoy.[20] From time to time, however, letters bubble over with emotion or declarations of affection, to a degree that might seem surprising in the late eighteenth century. One infantryman, stationed with his unit near Collioure, finished an account of his regiment's exploits in 1794 with an effusive statement of his love and devotion that may have astonished even him. 'You are my mother', he wrote,

> and I have no need of any other ... always I shall remember the good education you gave me from my very earliest years, and the good principles in which you raised me, in spite of all the problems I have had and will have in the future, you can believe that you will never be forgotten by a child who is full of respect and gratitude for your goodness.[21] *

He rambled on further in this vein, either in a spontaneous effusion of filial devotion or, and this is perhaps more probable, as a consequence of the painful insecurity and loneliness felt by a young man from the Beauce exiled to the inhospitable mountains of the Roussillon.

Outpourings of this kind are further evidence of the tendency to depression and *nostalgie* which we have already noted, and which undermined soldiers' morale even as it sapped their physical strength and vitality.[22] This could easily be triggered by the familiar everyday sights and sounds which reminded them of home – the lowing of cattle, the ringing of church bells, or their first glimpse of a great river or of the Mediterranean. For whatever they might say publicly, whatever terms of bravado they might resort to, the fact was that many of the soldiers had never really come to terms with their new life or with the sufferings to which they were exposed. This is not really very surprising. Conscription

---

* Vous êtes ma mère, je n'en ai pas besoin d'autre, mais soyez tranquille sur mon compte, et toujours je me souviendrai de la bonne éducation que vous m'avez donné dès mon bas âge ainsi que des bons principes malgré toutes les travers que j'ai daija esuyé de part et d'autres et que je suierai ancore, vous pouvez croire que jamais vous ne serai oublié d'un enfant qui est rempli de respect et de reconnaissance à toutes vos bontés.

was a condition which necessarily compounded male suffering, exposing
the soldier to danger and exhaustion, subjecting him to public scrutiny,
to unaccustomed nudity and possible humiliation, and providing an
unrelenting examination of his strengths and his stamina.[23] In the service
of the army his body was constantly strained and tested, both by
the physical fatigues to which he was subjected and by the damp, fever-
ridden conditions in which he was forced to live. This did not occur by
chance. The army set out to create a cult of the warrior, glorying in
those qualities of physical strength and bravery which underlined the
heroic, and demanding qualities of manliness and virility from the troops.
While many of the officers revelled in that culture, eighteenth-century
peasant boys did not necessarily find it easy to accept, and their unease
is reflected in their stream of complaints about the wearying tedium of
the exercise regime and the insistence on parade-ground drills to educate
their bodies and prepare them for the demands of battle. The anxiety,
the embarrassment, the fear of failure in front of their fellows all added
to the psychological burdens placed upon them and contributed in turn
to the spread of depression and *mal du pays*.[24]

In their letters soldiers talked more often of the causes of their
depression, their isolation from other young men from the *pays* and
their deep, gnawing desire to return home, than of its symptoms; and
they attributed their illnesses to fevers rather than to any psychological
difficulties. But they did admit to feeling lost, bewildered and even ill.
In his first letter home from Lille in 1809, Griveau admits that when he
got there – he had marched across France from the west – he had felt
abandoned and demoralised, 'like a tree that has been uprooted', and
that it was only the presence of his comrades that had saved him from
utter misery.[25] Others go further in describing their physical ailments.
In Year III a young Burgundian, Antoine Merat, noted how his journey
away from his home had been punctuated by attacks of distress: 'we felt
greatly troubled on leaving Auxerre ... we had to leave the coach at
Montereau because we were sick with grief ... we were obliged to spend
two days in Melun'.[26] Even more explicit is the journal kept by Sergeant
Fricasse in 1792. It was in Metz, with the Army of the Sambre-et-Meuse,
he explained, that he first came within inches of death, though this had
nothing to do with the battlefield. He suffered from a lingering fever
that drained his spirit and condemned him to six weeks in hospital.

And why? He attributed his piteous state to a combination of two things: fetid town air on the one hand, and his own gloom and state of depression on the other.[27]

If the soldiers' thoughts turned easily to home and to their parents' lot, so too they embraced the girls they had been forced to leave behind when military service had called. For if some noted the charms of local girls they encountered on their travels, even, in some instances, promising to return with foreign wives and mistresses when the war was over, others remained touchingly loyal to the memory of the village girls they had loved in civilian life. Perhaps because of the unease which writing letters to their parents caused them – and we have very few letters written directly to fiancées – many were prudent in what they said about lovers and girlfriends, limiting themselves to rather staid requests that their mother send on their compliments or enquire about their health. Standardised requests to pass on their regards to all who asked after them might well involve coded messages to the girls they had once loved. But some went further, enclosing a note or promising to kiss their beloved should they be spared to return. 'You will pass my compliments to my dear girlfriend', wrote Henri Baré of Milmort, near Liège, 'for I love her with all my heart. I am hers for life. When I go to bed of an evening I always wish to find my beloved by my side.'[28] Of course, with the passage of time, doubts began to creep in, and with them just a soupçon of jealousy towards the men left behind in civilian life. Another Liégeois, Gérard Jacquet, let slip that he had some doubts about his girl's constancy during his long absence at the front. 'I would ask you to watch over the conduct of my girlfriend', he wrote, 'and let me know if she is a behaving herself towards me.'[29] More explicit were the instructions sent home by a gunner from the Puy-de-Dôme who, after passing his regards to his *bonne amie*, added a word of general advice: 'Tell the girls of the *pays* that they should refuse to be kissed by the cowards who have stayed at home and were afraid to go off to fight.'[30] His words betray more than a sense of moral outrage, for the soldiers were well aware that the patience of their womenfolk could wear thin, while the 'cowards' hiding in the woods and the *garrigues* provided ample temptation. As one soldier told his brother and sister in 1808, he counted on them to 'let me know the name of anyone who makes love to my mistress'.[31]

Natural modesty, or unease at discussing such matters in front of their parents, may have served to reduce the number of references to village girls that we find in their correspondence. They showed less reserve in asking about their friends, about the village boys with whom they had grown up and who might now in turn be facing the prospect of conscription. Were they married? Had they found employment? Were they still frequenting the same haunts back in the village? Their anxieties on their friends' behalf clearly became more acute with the arrival of each recruiting season, when they knew that they risked having to go through the same ordeal as they themselves had done, the same uncertainty about their future, the same medical visits, the same lottery of balloting. Letters home seek information about the *tirage*, about who has been lucky in the draw, who has managed to buy a replacement, and who has had to leave for the front. And though they did undoubtedly appreciate the company of others from their region – their *pays* who spoke of familiar things and who did so in a familiar *patois* – they show a touching selflessness when discussing the fate of their friends. They would like them to be there at their side, of course, but they have no desire to see them conscripted. Thus René Vilain, himself a conscript from Arras, wrote of his concern about the weight of the 1813 levy in his home town, adding, almost casually, that he 'would be greatly upset if a lot of boys from our *pays* were forced to leave'.[32] When talking of their friends they tend to show sympathy and fellow-feeling, dropping all pretence that army life was attractive or desirable. 'You tell me that the levy has taken place,' one soldier wrote to his father, a peasant near Senlis, 'and that Jean-Louis and Libert lost out at the ballot. It makes me very sorry to see them reduced to such a pitiable fate.'[33] They knew only too well what awaited them once they had left the village, and in these circumstances few were inclined to pretend that army life was other than what it was.

In similar vein they often spared a thought for their younger brothers, those who would soon reach their eighteenth birthday and might soon find that they in turn had been consigned to military service. Here, too, they were anxious for news, desperate to know whether they had drawn a low number or had qualified for an exemption. Faced with the draft, families pulled together, and it is noticeable how few elder brothers chose to preach obedience and patriotism in these circumstances. Such instances as there were mainly occurred at the height of the Jacobin period, when government propaganda took a high moral tone and when ideological beliefs were more likely to take precedence. In August 1793, for instance, we find a soldier who was himself highly politicised and horrified by the indifference which his younger brother was showing, rhetorically urging his brother's wife to go to the butcher's to buy some heart to give him to eat, 'as he has none, since if he did have he would have left to defend the rights of equality like the rest of us'.[34] Occasionally, too, we find sober homilies about submissiveness and duty, though even then their tone could be muted in the light of what the soldier knew lay ahead. In one case an infantryman from Liège urged his father to exercise less tight discipline on his brother during what might prove to be his last weeks of freedom. He should be allowed to enjoy such leisure as remained, he suggested, since life would be much harsher in the regiments. 'You know that youth must be allowed to partake of its pleasures just as those of mature years partake of theirs.'[35]

But such instances were rare. More generally, men found ways of expressing their reservations, offering advice to their siblings about measures they might take to avoid the military. Even those soldiers who claimed to enjoy army life and who shared in the nationalistic language of the period could be racked with self-doubt when it was their own flesh and blood that was threatened with conscription. It was then, more than at any other time, that they urged caution, alluding to the high death rates in the ranks and begging their parents to spend their life-savings on finding replacements. Some were brutally unambiguous in their advice, like Telan, from Aiguebelle in Savoy, who, after passing his love to his brothers and sisters, concentrated on the matter that was troubling him and pleaded with his parents to 'try to prevent my brother from leaving, for we have too much misery in the ranks'. He was writing from bitter experience, and he had not yet advanced beyond Cambrai.[36] 'If I had thirty-six brothers', wrote one Belgian conscript with just a hint of hyperbole, 'I should not advise any of them to serve, for in truth it is a miserable way of life.'[37] Others desperately sought the certificates from their units which, they believed, would gain exemptions for their younger brothers. Increasingly, though, this became a forlorn hope as the demands of the war became ever greater, and the soldiers' attempts, and their language, showed all the signs of frustration. In 1809, for instance, young Fontaine wrote home to Compiègne desperately anxious about the fate of his brother, the delightfully named Charlemagne. He had asked his commanding officer for certification in the approved manner, to be told that only his municipality could grant exemptions, and that such a certificate would be valueless. He would, he wrote, be devastated if he learned that his brother had been conscripted, and he reminded them that they could use his last letter, postmarked in Spain, as evidence of his service. 'I pray to God every day that he favour you with his grace', he concludes, 'that you should all be happy, and that Charlemagne is allowed to stay, for then he will stay away from the many ills which we are all suffering on this campaign.'[38]

The advice they gave took different forms, but the purpose was essentially the same. A number of soldiers urged their brothers to marry without delay, believing that they would find in marriage a proven mechanism for avoiding the draft. 'You should tell our brother that he ought to get married as quickly as possible for his own good', wrote Louis Goddos unequivocally in 1813.[39] It was a commonly held belief, and many were convinced that their brothers should heed it, whether or not they had discovered their village sweetheart. Speed was of the essence here, since the law could change at any moment, and it might be that they had to take their chance with any woman available, even if she was old or palpably unsuitable. There was no hint of condemnation of those who had married women of sixty, seventy, or even on occasion eighty in an undisguised bid for freedom. And if they could not find a bride, the next best thing might be a trade. Soldiers eagerly advised their brothers to continue with their education, to gain craft skills or enter an apprenticeship, all seen as potential buffers against conscription. Daniel Griveau, on learning that his brother had been taken on as a *compagnon*, did not attempt to hide his joy, and he urged him to stick to his craft rather than be tempted by the army. A few months later, in response to the news that he had changed masters and was now employed in a different workshop, Griveau wrote, half-humorously, that the change sounded healthy and that he only wished he could do the same.[40] Such regrets were not confined to conscript soldiers. Even some of those who had taken money to go as *remplaçants* on behalf of others came to admit to their mistake when a younger brother showed signs of following in their footsteps, taking care to fill in all the necessary papers that would guarantee him an exemption.[41]

While advice of this kind was often given without qualification, the soldier having no problem with admitting to his unhappiness and urging his sibling to avoid the same fate, at other times the correspondence to and from the battalion could prove more delicate, as men tried to avoid the unwelcome attentions of the censor or the risk that they would spread alarm and discouragement at home. Through a rash or tactless reference, anxiety could be communicated to parents who had believed their sons to be happily integrated in the ranks and might suddenly wake up to a disturbing truth. Some pointed to a difference in character, arguing that, whereas they themselves were natural soldiers, their brothers were more timid, or more sensitive, or simply were not cut out for army life. This in turn allowed them to suggest that their parents look around for a possible replacement while there was still time to do so.[42] But there were also instances where it was the younger brother who sought to eschew the military and who himself made the case for remaining in a civil occupation. Charles Ignon was a printer to trade, and his elder brother was the official printer to the Prefecture of the Lozère, when in Year XII he wrote begging for help to buy a replacement. Perhaps because of his administrative position the elder brother refused, and Charles was left to plead his case. He has a good job in Bagnol, he argues, which he would have to give up in order to 'enter a service which I could not tolerate on account of my flawed temperament'; he has little hope of getting a medical exemption, though he has taken the precaution of arming himself with certificates from doctors in both Viviers and Montélimar; and if he cannot find the money to buy himself out, he has decided to enter the *vélites* rather than an ordinary infantry regiment. 'It is pretty costly', he moaned, 'but at least I would have to pay out ten francs every three months rather than a thousand francs all at one go.'[43]

Many of those already in uniform wanted only to get out, to gain the home leave they craved, to see the family and the farm they missed so deeply. If *mal du pays* made them sickly and disgruntled, a prey to every virus and fever that swept their unit, it also threw them open to temptation, above all to the temptation of desertion. Sunk in the depths of despond, their thinking dulled by fear and by the constant sound of gunfire, or their mood blackened by weeks spent in hospital, men talked of the regret they felt at having ever left home at all. In these expressions of regret there is more than a tinge of self-flagellation, a tendency to blame themselves for their misfortune. 'God knows how miserable I am', Marie-Antoine Lemaire acknowledged to his mother in 1811, 'and it is all my own fault. I should so like still to be with you at home. I recognise how stupid I was to leave you.'[44] Many of them indicated that they felt trapped in the army, unable to return home without risking a charge of desertion, unable to continue in the ranks without slipping still further into the deep slough of despond. They dreamed of a *congé*, of the simple piece of paper which would give them a legitimate means of returning home to do those familiar things they missed so badly, to see their parents, breathe in the fresh country air, fondle the cat, or hear the happy chatter of their friends. Their dreams were so touchingly limited, to be allowed the simple pleasures of youth which other boys in other generations took for granted. Occasionally letters tell triumphantly that they have been granted home leave; but far more often they report failure and disappointment, the news that they have first to serve three more months; the frustration of dealing with endless and unyielding bureaucracy; their acceptance that the queue is long and that their turn may be a long time in coming. And with every disappointment their dream was pushed further away, while the trough of their depression was deepened.

Sometimes their parents tired of their role as impotent bystanders and tried to intervene, pressing their sons' case with officialdom or directly with their commanding officers in an attempt to get them home. That they did so with the best of intentions is not in doubt, though for their sons the result could be embarrassment and on occasion consternation. Parents, after all, did not always understand the realities of army life or the sheer awkwardness of special pleading. Alexandre Ladrix begged his father not to force him to do something which he considered deeply shaming, interceding with his superiors to seek their protection, or taking advantage of a family friendship in order to steal a march on others. 'You must accept', he wrote, 'that it is simply not decent for me to go to my commander to solicit a special favour.'[45] Besides, the grant of home leave was very tightly regulated. A certificate had to be produced, demonstrating that the soldier's presence at home was imperative, and the case had to be accepted by the Ministry of War. And there were so many with even stronger claims! When peace was signed in 1801, Louis Godeau could hope for his *congé*, but, he told his parents, he would still have to wait since his claim was one of many: around one-eighth of the men and one-fifth of their officers had leave entitlement, and they could not all lay down arms at once.[46] It is noticeable, indeed, that in many instances the parents seem more enthused by the idea of intercession than their sons, whose experience of the army has instilled in them a certain fatalism. They were deterred both by embarrassment and by the punishments with which they were threatened. As Jean Floizac wrote to his parents in 1795 from his unit in Nice, their demands were simply unrealistic. Of course he would like to come home and to obtain his *congé* within the next fortnight, as they have pressed upon him, but he cannot do so. 'I should be the first to ask for one to have the satisfaction of coming to embrace you, but it is forbidden on pain of severe punishment. I am more pained by this than you can possibly be.'[47]

Some parents went further, urging their sons to come home without permission, to defy military discipline and desert. Their letters seldom survive, having doubtless been lost in the chaos of the march or burned surreptitiously in the flames of the camp fire. But we know from the replies which their sons wrote that parents often gave them encouragement and held out the promise of a warm welcome when they arrived. There was little sense of shame, little distinction drawn between right and wrong, and there was little reason to fear that they would be treated as social outcasts in their home communities. Some parents, encouraged when they saw other boys of military age disporting themselves openly in the village while their own sons remained in uniform, sought to put moral pressure on them to take the law into their own hands. Did they not love their mother sufficiently to seek home leave? Were they not concerned that their father was growing old and would soon be unable to care for the farm? Were they so heartless as to abandon their family when Jean-Pierre or Antoine was already back in the village, untroubled by the authorities and helping to sustain their parents in their failing years? These pleas did trouble their sons in the regiments, many of whom wanted neither to desert nor to increase their parents' anguish, and who felt tortured by the moral dilemma that was presented to them. 'Each letter that you write breaks my heart', wrote Louis Godeau in

response to a barrage of abuse from home, before trying to point out
the illogicality of their demands that he desert. 'You cite the example
of several boys who have returned to their homes by fleeing from their
units, living in fear of recapture. As soon as they return home they are
continually harassed and forced to hide in the forests.' Was that really,
he asked, a solution which they wanted to see for him?[48] Or else they
replied by asking tentative questions about the degree of policing in the
village, scarcely believing that conscripts could live openly in the community when they knew how harshly they were dealt with in the army.
They pressed for further information, seeking to gauge the risks which
a deserter might incur and making unspoken mental calculations about
their chances of success. Had troops been garrisoned in the area, they
asked. Did deserters really living normal lives, or were they forced to
cower like wild animals in the woods and thickets? And what was really
being done to control and arrest draft-dodgers?[49] More and more of
the soldiers began to harbour such doubts, as they found the accounts
in letters from home hard to correlate with the orders posted by the
army and with the evidence of their own eyes.

   Discussions of this sort between soldiers and their families provide
graphic proof of the temptations with which the young men were
struggling, and which they did not always resist. The call of the village
was siren-like, and it was all too easy, as they watched the sun playing
on the vines of northern Italy or rain clouds scudding across the
open skies of Westphalia, or when the wind blew the smell of harvest
into their nostrils, for young men to turn for home. But if they knew
this, so too did the military police and the censors whose job was to
intercept family mail and prevent military demoralisation. They were
not, as we have seen, either very systematic or particularly efficient,
but they were on the look out for seditious prompting at certain key
periods of the year, and they were more concerned by the advice coming
in to the troops than ever they were by the letters they sent out. There
were therefore dangers for the soldiers in discussing desertion or in
admitting that they had been toying with the idea of returning home,
and since letters sent to them were the ones most likely to be intercepted, parents had to be warned that their loose language on the subject
could easily bring trouble for their sons. The correspondence between
Jean Costedouat, a conscript of Year VII, and his father in Banos in the

Landes illustrates the point perfectly. Costedouat *fils* had asked about the levels of policing in the village and about the numbers of deserters who might be hiding there. His father tried to reassure him, pointing out that if the police descended, there would always be time to get away. He urged him to come at once, promising a rich celebration to greet him if he arrived by the following Saturday. But, he added, Jean should avoid drinking in the inn since the innkeeper 'is the agent of the commune, he is a devil, and you would be sure to be arrested'. In this case the letter was intercepted and Costedouat questioned; he had feared that it would be passed to the general and that he would risk retribution, though in the event a member of his company intervened and no further action was taken. The army probably felt that the point had been made and that no punishment was needed, since Costedouat had a good disciplinary record and had been considerably frightened by the incident.[50] Others did not escape so lightly.

Large numbers, of course, did desert – one letter describes how in Italy men were deserting in hundreds daily[51] – and many more considered it as a serious option, sometimes going so far as to admit the inadmissible, talking openly to their parents about their qualms over desertion and outlining the risks that they would have to run. It is, indeed, surprising how many of the men in the revolutionary and especially in the Napoleonic armies seem to have considered the option of deserting at one time or another. For most of them the issue was far more a practical than a moral one, and it was only fear of the terrible penalties that could be imposed on deserters – long years in gaol, forced labour, and the remote if ever-present threat of the death penalty – that made them grit their teeth and stay in their units. Yet there were times when almost any means of escape could seem attractive; and it could take very little, in the morose and depressed state in which so many of them found themselves, to make desertion seem a worthwhile option – a spell in hospital, the loss of a friend in battle, a mother's failure to reply to a letter, homesickness exacerbated by uncertainty. In 1793 Rémy Thirion described how he and his friends had been in trouble for slipping away from their unit without getting permission and that for their pains they had spent some time in prison at Longwy. Now they had been released, taking the places of men who were sick or absent when their unit was reviewed, but there is a just whiff of regret in his account. 'I am quite happy to be back in the battalion for the moment, but we are encamped in the most miserable weather; we are in the middle of ploughed land and endless mud.' The words do not suggest great constancy of purpose: it is striking, indeed, that Thirion expressed no contrition for his actions, preferring to look forward to the next chance they might get, when they would take better care not to get caught.[52] Men were not naive, and they knew only too well the risks that were involved, but some would always feel that these were worth taking as the price of their freedom, while others could console themselves with the thought that if they were caught there would soon be another amnesty to cut short their penance. Sadly, that amnesty did not always come, and some would pay dearly for their moments of indiscretion.

As time passed, it was desperation as much as hope that drove men to desert, as news and rumour infiltrated the ranks and a truer picture of the reality of life on the run began to take hold. Joliclerc was one who had a somewhat lurid view of the perils faced by men fleeing the army and who found his mother's blandishments relatively easy to dismiss. Though a staunch republican, he acknowledged that the army was not the best way in which to spend his youth. It was hard and brutalising, yet perhaps it was not the worst either. To drive home his point, he painted this image of the fate reserved for those who either dodged the draft or deserted from their units, who were reduced to skulking around the periphery of civil society.

> Would you prefer me to pass my life in exile, in Switzerland or Germany or England? I am at my post and I am staying at it. Would you rather I led the life of a bandit in the woods at Salins, down by the coast; to be chased by the police or forced to rob some traveller on the highways? For that is the sort of life which many conscripts do lead. *

---

* Aimeriez-vous mieux que je la passe, cette vie, en Suisse, en Allemagne, en Angleterre? Je suis à mon poste, j'y tiens. M'aimeriez-vous mieux à faire le bandit dans les bois de Salins, par la côte; à être poursuivi par les gendarmes ou bien à être obligé d'aller détrousser quelque passant sur les chemins? Voilà cependant la vie que bien des jeunes gens de la réquisition mènent. La trouvez-vous belle? Ils déchirent le sein de leur mère-patrie, ils versent le sang de leurs frères, ils désolent le pays à l'instigation de quelque scélérat de prêtre, de coquin, de vaurien royaliste, qui ont envie de nous remettre dans les fers; et vous osez me dire de m'en aller?

It is, he goes on, a precarious hand-to-mouth existence which can only bring misery and dishonour.

> They tear out the very heart of their motherland, they spill the blood of their brothers, they lay waste the country at the instigation of some scoundrel of a priest, a criminal, or good-for-nothing royalist who would like to see us all in chains; and you dare to tell me to desert? [53]

By the early imperial years, the dangers faced by deserters were greatly increased as the police presence was stepped up in rural areas and brigades of soldiers were sent to conduct *battues* in those areas where deserters congregated. Policing, indeed, would prove to be Napoleon's trump card in trying to break the will to desert, policing which was not confined to the soldiers themselves but which threatened their relatives and those who protected them. Here the billeting of troops on the parents of deserters was a master-stroke by the authorities which did much to break the bond of mutual interest between the fugitives and their families. Faced with the prospect of having *garnisaires* imposed on them, parents became less willing to welcome their sons home and less likely to encourage them to desert. Some, indeed, were driven to insist that they stay in their regiments and turned them away when they returned home illegally. One widowed mother, learning that her son was listed as a deserter and believing that 'the brigade' might be used against her, was sufficiently frightened to ask her 'dear cousin' to take the place of the boy's father and persuade him to return to his unit. Her letter, written from her sick-bed and signed in a barely literate hand, is poignant testimony both to her fear, exaggerated as it may have been, and to the potency of government propaganda in the villages of rural France.[54]

Those who did get away and who escaped the attentions of the troops posted to the army's rear did not always achieve happiness; nor were they sure to reach their goal and return to the bosom of their family. Life on the run was rarely easy, as they were forced to scrounge for food and entrusted themselves to an unfamiliar landscape. Many were intercepted by gendarmes or arrested by gamekeepers as they crossed unfamiliar fields; others were betrayed by people who befriended them; and they were often badly treated as they were passed from force to force on their way to stand trial. Of the letters written by deserters many come from men who have already been condemned, either to prison or to forced labour on the hulks. In the south, for instance, substantial numbers of deserters were sent to Corsica or herded into the citadel at Blaye. Conditions were miserable: men complained of damp cells, poor food and decaying clothing; often they had been robbed of such money as they had had and were at the mercy of their gaolers; and there was a terrible uncertainty about their future, condemned as they were to terms of seven or nine years in prison or to labouring on public works projects. Even if some consoled themselves with the thought that they were spared the terror of the front line, they had little sense of what the future held and knew that at any moment they might be sent back to battle. Men from Savoy reported on the harsh conditions in which they were held, and all expressed their regret that they had fallen to this: one talked of the 'slavery' of forced labour on the Canal Saint-Quentin; another of the diet of bread and water to which they had been subjected; a third described the humiliation of being led from prison to prison with chains round their necks and their hands manacled.[55] In their writings there is a terrible sense of loss and pathos. They had deserted in order to return home, to see their parents. Now they found themselves humiliated and stripped of all their resources, such little money as they had owned now spent on the cost of organising their defence. They called out for pity rather than retribution, their military careers ended in dishonour, and their dream of rejoining their families dashed, seemingly forever. Their mood of defiance often turned to regret as they contemplated the long years of misery that stretched before them as a consequence of a moment of foolhardiness. 'I assure you, my dear parents, that I will not cause you any more grief', wrote one repentant son from prison in Besançon, adding that he was now 'quite content to leave for Russia'.[56]

Where soldiers had such desperately ambivalent views of their own service they could scarcely be expected to share the army's institutional contempt for those who showed no stomach for the military way of life. Here we must distinguish between a sympathy born of suffering on the one hand, and an intolerance of shirkers on the other. For serving soldiers often showed great bitterness towards men who had avoided the draft through influence or education, those sons of influential parents or municipal officials who had managed to obtain exemption thanks to favours and special pleading, and who had found administrative or clerical posts back home while others risked their lives for France. Joliclerc for one had nothing but contempt for such departmental bureaucrats. 'If we were able to do so', he wrote, 'I think we should get ourselves to Lons-le-Saunier and put them to the sword, for they are our most cruel enemies.'[57] His intemperate language is all the more striking when we read soldiers' reactions to those convicted of desertion. In the eyes of many conscripts, desertion was not a crime that merited repression, as their officers insisted, but rather a natural impulse in a soldier, a viable means of escape which had been the resort of discontented troops of all nations from time immemorial. They understood, even if military regulations and the judges who sat on courts-martial could not, what it was that had driven so many of their comrades to walk away from the war, and in the main they hesitated to condemn. They had been there too, and many, as we have seen, had been tempted. So towards those of their friends who did desert and who then succeeded in reaching home safely, there was little evidence of malice or disapproval. Writing of a *copain* who had got back safely to his village of Thône in Savoy, Jacques Vairat merely observed that the news gave him considerable pleasure, though he remained concerned for his friend's safety and urged him to remain vigilant.[58] Well might he, since the soldiers knew that judges could be fickle and that sentencing for desertion could vary enormously. If there were long periods when the government's main objective to was to get the men back into uniform, and hence when sentences were relatively lenient, there were others when examples were made of individuals in order to impress the troops, who would be lined up on the parade-ground to witness their execution. There is no doubt that this left a deep mark on those present. Writing to his parents in 1806, Guillaume Brunel asked after one of his friends who had deserted and who, he hoped, had returned safely to his village in the Lozère. It is clear that he was anxious, since he added that he had seen a soldier shot for the crime and that he himself would never take that risk.[59] More poignantly, another soldier commented on the shooting of a deserter during the Italian campaign. The sympathy and fellow-feeling shone through his simple, rather frightened words, a sympathy born of the fact that the troops all shared the same heartfelt goal of getting out of the war and returning home. 'We shot one of our comrades', he wrote, 'and yet that saddened me greatly, for he had not done any harm, he had only deserted.' [60]

8

From One War to Another

The attitudes expressed by those revolutionary and imperial troops whose letters and journals we have sampled remained largely unchanged across over twenty years of war. The things they wished for were, in the main, such ordinary things, the basic routines of day-to-day existence which they had taken for granted in their childhood and which other boys would grow up to have. They wanted military victory, certainly, and they dreamed of returning in triumph to their home towns and villages, of being treated as heroes after years of deprivation. And particularly in the early months, when the army consisted of genuine volunteers who believed in the revolutionary cause, many of them also wanted to see the Revolution victorious, the Revolution which had brought them such palpable benefits as the abolition of feudalism and equality before the law. Some of the young officers and NCOs, in particular, were politically aware and had joined the army to further their ideological goals as much as to advance the cause of French arms. By 1795, moreover, some ex-Jacobins, hounded out of civil offices at home, had come to seek refuge in the army, where they would be judged more for their competence and tactical skills than for their political opinions, and where they felt they could best serve the Republic.[1] But it would be misleading to think of the majority of the soldiers as being in any way political. If they dreamt of victory, it was victory for its own sake, to assuage their pride and self-respect. Few, it would appear, would have opted for victory at any price; many simply longed for peace and an end to fighting, and they assumed that it was through victory that peace could be achieved.

There was no suggestion of disloyalty or of political rejection in this attitude. On the contrary, the troops come across in their writings as being intensely loyal to their country, to their regiments, and to their comrades, most especially, perhaps, to their comrades, to those other soldiers on whose companionship and support they were so dependent. But that is very different from a commitment to the army as an institution, or to victory as a cause to which they were utterly dedicated, in the interests of which they were prepared to contemplate any sacrifice. There were, of course, soldiers who shared such a commitment, and their patriotism and their military values shine through in their writings. But they were never more than a small minority, concentrated heavily amongst the officers and those career-soldiers who had come to look on the army as a profession and as a substitute home. Their views found little echo in the mass of the young conscripts who made up the regiments of the Directory and Consulate, or of those who marched with Napoleon's *Grande Armée*. These men showed little love for soldiering as a way of life, and even less desire for the war to be prolonged unnecessarily. Indeed, they longed for the day when they would be able to return home, to see their families and embrace their loved ones. They sighed for things that were familiar and ordinary, for a calm and measured existence marked by such reassuring fixtures of everyday life as laughter in the workshop, the cows being brought in from the fields, an evening drink with friends in the cabaret or the periodic ringing of the bells of the village church.

It is this very ordinariness which is so striking, and which contrasts with the heroic representations to which both revolutionary and Napoleonic governments were so addicted. With some exceptions, the soldiers of these letters and journals were not the patriotic heroes beloved of Jaurès and Michelet and encapsulated in the pedagogy of Ernest Lavisse, the willing martyrs whose image would become a central plank of the Republican and Bonapartist myths which played such a powerful part in the shaping of modern French memory.[2] They might believe sincerely in their cause and dearly love their country, but they come across in their writings as human and vulnerable, fallible, utterly believable men with all the doubts and fears of humanity at large. And that, too, is reassuring. For these were not the cardboard figures of nineteenth-century *images d'Epinal*, eternally smart and elegant, proud and chivalrous, gallant to every woman they met, unflinching in their sense of duty and honour. Rather they were a representative sample of their generation, peasant boys and artisans' sons, who had been caught up in great events of which they knew little, and who had been denied the irresponsible years of their youth by the ambitions of their rulers and by the failure of European diplomacy. In their writings the multi-faceted character of the troops becomes apparent – men who were prepared for the worst, willing, if need be, to die for their country or in the service of the Emperor, but who still yearned for their lost youth and who were by turns fearful and irresponsible, romantic and affectionate, fun-loving and dissolute, all qualities which emphasised their essential humanity and which helped to steer them through the worst horrors of the battlefield. The vast majority of them had no liking for war, and if they made the most of the comradeship which the army offered, they craved for peace and for a return to some vestige of normality.

In 1914, a hundred years after the end of the Napoleonic Wars, a new generation of young Frenchmen would find themselves called to the colours in a conflict that was to prove even more bloody and murderous. Once again the call to arms was shrouded in republican rhetoric and in a romanticised vision of the armies of the Year II. No one could feign surprise. The people had been well prepared by an unremitting barrage of patriotic propaganda during the previous months; and the young, in particular, had been inducted in both nationalism and repub-lican dogma in the schoolrooms of the Third Republic, a patriotic education which would be transferred to the battlefield by way of the many gymnastic and shooting clubs where so many boys had honed their skills in marksmanship or had developed their prowess in field sports in preparation for the day when France would avenge the loss of Alsace and Lorraine. The government itself became more active in championing sports, giving subventions to sporting clubs and associ-ations. And if within the traditional French *lycée* physical education teaching remained something of a joke, in the country as a whole new efforts were made to encourage physical exercise and to infuse sports with the dominant militaristic and nationalistic values of the period.[3] It is striking, indeed, how in popular memory such a large part of the long hot summers of 1912, 1913 and, more fleetingly, 1914, was spent in running, fencing, cycling, boxing or swimming; and equally striking that when war was finally declared, the young of France marched off with unparalleled optimism to seek out the enemy.[4]

The propaganda of schoolmasters and sporting clubs had comple-mented that of politicians to the point where the young were prepared to offer themselves willingly, even enthusiastically, for the defence of France. And not just for France, but for the Republic, for an ideal of republican liberty which provided the generation of 1914 with their own degree of ideology, at least initially, before the hopelessness and the fatuity of the war came home to them. It was a commitment on which recruitment posters and government propaganda agencies played mercilessly throughout the war years, emphasising not only the supposed cruelties and atrocities committed by the other side, but also a certain idea of France that was firmly grounded in republican values. The allegorical presence of Marianne in French war imagery helped encourage the young soldiers to believe that they were fighting for a way of life, a set of institutions, a part of their national heritage that dated back to the Revolution. Marianne, stern and unsmiling in her Phrygian cap, the *bonnet rouge* of the sans-culottes of 1793, was ever-present in war propaganda, a symbol of both liberty and fraternity, and of the popular enthusiasm for the ideal of liberty. Indeed, Marianne represented France in the Great War far more than the other allegorical figures which symbolised European nations; increasingly she had become France, a unifying symbol of the nation rather than that of a republican faction, a symbolic image draped less in red than in the colours of the nation, the red, white and blue of the *tricolor*.[5]

Nor, when war broke out, was there any question of how the army should be recruited. In contrast to countries like Britain, where there was strong resistance to the idea of compulsion, the French seemed agreed that only by introducing conscription could the necessary manpower be found, since, in the best traditions of the Republic, a national emergency demanded the efforts of all: men should not be allowed to shirk their responsibilities simply because they were rich, or educated, or well-connected. In the spirit of the revolutionary *levée en masse*, no provision was made for men to buy themselves out by producing substitutes to serve in their stead; in 1914, just as they had done in the two most radical of the revolutionary *levées*, in 1793 and 1799, the French demanded service in person and insisted on a transparent equality of sacrifice. And though the idea of civic equality was central to the republican idea of France, this should not be dismissed as ideological dogma. It was also deemed to be vital for the morale of the troops and hence for their effectiveness as fighting men: no soldier likes to feel that he is making a huge sacrifice for others while at home the more fortunate, or the more cosseted, of his fellows are allowed to flourish in the safety of a school classroom or a government office. Equality was seen as essential if the army was to offer itself generously and willingly in the service of the nation, and was to fight to the limit of its powers. As the philosopher Henri Bergson explained in 1914, the fact that France based her defence on the collective strength of the people gave her added moral force. 'The conflict before us', he wrote, 'is between two opposing forces – the force which wears itself out because it is not supported by a higher ideal, and the force which can never be spent because it rests upon an ideal of justice and liberty.'[6] Just like the soldiers of the Revolution and Empire, he believed, France's troops in the Great War enjoyed a degree of self-belief which would carry them to victory.

By 1918, when that victory could finally be celebrated, some eight million men had been mobilised, of whom a quarter – over two million – never returned. The carnage, both in the ranks and in the many communities that were engulfed in the battle zones of the north and east, would have been unimaginable to the generation of 1913 or to the many families whose sons were swallowed up in it. Yet still, through all the destruction and obliteration of human life, the anger of the troops and the mutinies of individual units, the public face of France remained unchanged: still Marianne demanded sacrifices, and still official optimism was maintained. Between 1914 and 1919, indeed, the French government's propaganda offensive remained so intense that it risked bringing discredit on the papers and the journalists who unquestioningly printed the official line, obfuscating news, concealing military setbacks, and peddling the pretence that the soldiers shared the blind faith and commitment of their leaders. Throughout these years France was the only one of the major belligerent nations where it was strictly forbidden to make public the levels of losses, in the belief that public order depended on it, and that the French people must be shielded from a truth too terrible to be borne stoically.[7] Newspapers were, whether consciously or unconsciously, vehicles for patriotic propaganda, tightly censored and forced to place a single-minded emphasis on the heroism and the determination of France's soldiers in the face of adversity. Officers and NCOs were lionised as heroes, as were aviators, well-known sportsmen, and a few ordinary soldiers, those *héros poilus* whose exploits singled them out from the nameless masses in the trenches. For the first time some papers were able to make use of photographic illustrations, and these, too, tended to give prominence to classical ideals of military heroism.[8] Thus the soldier became an icon, symbolic, noble-minded and pure, while the real *poilu*, like the volunteer of 1791 before him or the conscript of the Napoleonic Empire, was given little opportunity to voice his feelings, being allowed to speak only in patriotic clichés, trusting in victory and looking to exact vengeance for the loss of Alsace and Lorraine. It is this which helps explain the rancour felt by many soldiers towards their own press. Their fears and hopes, along with the intensity of their day-to-day feelings, remained unexpressed, deliberately hidden, silenced and excluded from the public sphere.

Where these feelings did find expression, as during the Revolution and Empire, was in the soldiers' private writings, whether the letters they sent home in astounding quantities from the front or in the diaries and journals which many of them wrote up each evening, private documents in which their doubts and despair could be expressed with the same freedom as more acceptable sentiments of pride and patriotism, and where the details of their daily existence could be logged for posterity. By the early twentieth century, of course, France had undergone a major social and cultural change, in that literacy had spread even to the remotest villages and hamlets. The vast majority of the troops could read and write and could do so with ease, without referring to their comrades for help or struggling to express the thoughts which they wanted to convey. Indeed, it would be no exaggeration to say that the men who went to war in 1914 were the first truly literate generation, children of the Third Republic who had been subjected to compulsory primary schooling, a crucial change which was reflected in a far greater fluency and in a mastery of French spelling and syntax. They could write with bathos and lyricism, with deep feeling and acute description, in short, with a range of linguistic subtlety which previous generations simply could not command. In their letters we can find little evidence of the frustrations which we saw expressed by those revolutionary and imperial soldiers who felt cut off from their families and their villages by their inability to communicate, and who faced artificial isolation because of their educational shortcomings. Writing came naturally to them in circumstances where they craved an audience for their sufferings. And if they could write, it is striking how often they wrote, how compulsively (some might feel tempted to add how obsessively) to their parents and brothers and loved ones, their thirst for news seemingly unquenchable. For this reason we know far more about the private feelings and psychology of the men who served between 1914 and 1918 than we know of the soldiers of any previous war. They expressed twentieth-century fears and aspirations and were less afraid than their forebears to admit to emotions. They did so, moreover, in a language that boasted a spontaneity and an immediacy that the more laboured prose of the late eighteenth and early nineteenth centuries could not hope to match.

The scale of letter writing in the First World War was quite staggering. Each day the military posts carried some four million letters from the front to the villages of the interior, keeping open the vital link between families which played such an important part in maintaining morale.[9] Each day men would devote the greater part of their free time to letter writing, driven by the need to inform and the desire for information from the outside world. This was, of course, a new experience for many of them, for if they undoubtedly had the necessary skills and literacy, the majority of them had not, in their civilian lives as farmers or stonemasons or carpenters, had the slightest need to write, or the least inclination to consign their thoughts to the written page. Far from being a practised art, writing was a pastime occasioned by the exigencies of the war itself. From time to time, of course, the flow would be interrupted to take account of enemy shelling, but it would resume when the guns fell silent. Their correspondence was unremitting, with many men writing and receiving letters every day, writing out of a sense of duty when the day's work was over, writing out of an exploding desire to communicate pent-up feelings and emotions, writing as a matter of routine, in a desperate quest for something akin to normality in the midst of a strange and alienating barbarity. They needed to write, and in turn they would be bitterly aggrieved when letters failed to arrive, when they were left without the news which they craved.

As the war ground on they might make use of other, more immediate forms of correspondence which new technology had made available and which the army actively encouraged. Some filled in brief form-letters in minutes snatched between duties, which could do little more than tell of the progress of the army or confirm that they were in good health. Others took advantage of the new vogue for picture postcards, which again allowed for only a short message but which conveyed visually something of their own experience, something which few would have been capable of conveying in words. Relatively few of these cards were openly militaristic in tone, though some tried to lift morale by conveying patriotic images or caricatured visions of the Germans; others would portray a *poilu* standing proudly in uniform, emphasising his bravery or his cheerful demeanour and encouraging the reader to imagine their own son or brother standing there in his stead. Overall, however, the proportion of cards which chose to portray patriotic or specifically military themes, such as anti-German caricatures or nationalistic icons, did not exceed ten per cent of the cards which soldiers sent, whereas the vast majority carried photographs of local landscapes, of gloomy northern towns or of the countryside of Flanders or Picardy, scenes chosen by the troops to give their parents in Languedoc or the Auvergne some impression of the region in which they were fighting. In this way men tried to share something of their experience in the trenches with families who probably had never left the vineyards of Burgundy or the *garrigues* of the Gard. Postcards could supplement, in a far more personal way, the photographs of the war zone that were beginning to appear in the national press. They constituted a powerful aid to the imagination, and the soldiers appreciated them for that reason.[10]

But we should be careful not to exaggerate the impact of photography or other forms of technical innovation on day-to-day communication. The handwritten letter remained the staple form of communication between army and village, soldier and civilian; the letter that might be written every day or even several times in a day, whenever leisure permitted or boredom dictated. Some picked up their pen at every opportunity. Jean Robin from Nice, for instance, was an avid correspondent during the one hundred and four days he spent at the front in 1915, and there is no reason to suppose that he was in any sense exceptional. Each day he would write three or four letters, receiving two or three in his turn. In all, he sent his family 390 cards or letters during that period, often, it is true, in fairly brief snatches of less than twenty lines. But that must not be allowed to detract from their value, either to Robin himself or to those who read him.[11] Letters were important in the Great War for the same reason that they had been important under Napoleon: they had a crucial affective value, providing material evidence of the ties that bound the young men to their loved ones. The failure of parents to write back, in 1916 as in 1794, produced long periods of gloom and depression – the deep and self-destructive *cafards* of the trenches which afflicted so many and which were the Great War's equivalent of *nostalgie* and *mal du pays*. The symptoms were largely the same; only the medical terminology had changed. The army recognised the importance of letters in combatting depression, and it responded by placing a high priority on the military postal service. And the soldiers in turn understood what it would be like to be bereft of such contact, regarding the absence of mail as one of the most intolerable of conditions. What had changed since the 1790s was not the function of the letter, but the circumstances in which it was written – levels of literacy, the speed of communication, the efficiency of the mails, the acceptance of postal communication as being somehow ordinary and routine.

Sending and receiving letters had profound implications for military morale in the Great War. Men wrote because they felt a profound need to communicate with their families, with those they loved, with people who were continuing to enjoy the rhythms and rituals of civilian life with which they could identify, who injected an element of sanity into the miseries of life in the trenches. Many admitted to feeling a physical need to make that contact with the outside world if they were not to lose all hope of returning to a normal existence. And if they felt the need to write, they experienced an even greater joy in receiving letters and parcels from home, proof that their loved ones still cared for them, of course, but also that glimmer of the familiar, of life as it should be lived. Their enjoyment of parcels is particularly instructive in this respect, for it was the familiarity of the food they were sent, almost as much as the taste, which aroused comment and appreciation – local delicacies which reminded them of home, the cakes their mothers baked, the ham or sausage from their region, part of their culture, of their past. They were delicacies to talk about, to boast of, above all to share with their new comrades from other parts of the country.

When André François, a country boy who was captured by the Germans and held prisoner from the first months of the war, gratefully acknowledged the parcel his uncle Auguste sent him in June of 1915,

'containing bread, figs, sugar, sausage, cigarettes and soap', he added, 'I
can tell you that that gave me the greatest pleasure'.[12] It was a sign that
life was continuing normally at home, in his family of olive-growers in
the Midi; it was also an indication of his own morale, his continued
pleasure in partaking of that life. When that pleasure dimmed it was
evidence of sickness and demoralisation. In May 1917, when he was
attacked by a fever and suffered a second serious abscess, André did not
try to conceal the fact that his health was failing. Writing to his parents
from his hospital bed, he even discouraged them from sending further
food parcels. 'I don't know what becomes of them, I haven't touched
any of them since 23 March, it's hardly worth it just to fatten up someone
else.'[13] Predictably, perhaps, this was to be André's last letter home.

In war memoirs and novels written after the First World War one
can find innumerable references to that most important moment of the
day when the troops underwent the ritual of the distribution of the
mail, the moment which was most eagerly awaited and which, for many
men, gave meaning to their lives for the next twenty-four hours. A shout
of expectation greeted the distribution, an expectation that was at once
individual and collective; men left their shelters and rushed forward,
sometimes at considerable risk to their lives, as everything else became
secondary to receiving, and opening, and burying oneself in a letter.[14]
The news which it contained might be uplifting or deeply depressing;
more often it was simply mundane, the act of keeping open a channel
with the outside world. But its importance did not rest there. Through
their letters the men also got to know one another, as the interminable
hours in the trenches were punctuated by conversation about their
families, about the state of the harvest at home, or the health and beauty
of their wives, or the latest achievements and escapades of their children.
Some were making progress at school, others might be wild, unruly,
adventurous; but all were the source of pride and reassurance, a welcome
reminder of normality, of a life beyond their immediate hell.[15] The vast
majority of the men did receive letters on a regular basis, though some,
of course, missed out – those without wives or girlfriends, those whose
parents had died or split up, the victims of family quarrels. They could
not but feel isolated and abandoned as they watched their comrades
open letters and parcels, exchanging news of their families or gossip
about their children growing up. The real mystery, indeed, was how

those men who never received mail managed to deal with the dreadful solitude of their lot.[16] For without stories of home, tales of harvest and childish escapades, men were denied not just personal solace, but a whole slice of that very intense camaraderie which developed in the trenches. They might feel mildly envious or simply unloved and rejected, but in any event they felt excluded and terribly, desperately alone. The army recognised that it had a problem here, and volunteers were organised to adopt and befriend those soldiers who were single, solitary, or abandoned by their families, those who had no parents or who had been the product of children's homes. By the time of the Great War, mail, which was already such a source of solace in the semi-literate society of the Napoleonic Wars, had come to be seen as an essential prerequisite for maintaining military morale.

If the act of writing was itself therapeutic, so was the opportunity which it provided to talk, to tell of their experiences and pour out their feelings, and at times to admit to parents and loved ones sentiments, regrets or personal failings which could not be freely admitted in the regiment. Just as they had done during the Revolution and Empire, the majority of soldiers showed great patience with the war and tolerance of the terrible conditions in which they were forced to live; they remained patriotic, were loyal in support of the Republic, and generally believed that the cause for which they were fighting was just. Their letters are punctuated by outbursts of nationalistic rhetoric, at least in the early months, and there is little reason to doubt that, if they had been pressed, they would have wished for the restoration of Alsace and Lorraine, for a just peace to end a just war. That was the picture which the government liked to give of the *poilu*, the picture of the valour and patriotism which was painted repeatedly in official communiques and in the pages of the military press. But is it a picture that ought to be taken at face value? The troops were not dupes, and we know from their own accounts that newspaper reports elicited groans of disbelief and derision as often as nods of agreement; they were seen as propagandist and heavily censored, presenting the view of the armies which the government wanted to convey, but they were still welcome in as far as they allowed the individual soldier to have a glimpse of what was happening elsewhere, and to effect a momentary escape from his own constricted sector of the battlefield. Besides, the *journaux du front* generally humanised that image by a widespread resort to humour, a mocking, satirical humour which, the military editors believed, was necessary if French morale were to be sustained in the face of such terrible dangers.[17] The humour may have left a deeper impression than the more predictable expressions of patriotism.

In their personal letters – and this despite the fact that they knew when they were writing that they were subject to censorship – we find only occasional references to the supposed valour, gallantry or gaiety of the troops, and few acknowledgements of the cause in which they were fighting. Personal correspondence was not the place for outpourings of patriotism or commentaries on public policy, and most of the men were careful to distinguish between the public and the private. In letters home they had other, more pressing priorities; they had little time for patriotic effusions, even if we do make the assumption that soldiers retained any appetite for them after their first optimistic outpourings of 1914, before they had been thrown into the reality of battle.

For the greater part of the war years that assumption is surely quite unjustified. In spite of official censorship, the civilian population was not left in total ignorance of what was going on at the front. Press reports and letters from serving troops brought to every town and village of France a more sombre vision of the trench warfare in which they were engaged, so that within a few months it had become clear to most recruits what was the nature of the fighting and the scale of the suffering ahead. So, too, did the solemn, almost embarrassed visits paid by local mayors to those families who had lost sons or relatives in the war, breaking the news of their deaths in action, moments of heartbreak which finally ended all uncertainty and were the signal for long periods of family mourning and grieving.[18] As a result, the heady optimism of the summer of 1914 could never recur. The young men of France knew long before they were called up that their experience of war would have little of the romantic about it, that this war would be harsh and detestable like no other, a war in which there were few opportunities for individual combat or heroism. Soldiers killed and were killed anonymously, by the firing of shells and canons at long range into the mud of the trenches.[19] And while their officers and political leaders continued to claim that they were inspired by patriotism and by a burning love of the French Republic, by a hatred and loathing of their German enemies, in their writings there is little evidence to support it. If patriotism was present, it was scarcely a key driving force. Often there is even a grain of sympathy for the Germans, who come across not as ogres but as honest young men like themselves, condemned to the misery of war by forces beyond their control, by the brutality of their officers, the intransigence of their government, the ambitions of their generals, or the greed of their capitalists. The soldiers were victims, just as they were.

In the circumstances of the Great War combat morale was not shaped by patriotism or by the great projects of statesmen. And it is arguable that it had relatively little to do with the institution of the army as a whole. Rather it depended on those small groups of men forced by circumstance to fight and live and die together in their trenches, men on whose sense of duty each soldier depended for his own safety – their section rather than their regiment, the men of the immediate *escouade* of which they were part. Louis Barthas, the village barrelmaker from the the Minervois who wrote such a telling commentary on his day-to-day experiences in his *Carnets de guerre*, leaves us in no doubt as to where he felt his loyalties lay.

> The section forms a little family, an affective grouping whose members are bound by strong feelings of solidarity, devotion and intimacy, and from which the officer and even the simple sergeant are excluded; the soldier does not confide in them, he remains distrustful, and any officer wishing to describe, as I have done, the strange way of life of the trenches, could never know, except on odd occasions when he might take his men by surprise, the true sentiments, the real spirit or the plain language of the soldier, nor his deepest thoughts.[20] *

The section became, for the duration of their shared miseries, a substitute family, a group of comrades, of mates, those about whom they really cared. They would be intensely loyal to one another, sharing their fears

---

* L'escouade est une petite famille, un foyer d'affection où règnent entre ses membres de vifs sentiments de solidarité, de dévouement, d'intimité d'où l'officier et le simple sergent lui-même sont exclus; devant eux le soldat ne se livre pas, se méfie, et un officier qui voudra tenter de décrire, comme moi, cette vie étrange de la tranchée n'aura jamais connu, si ce n'est quelquefois par surprise, les vrais sentiments, le véritable esprit, le net langage du soldat, ni son ultime pensée.

and despondency, and willing in the final analysis to suffer, even to sacrifice their lives for their friends. That, more than anything, was what made men accept the miseries they encountered, made them stay at their posts rather than run from the front line. And it was that in turn which made the sociability of the trenches – a sociability that transcended rank and seniority – so vital to the battle effectiveness of each unit.[21]

That is not to deny that patriotic sentiment existed, or that it helped stimulate the troops to ever greater efforts. Patriotism, the love of France and of its republican creed, did doubtless have its place in the consciousness of the average soldier during the First World War. It certainly had been a major motivating force in the first months of the war in encouraging men from all backgrounds to offer themselves to the *patrie*. But their experience of warfare once they became engaged in it quickly caused their initial enthusiasm to wane, and after 1915 the soldiers' writings seldom make any mention of patriotism, giving force to the view of wartime novelists like Henri Barbusse that its place in the daily lives of the troops was a limited one, easily pushed aside by more immediate considerations such as friendship or the desire for survival.[22] They talked, as their forefathers had talked in 1800, of the family and the harvest, the appearance of the countryside and the state of the crops. They discussed the material conditions in which they were forced to exist, the state of the trenches, the food and the rats and the scale of the losses they had suffered. And despite their greater fluency, they, too, passed over certain experiences in silence – the horror and the stench of battle, for instance, the disfiguring effects of shellfire, the cold, numbing fear of trench warfare. They condemned the indifference which they detected in public opinion, feeling that they were increasingly being left to their fate and revealing a degree of contempt for those who had dodged the draft or found safety in reserved occupations. And they were angered by those civilian newspapers they came across, which, they felt, were concealing an important part of the truth from the French public by playing down the losses they were suffering and pretending all was well when they knew very well that it was not. In short, among the *poilus* disillusionment with the war quickly set in, a disillusionment which meant that men cried out for peace not as a source of glory but as a simple end to hostilities, the opportunity which they craved to end a hateful war and return to civilian life.

By 1916, the last traces of the blithe optimism which had helped propel the armies in the early days had all but disappeared, and with it went the cult of victory which the politicians and the military high command were so eager to encourage. In the words of one thoughtful infantryman, written to his parents on 25 May 1916,

> All the soldiers, with the exception of a few idiots, want peace at any price. We are forced to stay there, forced to massacre one another, to kill Germans who have never done us any harm. Three-quarters of the officers think as we do, but they do not dare say anything. We are all fighting this war reluctantly and against our wishes.[23] *

His bitterness and desperation, repeated time and again in the letters of his comrades, reflected the terrible lassitude which swept through the armies. The tenor of these remarks is clear, the same sentiments repeated spontaneously by thousands of individual soldiers. Only the forcefulness varied. 'If our wives and mothers knew exactly the extent of our sufferings', wrote one man with unusual venom, 'then the war would undoubtedly be brought to a speedy conclusion.'[24] More commonly the young soldiers expressed themselves more cautiously, keeping one eye on the censor and holding back from describing their sufferings to those who had not shared them, who could not know.

If there is a single word that can sum up the mood in the trenches of the Great War, it is perhaps resignation. The soldiers knew that they that they had no choice but to fight; it was, they insisted, their duty to do so, and the word 'duty' (*devoir*), spelt by some with a capital letter, recurs frequently in their despatches from the front. Indeed, they mentioned it constantly, their duty to the motherland, to their parents and the honour of their family, the duty of sacrifice, of suffering, of obedience, the duty, in the final analysis, to accept whatever fate might await them. They spoke of it with a certain sense of inevitability. It was, as they had learned in their school classrooms, no more than what they owed to France.[25] Yet most would have agreed with that great pacifist

---

* Tous les soldats, à part quelques idiots rares, veulent la paix à tout prix. On nous force à rester là, à nous massacrer mutuellement avec les Allemands qui ne nous ont rien fait. Les trois-quarts des officiers sont comme nous, mais ils n'osent rien dire. Nous faisons tous la guerre à contre-coeur.

writer of the inter-war years, John Norton Cru, that there was little
glorious about the fighting, and that the mythification of war was a
crude tool in the hands of generals and politicians of which they were
the victims. The war, claimed Norton Cru in his belligerently anti-
Establishment pamphlet, *Témoins*, in 1929, was hated because of what
it did to men, what it did to their bodies and their minds. Only those
who did not have to fight – the cabinet ministers, the civil servants, the
publicists and schoolteachers and armchair philosophers – could afford
to idealise the war and to praise the dignity and heroism of its soldiers,
and they could do so becaue of they had no first-hand knowledge of
what went on.

> The almost undivided testimony of the combatants proves that war is hateful
> to those who fight it, unreservedly hateful, and that no appetite for risk can
> survive either in attack or under bombardment. The combatant has lived
> through the reality of which he speaks, and it is he, not some armchair
> philosopher, who is right.[26] *

The Great War, he believed, was uniquely hateful because of its exaggerated violence, the fact that there was little one-to-one combat, little
opportunity to pit one's strength or subtlety against an adversary.
Soldiers' bodies were vulnerable as never before to the assault of the
other side, sustaining terrible wounds as heads were blasted off by
shells and entrails spilled across the mud of the trenches. And their
spirit was condemned to a numbing fear and helplessness. It was this
kind of war that forced doctors to recognise the psychological damage
caused by action, the traumatic shock which drove men mad and
which in English would create a new word in the medical lexicon, 'shell
shock'.[27] In consequence, 'no section of trench, long or short, manned
by the best platoon, company or regiment in the whole army, can
be held if the enemy chooses to use enough artillery against it. No
heroism will help to avert the doom. The fate of the occupants is
sealed. There is a fatality about it which never existed in past military
history.' That fatality, in turn, created fear in the participants which was

---

* Le témoignage à peu près unanime des combattants prouve que la guerre
est haïssable, sans réserve, à celui qui la fait, et que le goût du risque n'existe
ni à l'assaut ni sous le bombardement. Le combattant a vécu la réalité qu'il
affirme et il a raison contre le philosophe de cabinet.

translated into those expressions of futility and helplessness which litter the personal writings of the soldiers of the period and which Norton Cru identified as 'truth'.[28]

It is certainly tempting to view the First World War as being different in kind from previous wars, and as placing unparalleled strains on the individual soldier and on his continued morale. After all, in the four years from 1914 until 1918 France lost nearly nine hundred soldiers every day to wounds and disease, deaths that were a direct consequence of the war.[29] It is this chilling fact which has led twentieth-century historians to concentrate so much attention on the issue of morale, and to ask why men accepted this level of sacrifice and suffering, why they did not turn more to desertion and mutiny. In the French case the preferred answer seems to be that by 1914 the sense of nationhood was of long standing, and the implications of citizenship well understood. The French people 'accepted the war because they were part of one nation and they tolerated it for the same reason'.[30] While this is undoubtedly true of the soldiers and their families in the early part of the twentieth century, it cannot apply with the same resonance to those who went before them under the Revolution and Empire. The traditions of the nation were still in the process of formation; and both the Republic and Napoleon aroused strong opposition among royalists and Catholics even as they cemented deep loyalties among their supporters. Yet the young Frenchmen of the 1790s and 1800s also stood firm, and also seemed moved by the call of the nation and by loyalty to the Republic or to the Emperor. As their letters and journals make clear, they shared many of the same emotions as those in the trenches of the Somme, the same pride and devotion to their cause, the same fears and tribulations, the same homesickness and *mal du pays*. In their most intimate moments *grognards* and *poilus* spoke with a common voice. Their emotional responses, their cares and priorities, seem to have been very similar.

Soldiers' writings, despite their persistent reticence on matters that might cause embarrassment or outrage, provide a more coherent insight into the psychology of a generation at war than any other archival source available to us. For that generation which was called upon to fight and die for the Revolution and Empire, to fight a war on an unprecedented scale across the entire European continent, they also offer a unique

insight, and one that would inspire Republicans and Bonapartists alike
throughout the following century. For twentieth-century warfare historians can turn to other kinds of material to establish the reality of the
ordinary soldier's experience. The troops of the Great War, themselves
more at home with the written word and often rather older than the
revolutionary and Napoleonic conscripts, left behind a far richer variety
of writing, more subtly expressed, more carefully crafted to describe the
most harrowing moments of their lives. Among their number were poets
and novelists who provided inter-war Europe with searing images of
the day-to-day reality of the trenches and contributed to the growth
of pacifism amongst the young. War correspondents were employed to
offer images of war on the ground to the readers of national newspapers;
photography provided compelling visual evidence unavailable to previous generations; and battle scenes in the mud of Flanders were caught
for posterity on early newsreels. Just as important was the effort of the
post-1918 world to memorialise and commemorate war, to guarantee
that the sufferings of the trenches were not forgotten and to help focus
the grief and the mourning of those left behind. Veterans' associations
were formed to bring pressure on government and to keep the sacrifice
of the *poilu* in the public eye. The process of remembrance achieved an
official status unparalleled in the wake of previous wars. Public opinion
demanded that it should be so, as local communities throughout France
clamoured to be allowed to remember their dead on plaques and war
memorials, in cemeteries and on village squares, memorials on which
the soldiers were often depicted through commissioned sculptures and
works of public art. France in the early nineteenth century seemed to
share few of these concerns. It was, of course, a less democratic society,
less concerned to resurrect the lives of ordinary soldiers than to preserve
the memory of their leaders.[31] It was also a less affective society than
that of the twentieth century, less given to public shows of grief and
mourning. If parents and loved ones chose to grieve – as they surely
did – they were left to do so privately. In similar vein, the soldiers' war
was largely left to private memory and reflection, to the conversations
of old comrades, or to reading the jottings they had made in diaries
and in the piles of yellowing letters that lay half-forgotten in attics. It
is this, as much as the intrinsic interest of the thoughts expressed by
what was still a semi-literate society, which makes these writings so

valuable if we are to reconstruct something of their everyday experience, of their private thoughts and sentiments, and of the state of their morale in battle.

Notes

Notes to Introduction

1. Robertson Davies, *Fifth Business* (Toronto, 1970), reissued as *The Deptford Trilogy* (Harmondsworth, 1983), pp. 65–66.

Notes to Chapter 1: The Armies of the Revolution and Empire

1. British and American historians have been more prone to challenge the classical republican interpretation of the revolutionary wars, which has survived more robustly in France. See, for instance, T. C. W. Blanning, *The French Revolutionary Wars, 1787–1802* (London, 1996); Jeremy Black, *European Warfare, 1660–1815* (London, 1994); and especially Paul Schroeder, *The Transformation of European Politics, 1763–1848* (Oxford, 1994). A highly revisionist account of the conduct of the wars can be found in Paddy Griffith, *The Art of War of Revolutionary France, 1789–1802* (London, 1998).
2. J. M. Stewart, *A Documentary Survey of the French Revolution* (New York, 1951), p. 403.
3. These examples are all drawn from the archives of one *département*, the Cantal. For more detail, see Alan Forrest, *The French Revolution and the Poor* (Oxford, 1981), pp. 146–47.
4. J. M. Stewart, *Documentary Survey*, pp. 472–74.
5. A good discussion of this process is J.-A. Castel, *L'application de la Loi Jourdan dans l'Hérault* (mémoire de maîtrise, Université de Montpellier, 1970).
6. René Bouscayrol, *Cent lettres de soldats de l'an II* (Paris, 1987), p. 9.
7. Richard Challener, *The French Theory of the Nation-in-Arms, 1866–1939* (New York, 1955), pp. 58–59.
8. John Horne, 'From *Levée en Masse* to "Total War": France and the Revolutionary Legacy, 1870–1945', in Robert Aldrich and Martyn Lyons (eds), *The Sphinx in the Tuileries and Other Essays in Modern French History* (Sydney, 1999), pp. 319–21.

9. These cases are examined in Daniel Moran and Arthur Waldron (eds), *The People in Arms: Military Myth and Political Legitimacy since the French Revolution* (Cambridge, 2002). For a more detailed examination of the Vietnamese army see Greg Lockhart, *Nation in Arms: The Origins of the People's Army of Vietnam* (Sydney, 1989).

10. Carl von Clausewitz, *On War* (London, 1968), p. 219.

11. Charles J. Esdaile, *The Wars of Napoleon* (London, 1995), pp. 40–41.

12. Gunther E. Rothenberg, *The Art of Warfare in the Age of Napoleon* (Bloomington, Indiana, 1978), p. 127.

13. Annie Crépin, *La Conscription en débat, ou le triple apprentissage de la nation, de la citoyenneté, de la république, 1798–1889* (Arras, 1998), p. 19.

14. Alan Forrest, *Conscripts and Deserters: The Army and French Society during the Revolution and Empire* (New York, 1989), p. 41.

15. Jean-Pierre Gross, *Saint-Just: sa politique et ses missions* (Paris, 1976), pp. 173–74.

16. Robert Devleeshouwer, *L'arrondissement du Brabant sous l'occupation française, 1794–95* (Brussels, 1964), pp. 156–57.

17. Esdaile, *The Wars of Napoleon*, p. 13.

18. Georges Lefebvre, *Napoleon: From 18 Brumaire to Tilsit, 1799–1807* (London, 1969), p. 193.

19. Charles J. Esdaile, *The Spanish Army in the Peninsular War* (Manchester, 1988), pp. 75–76.

20. Stuart Woolf, *Napoleon's Integration of Europe* (London, 1991), p. 233.

21. A good modern narrative of Napoleon's military exploits is to be found in David Gates, *The Napoleonic Wars, 1803–1815* (London, 1997).

22. Robert M. Epstein, *Napoleon's Last Victory and the Emergence of Modern War* (Lawrence, Kansas, 1994), pp. 178–79.

23. Emmanuel de Las Cases, *Mémorial de Sainte-Hélène* (2 vols, Paris, 1962), ii, pp. 252–53; Jean Tulard, 'Les historiens de Waterloo', in Marcel Watelet and Pierre Couvreur (eds), *Waterloo, lieu de mémoire européenne, 1815–2000* (Louvain-la-Neuve, 2000), pp. 15–17.

24. Jean et Nicole Dhombres, *Lazare Carnot* (Paris, 1997), esp. chapter 4.

25. Peter Paret, *Clausewitz and the State: The Man, his Theories and his Times* (Princeton, 1985), p. 33.

26. Louis Bergeron, *France under Napoleon* (Princeton, 1981), p. 59.

27. Ibid., p. 64.

28. Ibid., p. 69.

29. Donald Horward, 'Jean Lannes', in David Chandler (ed.), *Napoleon's Marshals* (London, 1987), p. 192.

30. Martyn Lyons, *Napoleon Bonaparte and the Legacy of the French Revolution* (London, 1994), pp. 167–68.

31. Archives Nationales (AN), AF IV 1123, Hargenvilliers, 'Compte général sur la conscription depuis son établissement', 1808.

32. Michael Rapport, *Nationality and Citizenship in Revolutionary France: The Treatment of Foreigners* (Oxford, 2000), p. 218.

33. Owen Connelly, *Blundering to Glory: Napoleon's Military Campaigns* (Wilmington, Delaware, 1987), p. 159.

34. Georges Blond, *La Grande Armée* (Paris, 1979), p. 558.

35. Esdaile, *The Wars of Napoleon*, p. 260.

Notes to Chapter 2: The Soldiers and their Writings

1. Jay Winter, *Sites of Memory, Sites of Mourning: The Great War in European Cultural History* (Cambridge, 1995), p. 223.

2. Samuel Hynes, 'Personal Narratives and Commemoration', in Jay Winter and Emmanuel Sivan (eds), *War and Remembrance in the Twentieth Century* (Cambridge, 1999), pp. 218–19.

3. Emmanuel de Las Cases, *Mémorial de Sainte-Hélène* (Paris, 1823). The *Mémorial* is described by Jean Tulard, without exaggeration, as 'probably the greatest best-seller of the nineteenth century'.

4. Sergio Luzzatto, *Mémoire de la Terreur* (Lyon, 1988), esp. pp. 179ff.

5. For a discussion of the creation of republican and Bonapartist memory, see Robert Gildea, *The Past in French History* (New Haven and London, 1994), and Bernard Ménager, *Les Napoléon du peuple* (Paris, 1988).

6. Jean Marnier, *Souvenirs de guerre en temps de paix, 1793 – 1806 – 1823 – 1862* (Paris, 1867), p. 23.

7. Samuel Hynes, *The Soldiers' Tale: Bearing Witness to Modern War* (London, 1997), p. 2.

8. Frédéric Rousseau, *La guerre censurée: une histoire des combattants européens de 14–18* (Paris, 1999), p. 21.

9. On the intricacies of the sales of *biens nationaux* in rural areas, see Peter Jones, *The Peasantry in the French Revolution* (Cambridge, 1988), pp. 154–61.

10. Alan Forrest, *Conscripts and Deserters: the Army and French Society during the Revolution and Empire* (New York, 1989), pp. 208–11.

11. Jacques Staes, 'Les minutes notariales, source pour l'histoire militaire pendant le Premier Empire', in *Neuvième rencontre historiens Gascogne-Adour* (Université de Pau, 1980), pp. 71–105.

12. Archives Départementales (AD) Oise, series R, Lettres de soldats de l'Empire à leurs familles, an VIII–1823. For a supplement to this collection, see Jacques Bernet, 'Document inédit: lettres de soldats compiègnois à leurs familles sous la Révolution', *Annales historiques compiègnoises modernes et contemporaines*, 2 (1978).

13. L.-J. Bricard, *Journal du canonnier Bricard, 1792–1802* (Paris, 1891).

14. Gustave Vallée and Georges Pariset (eds), *Carnet d'étapes du dragon Marquant: démarches et actions de l'Armée du Centre pendant la campagne de 1792* (Paris, 1898).

15. John Norton Cru, *Témoins* (Paris, 1929), p. 465, quoted in Lionel Lemarchand, *Lettres censurées des tranchées: 1917* (Paris. 2001), p. 18.

16. Melvin Edelstein, 'Le militaire-citoyen, ou le droit de vote des militaires pendant la Révolution Française', *Annales historiques de la Révolution Française*, 310 (1997), p. 585.

17. Maximilien Robespierre, quoted in Jules Leverrier, *La naissance de l'armée nationale, 1789–94* (Paris, 1939), p. 71.

18. Paddy Griffith, *The Art of War in Revolutionary France, 1789–1802* (London, 1998), passim and esp. p. 280.

19. James M. McPherson, *For Cause and Comrades: Why Men Fought in the Civil War* (New York, 1997), pp. 12–13.

20. Jean-Yves Leclercq, *Le mythe de Bonaparte sous le Directoire, 1796–99* (mémoire de maîtrise, Université de Paris-I, 1991), pp. 57–91; see also Marc Martin, *Les origines de la presse militaire en France à la fin de l'Ancien Régime et sous la Révolution* (Vincennes, 1975), pp. 339–41.

21. Christopher Prendergast, *Napoleon and History Painting: Antoine-Jean Gros's 'La Bataille d'Eylau'* (Oxford, 1997), pp. 129–31.

22. Rab Houston, *Literacy in Early Modern Europe: Culture and Education, 1500–1800* (London, 1988), p. 132.

23. Michel Vovelle, 'Y a-t-il eu une révolution culturelle au dix-huitième siècle? A propos de l'éducation populaire en Provence', *Revue d'histoire moderne et contemporaine*, 22 (1975), pp. 89–141.

24. Roger Chartier, *The Cultural Uses of Print in Early Modern France* (Princeton, 1987), pp. 256–57.

25. A. Gazier (ed.), *Lettres à Grégoire sur les patois de France* (Paris, 1880), p. 146, quoted in Chartier, *Cultural Uses of Print*, pp. 260–61.

26. Jack Thomas, *Le temps des foires: foires et marchés dans le Midi toulousain de la fin de l'Ancien Régime à 1914* (Toulouse, 1993), pp. 18–21.

27. Nicole Garnier, *Catalogue de l'imagerie populaire française* (2 vols, Paris, 1990 and 1996).

28. David Hopkin, 'Changing Popular Attitudes to the Military in Lorraine

and the Surrounding Regions, 1700–1870' (Ph.D. thesis, University of Cambridge, 1997), esp. pp. 16–36.

29. François Furet and Jacques Ozouf, *Reading and Writing: Literacy in France from Calvin to Jules Ferry* (Cambridge, 1982), pp. 16–19.

30. Among white soldiers on both sides the number who were classified as illiterate did not exceed 10–12 per cent; see McPherson, *For Cause and Comrades*, p. viii.

31. René Bouscayrol, *Cent lettres de soldats de l'an II* (Paris, 1987), p. 30.

32. Louis de Chauvigny, *Lettres inédites de Choderlos de Laclos* (Paris, 1904), p. 154.

33. Marcel Reinhard, 'Nostalgie et service militaire pendant la Révolution', *Annales historiques de la Révolution Française*, 30 (1958).

34. André Chabrol, 'La poste aux armées', in Maurice Bruzeau (ed.), *La poste durant la Révolution, 1789–1799* (Paris, 1989), p. 134.

35. Maurice Ferrier (ed.), *La poste aux armées: textes, documents, souvenirs et témoignages* (Paris, 1975), p. 50.

36. Ibid., p. 55.

37. André Chabrol, 'La poste aux armées', pp. 137–38.

38. Ph.-F. De Frank, *Les marques postales de la Grande Armée, par son histoire, 1805–08* (Paris, 1948), p. 24

39. Maurice Ferrier (ed.), *La poste aux armées*, p. 57.

40. Jean-Paul Bertaud and Daniel Reichel (eds), *Atlas de la Révolution Française*, iii, *L'armée et la guerre* (Paris, 1989), p. 38.

41. For the references which follow I am indebted to Jean-Paul Bertaud, who is writing a biography of Laclos and who kindly drew the documents to my attention.

42. Louis de Chauvigny (ed.), *Lettres inédites de Choderlos de Laclos*, p. 208.

43. Ibid., p. 154.

44. Bell Irvin Wiley, *The Life of Johnny Reb: The Common Soldier of the Confederacy* (new edition. Baton Rouge, Louisiana, 1978), p. 192.

45. McPherson, *For Cause and Comrades*, pp. 132–33.

46. AD Savoie, L1137, letter from Deleglise to his father in Saint-Jean-de-Maurienne, 25 August 1810.

47. AD Savoie, L1137, letter from Bonait in Corte to his father in Saint-Jean-de-Maurienne, 10 July 1809.

48. AD Vosges, 18R4, letter from Petit to his father near Chatel (Vosges), 15 January 1811.

49. Emile Fairon and Henri Heuse, *Lettres de grognards* (Liège, 1936), p. 376.

50. Capitaine de la Bastide, 'Lettres de soldats (an II)', *Carnet de la Sabretache*, 7 (1908), p. 382n.

51. AD Savoie, L1137, letter from François Morat from England to his father in Chambéry, 23 June 1813.

52. AD Loir-et-Cher, F2196, letter from Louis Godeau from his regiment in Ypres, 29 prairial II.

53. Roger Chartier, 'Introduction: An Ordinary Kind of Writing', in Roger Chartier, Alain Boureau and Cécile Dauphin, *Correspondence: Models of Letter-Writing from the Middle Ages to the Nineteenth Century* (Cambridge, 1997), p. 5.

54. André Palluel-Guillard, 'Correspondance et mentalité des soldats savoyards de l'armée napoléonienne', in *Soldats et armées en Savoie: actes du 28e congrès des Sociétés Savantes de Savoie, Saint-Jean-de-Maurienne*, 1980 (Chambéry, 1981), p. 198.

55. One excellent recent collection, with commentary, is the volume by Jean Nicot, *Les poilus ont la parole: lettres du front, 1917–1918* (Paris, 1998).

56. Hynes, *The Soldiers' Tale*, p. 283.

Notes to Chapter 3: Official Representations of War

1. The key text on the creation of a public sphere and on the inferences to be drawn from it is Jürgen Habermas, *The Structural Transformation of the Public Sphere: An Enquiry into a Category of Bourgeois Society* (Cambridge, Massachusetts, 1989). For eighteenth-century France, see Dena Goodman, *The Republic of Letters: A Cultural History of the French Enlightenment* (Ithaca, New York, 1994), esp. pp. 12–15; and Keith Baker, 'Defining the Public Sphere in Eighteenth-Century France: Variations on a Theme by Habermas', in Craig Calhoun (ed.), *Habermas and the Public Sphere* (Cambridge, Massachusetts, 1992), pp. 181–211.

2. Michel Vovelle, *La Révolution Française: images et récit* (5 vols, Paris, 1986), iii, pp. 50–51.

3. Ibid., iv, pp. 110–11.

4. Raymonde Monnier, 'Le culte de Bara en l'an II', in *Joseph Bara (1779–1793): pour la deuxième centenaire de sa naissance* (Paris, 1981).

5. James A. Leith, *Art as Propaganda in France, 1750–99* (Toronto, 1965), p. 107.

6. For a fascinating analysis of the painting, see the *catalogue raisonné* produced by the Musée Calvet on the occasion of a special exhibition held to mark the bicentenary of the French Revolution, *La mort de Bara* (Avignon, 1989).

7. Leith, *Art as Propaganda*, p. 95.

8. Jean-François Heim, Claire Béraud and Philippe Heim, *Les salons de peinture de la Révolution Française, 1789–99* (Paris, 1989), p. 47.

9. Ibid., pp. 59–60, 64.

10. Ibid., p. 63.

11. Jacques-Antoine-Hyppolite de Guibert, *Essai général de tactique* (Paris, 1772); Joseph Servan, *Le soldat-citoyen* (Paris, 1781); see also Jean-Paul Bertaud, *La Révolution armée: les soldats-citoyens et la Révolution Française* (Paris, 1979), pp. 57–59.

12. E.-G. Léonard, *L'armée et ses problèmes au dix-huitième siècle* (Paris, 1958), pp. 229–30.

13. Jean Chagniot, *Paris et l'armée au dix-huitième siècle: étude politique et sociale* (Paris, 1985), p. 525.

14. David M. Hopkin, 'La Ramée: The Archetypal Soldier', *French History*, 14 (2000), pp. 116–17.

15. John Lynn, *The Bayonets of the Republic: Motivation and Tactics in the Army of Revolutionary France, 1791–94* (Urbana, Illinois, 1984), pp. 13–14.

16. Melvin Edelstein, 'Le militaire-citoyen ou le droit de vote des militaires pendant la Révolution Française', *Annales historiques de la Révolution Française*, 310 (1997), p. 586.

17. Bertaud, *La Révolution armée*, p. 63.

18. René Baticle, 'Le plébiscite sur la constitution de 1793', *Révolution Française* 58 (1910), pp. 127–28.

19. Edelstein, 'Le militaire-citoyen', p. 600.

20. Archives Nationales, ADVI 74, decree of 8 February 1793.

21. Isser Woloch, *The French Veteran from the Revolution to the Restoration* (Chapel Hill, North Carolina, 1979), p. 84.

22. Françoise Deplace, 'L'assistance aux militaires et aux familles des militaires à Paris sous la Convention' (mémoire de maîtrise, Université de Paris-I, 1987), p. 9.

23. Ibid., p. 83.

24. Mona Ozouf, *La fête révolutionnaire, 1789–99* (Paris, 1976), passim.

25. Jean-Pierre Gross, *Saint-Just: sa politique et ses missions* (Paris, 1976), p. 85.

26. Alan Forrest, 'Robespierre, the War, and its Organisation', in Colin Haydon and William Doyle (eds), *Robespierre* (Cambridge, 1999), pp. 127–40.

27. *Oeuvres complètes de Maximilien Robespierre*, ed. E. Déprez and others (10 volumes, Paris, 1910–67), vii, p. 263.

28. M. Delarue, 'L'éducation politique à l'armée du Rhin' (mémoire de maîtrise, Université de Paris-Nanterre, 1968).

29. Joseph Vingtrinier, *Chants et chansons des soldats de France* (Paris, 1902), pp. 14–16.

30. Robert Brécy, 'La chanson révolutionnaire de 1789 à 1799', *Annales historiques de la Révolution Française*, 53 (1981), pp. 279–303; figures quoted

in Lynn Hunt, *Politics, Culture and Class in the French Revolution* (Berkeley, California, 1984), p. 20n.

31. Xavier Maeght, 'La presse dans le département du Nord sous la Révolution Française, 1789–1799' (thèse de troisième cycle, Université de Lille-III, 1971), pp. 321–22.

32. Antoine-François Lemaire, *L'Ami des Soldats: par l'auteur des lettres bougrement patriotiques* (Paris, 1790), issue 2, p. 13.

33. *La Soirée du Camp*, issues 1–39 (2 Thermidor II to 10 Fructidor II).

34. Delarue, 'L'éducation politique', p. 124.

35. Martyn Lyons, *Napoleon Bonaparte and the Legacy of the French Revolution* (London, 1994), p. 6.

36. Bonaparte's proclamation justifying the Brumairian coup, 10 November 1799, quoted in Malcolm Crook, *Napoleon Comes to Power: Democracy and Dictatorship in Revolutionary France, 1795–1804* (Cardiff, 1998), pp. 96–98.

37. *Bulletin de la Grande Armée*, Jena, 15 October 1806. This and the quotations that follow are drawn from French texts reproduced in Napoleon Bonaparte, *Proclamations, ordres du jour, bulletins de la Grande Armée* (Paris, 1964).

38. *Bulletin*, Potsdam, 26 October 1806.

39. *Bulletin*, Wilkowyszki, 22 June 1812.

40. *Bulletin*, Paris, 21 March 1815.

41. Jean-Paul Bertaud, *La presse et le pouvoir de Louis XIII à Napoléon Ier* (Paris, 2000), pp. 88–89.

42. Christopher Prendergast, *Napoleon and History Painting: Antoine-Jean Gros's 'La Bataille d'Eylau'* (Oxford, 1997), pp. 1–5.

43. Jean-Paul Bertaud, *Guerre et société en France de Louis XIV à Napoleon I* (Paris, 1998), p. 174.

44. Prendergast, *Napoleon and History Painting*, pp. x–xi.

45. Timothy Wilson-Smith, *Napoleon and his Artists* (London, 1996), p. 161.

46. Ibid., p. 150.

47. René Bouscayrol, *Cent lettres de soldats de l'an II* (Paris, 1987), p. 230.

48. Jean Barada, 'Lettres d'Alexandre Ladrix, volontaire de l'an II', *Carnet de la Sabretache*, third series, 9 (1926), p. 84.

Notes to Chapter 4: The Voice of Patriotism

1. Edmond Leleu, *La société populaire de Lille* (Lille, 1919), p. 82.

2. Jean-Paul Bertaud, *La Révolution armée*, pp. 312–13.

3. Archives de la Guerre (AG) Vincennes, MR1718, *Mémoires, infanterie: adresses à l'Assemblée Nationale des bas-officiers* (1789).

4. AG Vincennes, MR1718, address from the Régiment d'Infanterie de l'Aunis, 18 September 1789.

5. Eugène Maury (ed.), *Lettres de volontaires républicains, 1791–94* (Troyes, 1901), pp. 6–7.

6. M. Demay, 'Les volontaires auxerrois de 1792 aux armées de la République', *Bulletin de la Société des sciences historiques et naturelles de l'Yonne*, 28 (1874), p. 591.

7. L.-G. Pélissier, *Lettres de soldats, 1792–93* (Paris, 1891), p. 5.

8. G. Tholin, 'Mémoires et pièces diverses pour servir à l'histoire des volontaires du Lot-et-Garonne, engagés de l'an II', *Revue de l'Agenais*, 22 (1895), p. 258.

9. Alain Richard, 'Un journal d'armée sous la Révolution: *L'Ami Jacques, Argus du Département du Nord*' (mémoire de maîtrise, Université de Lille-III, 1978), p. 22.

10. Marc Martin, *Les origines de la presse militaire en France à la fin de l'Ancien Régime et sous la Révolution, 1770–1799* (Vincennes, 1975), pp. 150ff; also 'Journaux d'armées au temps de la Convention', *Annales historiques de la Révolution Française*, 44 (1972).

11. *Journal de l'Armée des Côtes de Cherbourg*, ed. J. J. Derché (Bibliothèque Nationale de France, Lc2.2583), 9 August 1793.

12. F.-X. Joliclerc, *Ses lettres, 1793–96* (Paris, 1905), pp. 20–21.

13. L. Duchet, *Deux volontaires de 1791: les frères Favier de Montluçon* (Montluçon, 1909), p. 65.

14. Emile Fairon and Henri Heuse, *Lettres de grognards*, p. 376.

15. AG Vincennes, Xw49 (Indre), letter of 23 Prairial II.

16. AG Vincennes, Xw7 (Ariège), letter of 1 Germinal II.

17. G. Tholin, 'Mémoires et pièces diverses', *Revue de l'Agenais*, 20 (1893), p. 359.

18. AG Vincennes, Xw49, letter from Gabriel Bourguignon to his parents, 26 Messidor II.

19. Demay, 'Les volontaires auxerrois', p. 550.

20. Ibid., p. 570.

21. Lorédan Larchey, *Journal de marche d'un volontaire de 1792: le journal du sergent Fricasse* (Paris, 1911), p. 4.

22. François Vigo-Roussillon, *Journal de campagne, 1793–1837* (Paris, 1981), p. 13.

23. Bell Irvin Wiley, *The Life of Johnny Reb: The Common Soldier of the Confederacy* (Baton Rouge, Louisiana, 1943), p. 25.

24. A. Pioger, 'Lettres de Pierre Cohin, volontaire à l'Armée du Nord, à des membres de sa famille', *Annales historiques de la Révolution Française*, 27 (1955), p. 131.

25. Archives Départementales (AD) Loir-et-Cher, F2196, letter from Louis Godeau to his parents in Pontlevoy, 27 Messidor II.

26. AG Vincennes, Xw49 (Indre), letter of 22 Ventôse II.

27. Joanna Bourke, *An Intimate History of Killing: Face-to-Face Killing in Twentieth-Century Warfare* (London, 1999), pp. 1–12.

28. AD Mayenne, L1028, letter from René Cécé to his parents, 11 Thermidor III.

29. AD Vosges, 18R4, letter from Jean Duhout to his father in Saint-Clémens, 16 July 1808.

30. John R. Elting, *Swords around a Throne: Napoleon's Grande Armée* (London, 1989), pp. 394, 713.

31. AD Lozère, F424, letter from Joseph Vachin to his uncle in Mende, 13 Thermidor XI.

32. Elzéar Blaze, *La vie militaire sous le Premier Empire* (Paris, 1888), p. 28.

33. AG Vincennes, Xw7 (Ariège), letter of 9 June 1793.

34. Jean Barada, 'Lettres d'Alexandre Ladrix, volontaire de l'an II', *Cahiers de la Sabretache*, third series, 9 (1926), p. 149.

35. AD Drôme, 20R1–2, letter from Béranger to his father in Saint-Vallier, 10 July 1811.

36. AD Finistère, 35J11, letters from François Avril to his father in Saint-Lô, 17 Pluviôse, 20 Pluviôse and 18 Ventôse XII.

37. AD Loir-et-Cher, F2196, letter of 10 Messidor IX.

38. Lieutenant Chevalier, *Souvenirs des guerres napoléoniennes* (Paris, 1970), p. 61.

39. John Lynn, 'Toward an Army of Honor: The Moral Evolution of the French Army, 1789–1815', *French Historical Studies*, 16 (1989).

40. Pierre-Auguste Paris, 'Souvenirs du 14e Léger, 1805–12, par un officier du corps', *Carnet de la Sabretache* (1904), pp. 104–5.

41. AD Finistère, 35J11, letter from François Avril to his parents, from Kelbruk, 16 Frimaire XIII.

42. AD Finistère, 35J11, letter from François Avril to his parents from Zimmern, 25 March 1806.

43. Vigo-Roussillon, *Journal de campagne*, p. 32.

44. AD Pas-de-Calais, 1J625, letters from soldiers, 1806–11.

45. One example among many can be found in AD Creuse, 2F81, letter from Léonard Peigne to his father, 2 April 1812.

46. Gustave Dupont-Ferrier, 'Trois lettres inédites d'un caporal-fourrier aux Armées des Alpes et d'Italie (1795–97), *Annuaire-bulletin de la Société de l'histoire de France* (1929), pp. 139–41.

47. AD Oise, R (non-classée), letter from Danserville to his uncle from Palma-Nuova, 20 December 1807.

Notes to Chapter 5: From Valmy to Moscow

1. For a comparison with Confederate soldiers in the American Civil War, see Bell Irvin Wiley, *The Life of Johnny Reb: The Common Soldier of the Confederacy* (new edn, Baton Rouge, Louisiana, 1978), p. 15. In the spring of 1861 many felt, in the words of a young trooper from Arkansas, 'like ten thousand pins were pricking me in every part of the body, and started off a week in advance of my brothers'. Their mood would be very different by 1863.

2. John Lynn, *The Bayonets of the Republic: Motivation and Tactics in the Army of Revolutionary France, 1791–94* (Urbana, Illinois, 1984), pp. 35–36.

3. Jean Barada, 'Lettres de Joseph Ladrix, soldat de la Révolution', *Carnet de la Sabretache*, third series, 8 (1925), p. 28.

4. Letter of Auguste, soldier of the Armée des Vosges, written from Bitche, 29 May 1793, in L.-G. Pélissier, *Lettres de soldats, 1792–93: extrait de la Revue Alsacienne* (Paris, 1891), p. 5.

5. G. Vallée and G. Pariset (eds), *Carnet d'étapes du dragon Marquant: démarches et actions de l'Armée du Centre pendant la campagne de 1792* (Paris, 1898), p. 8.

6. Baron Ernouf, *Souvenirs d'un jeune abbé, soldat de la République, 1793–1801* (Paris, 1881), pp. 3–5.

7. Archives Départementales (AD) Vosges, 18R4, letter from Chanal to his father at Corcieux, 13 Messidor XIII.

8. AD Oise, series R (non-classée), letter from Jean Mullier to his mother at Saint-Crispin (Oise), 7 August 1813.

9. AD Pas-de-Calais, 1J1237, letters from Ambroise Forentiez to his mother and brother, 16 April 1810 and 9 March 1811.

10. AD Seine-et-Oise, 1F256, letter from Pimon to his parents in Gambais (Seine-et-Oise), 8 Brumaire X.

11. For a fuller discussion of the prevalence of homesickness among the troops, and for a fuller treatment of soldiers' intercessions on their brothers' behalf, see Chapter 7 below.

12. Guy Citerne, 'Les soldats de l'an II: lettres de conscrits auvergnats', *Gavroche: revue d'histoire populaire*, 13 (1984), p. 14.

13. AD Vaucluse, 1J161, letter from Laurent Jaummard in Madrid to his father at Bonnieux (Vaucluse), 12 May 1808.

14. André Palluel-Guillard, 'Correspondance et mentalité des soldats savoyards de l'armée napoléonienne', in *Soldats et armées en Savoie: actes du 28e congrès des Sociétés Savantes de Savoie* (Chambéry, 1981), p. 201.

15. E. Fairon and H. Heuse, *Lettres de grognards* (Liège, 1936), p. 347.

16. Ibid., p. 275.

17. Archives de la Guerre (AG) Vincennes, Xw7, letter from Jean Douciet to his father, 5 February 1794.

18. AD Mayenne, 108J cj, letter from a soldier in camp at Embleteuse, 19 May 1809.

19. AD Indre, L778, letter from André Desbruères to his mother in Châteauroux, 7 Messidor II

20. Fairon and Heuse, *Lettres de grognards*, p. 366.

21. AG Vincennes, Xw66, letter from Rémy Thirion to his family at Beuvezain (Meuse), 2 Floréal II.

22. Philippe-René Girault, *Mes campagnes sous la Révolution et l'Empire* (Paris, 1983), pp. 17–18.

23. Lieutenant Chevalier, *Souvenirs des guerres napoléoniennes* (Paris, 1970), p. 66.

24. L. Hennet and E. Martin (eds), *Lettres interceptées par les Russes durant la campagne de 1812* (Paris, 1913), p. 18.

25. J.-R. Coignet, *Souvenirs d'un vieux grognard* (Paris, 1912), pp. 146–47.

26. Maurice Boulle (ed.), 'Un ardéchois soldat de la République: André Amblard de Lussas à Mayence, en 1793', *Revue de la Société des enfants et amis de Villeneuve-de-Berg*, 40 (1980), p. 27.

27. Vallée and Pariset (eds), *Carnet d'étapes du dragon Marquant*, p. 28.

28. Philippe-René Girault, *Mes campagnes sous la Révolution et l'Empire* (Paris, 1983), p. 158.

29. Eugène Maury (ed.), *Lettres de volontaires républicains, 1791–94* (Troyes, 1901), p. 24; Fairon and Heuse, *Lettres de grognards*, p. 14.

30. Archives de l'Etat, Liège, Fonds Français, letter from Nicolas-Joseph Halleux to his parents, from Veselle, 15 June 1813.

31. AD Mayenne, L1028, letter from René Jendry, from Simplé (Mayenne), 2 pluviôse II.

32. Baron Ernouf, *Souvenirs militaires d'un jeune abbé, soldat de la République, 1793–1801* (Paris, 1881), p. 36.

33. AD Finistère, 35J11, letter from Guidon, commander of the 36th Regiment, announcing the death of a fellow-officer, 12 January 1811.

34. M. Demay, 'Les volontaires auxerrois de 1792 aux armées de la République', *Bulletin de la Société des sciences historiques et naturelles de l'Yonne*, 28 (1874), pp. 546–48.

35. AD Haute-Loire, R5973, letters from Jacques Bourgeat and from Lac to their parents in the Haute-Loire, 1809–1810.

36. AD Mayenne, L1028, letter from Jean Cosnard to his brother in Ballée, 28 Brumaire III.

37. Boulle, 'Un ardéchois soldat de la République', p. 27.

38. F.-X. Joliclerc, *Ses lettres*, p. 24.

39. André Palluel-Guillard, 'Correspondance et mentalité des soldats savoyards de l'armée napoléonienne', p. 206.

40. AD Savoie, L1137, letter from Claude Lavit in Legnano, 5 August 1809.

41. AD Oise, series R (unclassified), letters of imperial soldiers to their families, an VIII – 1823.

42. AD Lozère, letter from Joseph Vachin to his uncle in Mende, 1 September 1808.

43. Jean Marnier, *Souvenirs de guerre en temps de paix* (Paris, 1867), p. 36.

44. 'Journal du Capitaine Amblard, sur les routes d'Europe', *Revue de la Société des enfants et amis de Villeneuve-de-Berg*, 42 (1982), p. 47.

45. AD Finistère, 35J11, letter from François Avril to his parents from Zamora, 26 July 1809.

46. Lieutenant Chevalier, *Souvenirs des guerres napoléoniennes*, p. 74.

47. Michel Chatry (ed.), *Turreau en Vendée: mémoires et correspondance* (Cholet, 1992), p. 20.

48. G. Pages, 'Lettres de requis et volontaires de Coutras en Vendée et en Bretagne', *Revue historique et archéologique du Libournais*, 190 (1983), p. 155.

49. AG Vincennes, Xw29, letter from Louis Primault to his mother, 10 Fructidor II.

50. R. Huetz de Lemps, 'Un témoignage sur les Guerres de Vendée: le journal de Nicolas Poincenet', *Revue du Bas-Poitou*, 71 (1960), p. 35.

51. Joliclerc, *Ses lettres*, p. 155.

52. AD Gironde, 12L1, letter from Boissé to the President of the Club National in Bordeaux, 24 September 1793.

53. Pages, 'Lettres de requis et volontaires de Coutras', p. 157.

54. Ibid., p. 158.

55. Hennet and Martin, *Lettres interceptées par les Russes durant la campagne de 1812*, p. 61.

56. Ibid., p. 171.

57. Ibid., p. 254.

Notes to Chapter 6: Everyday Life in the Armies

1. Paul Fussell, *The Great War and Modern Memory* (Oxford, 1975), pp. 72–74.

2. Gabriel Noël, *Au temps des volontaires*, p. 12, quoted in Jean-Paul Bertaud, *La vie quotidienne des soldats de la Révolution, 1789–99* (Paris, 1985), p. 142.

3. Marcel Reible, 'Lettres du grognard Michaud, natif de Villognon (Charente)', *Revue de l'Institut Napoléon*, 135 (1979), p. 51.

4. Pierre-Auguste Paris, 'Souvenirs du 14e Léger, 1805–12, par un officier du corps', *Carnet de la Sabretache* (1904), p. 115.

5. M. Demay, 'Les volontaires auxerrois de 1792 aux armées de la République', *Bulletin de la Société des sciences historiques et naturelles de l'Yonne*, 28 (1874), p. 553.

6. Archives Départementales (AD) Loir-et-Cher, F2196, letter from Louis Godeau to his parents, 23 November 1793.

7. AD Seine-et-Oise, IV. M. 1–6, letter from Louis Ruzé to his mother, 10 February 1813.

8. Archives de la Guerre (AG) Vincennes, Xw7 (Ariège), letter of 9 Ventôse II.

9. AD Oise, series R (non-classée), letter from François Bourbier in Metz, 13 May 1813.

10. AD Oise, series R (non-classée), letter from Martin-Louis Pottier in Cremona, 12 January 1807.

11. AD Alpes-Maritimes, R32, letter from Jean-Baptiste Depoulis in Navarre, 20 September 1808.

12. F.-X. Joliclerc, *Ses lettres, 1793–1796* (Paris, 1905), p. 35.

13. Emile Fairon and Henri Heuse (eds), *Lettres de grognards* (Liège, 1936), p. 205.

14. AD Oise, series R (non-classée), letter from Jean-Pierre Laine in Vilna, 23 July 1812.

15. AD Finistère, 60J99, letter from Sébastien Mevel in Augsburg, 18 July 1809.

16. Fairon and Heuse (eds), *Lettres de grognards*, p. 354.

17. Philippe-René Girault, *Mes campagnes sous la Révolution et l'Empire* (Paris, 1983), pp. 53, 97–98.

18. Alfred Darimon (ed.), *Mémoires de François Lavaux, sergent au 103e de Ligne, 1793–1804* (Paris, 1894), p. 328.

19. Jean-Michel Chevalier, *Souvenirs des guerres napoléoniennes* (Paris, 1970), p. 43.

20. AG Vincennes, Xw7, letter from Marie-Joseph Duport to his mother in Saint-Ybars (Ariège), 10 June 1793.

21. AD Oise, series R (non-classée), letter from Doré in Antwerp to his mother in Auger-Saint-Vincent (Oise), 26 September 1809.

22. Fairon and Heuse (eds), *Lettres de grognards*, p. 372.

23. AD Oise, series R (non-classée), letter from Brassard in Warsaw, 13 January 1807.

24. André Palluel-Guillard, 'Correspondance et mentalité des soldats savoyards

de l'armée napoléonienne', in *Soldats et armées en Savoie: actes du 28e congrès des Sociétés Savantes de Savoie* (Chambéry, 1981), pp. 202–3.

25. AD Haute-Loire, R5973, letter from Pierre Dupin to his brother from Genoa, 26 December 1812.

26. Jean Barada, 'Lettres d'Alexandre Ladrix, volontaire de l'an II', quoted in *Bulletin de la Société d'histoire et d'archéologie du Gers*, 28 (1927), pp. 235–36.

27. Pierre-Auguste Paris, 'Souvenirs du 14e Léger, 1805–12, par un officier du corps', *Carnet de la Sabretache* (1904), p. 117.

28. Gabriel Noël, *Au temps des volontaires: lettres d'un volontaire de 1792* (Paris, 1912), pp. 13, 88.

29. AD Loir-et-Cher, F2196, letter from Louis Godeau to his parents from Hockelheim, 8 Brumaire VII.

30. Demay, 'Les volontaires auxerrois', p. 542.

31. AG Vincennes, Xw73, letter from Demouchy in Rousbrugge to his brother in the Nord, 7 October 1793.

32. Girault, *Mes campagnes sous la Révolution et l'Empire*, p. 26.

33. G. Vallée and G. Pariset (eds), *Carnet d'étapes du Dragon Marquant*, p. 231.

34. Demay, 'Les volontaires auxerrois', pp. 565–66.

35. Ibid., pp. 585–86.

36. François Vigo-Roussillon, *Journal de campagne, 1793–1837* (Paris, 1981), p. 19.

37. AD Oise, series R (non-classée), letter from Joseph Gérard to his parents, from Hamburg, 28 June 1813.

38. Demay, 'Les volontaires auxerrois', p. 597.

39. E. Maury (ed.), *Lettres de volontaires républicains, 1791–94*, pp. 26–27.

40. L. Duchet, *Deux volontaires de 1791: les frères Favier de Montluçon* (Montluçon, 1909), p. 58.

41. Capitaine de Bontin and Lieutenant Cornille, 'Les volontaires nationaux et le recrutement de l'armée pendant la Révolution dans l'Yonne', *Bulletin de la Société des sciences historiques et naturelles de l'Yonne*, 66 (1912), p. 590.

42. Jean Barada, 'Lettres d'Alexandre Ladrix, volontaire de l'an II', *Carnet de la Sabretache*, third series, 9 (1926), p. 66.

43. AD Vosges, 18R4, letter from Sébastien Marie in Metz to his parents in Plainfaing (Vosges), 6 November 1813.

44. AG Vincennes, Xw61 (Maine-et-Loire), letter of 26 Prairial III.

45. L. Hennet and E. Martin, *Lettres interceptées par les Russes durant la campagne de 1812* (Paris, 1913), p. 228.

46. AD Lozère, F424, letter of Joseph Vachin to his uncle from Bruin in Moravia, 17 Frimaire XIV.

47. AD Corrèze, 2F81, letter from Léonard Peigne to his father in the Corrèze, 2 April 1812.

48. AD Savoie, L1137, letter from Bonnel in Parma to his father in Fontcouverte (Savoie), 1 June 1809.

49. Jean-Michel Chevalier, *Souvenirs des guerres napoléoniennes*, p. 43.

50. Letter from François Dumey to his mother in Verlinghem (Nord), 5 Floréal III, in 'Lettres de campagne du sergent-major Dumey de la 8e demi-brigade', *Carnet de la Sabretache*, third series, 1 (1913), p. 612.

51. L.-J. Bricard, *Journal du canonnier Bricard, 1792–1802* (Paris, 1891), pp. 113, 126.

52. AD Finistère, letter from Lieutenant Avril to his father from Midelheim, 28 Vendémiaire XIV.

53. AD Haute-Loire, letter from Lac to his father, an innkeeper in Le Puy, 1809.

54. AD Vosges, 18R4, letter from Jean Lallemant in Nancy to his parents at Tendon, near Remiremont, 14 December 1813.

55. AD Bouches-du-Rhône, L490, letter from Auguste to his comrades in the Jacobin Club of the Section de Quatre-Vingt-Douze in Paris, 29 May 1793.

56. AD Savoie, L1137, letter from Charles Favre in Parma to his mother in Saint-Jean-de-Maurienne, 30 August 1809.

57. Demay, 'Les volontaires auxerrois de 1792', p. 569.

58. Fairon and Heuse, *Lettres de grognards*, p. 361.

59. Guy Citerne, 'Les soldats de l'an II: lettres de conscrits auvergnats', *Gavroche: revue d'histoire populaire*, 13 (1984), p. 13.

60. Alfred Darimon (ed.), *Mémoires de François Lavaux, sergent au 103e de Ligne, 1793–1814* (Paris, 1894), pp. 315–16.

61. Archives de l'Etat, Liège, Fonds Français 1045, letter 346, letter from Alexandre Goffart to his parents from prison in Portsmouth, 10 June 1811.

Notes to Chapter 7: The Lure of Family and Farm

1. Bell Irvin Wiley, *The Life of Johnny Reb: The Common Soldier of the Confederacy* (Baton Rouge, Louisiana, 1978), p. 192.

2. Archives Départementales (AD) Mayenne, 108Jcj, letter from Daniel Griveau in Embleteuse to his mother in Courveille (Mayenne), 8 June 1809.

3. AD Oise, R (non-classée), letter from Jean-Baptiste Dourlens in Hamburg to his father in Songeons (Oise), 25 June 1813.

4. André Palluel-Guillard, 'Correspondance et mentalité des soldats savoyards de l'armée napoléonienne', p. 201.

5. 'Lettres de campagne du sergent-major Dumey de la 8e demi-brigade', *Carnet de la Sabretache*, third series, 1 (1913), p. 612.

6. G. Ermisse, 'Lettre d'un soldat de l'an II', *Société d'archéologie et de statistique de la Drôme*, 79 (1974), p. 203.

7. Emile Fairon and Henri Heuse (eds), *Lettres de grognards*, p. 356.

8. Le capitaine de Bontin et le lieutenant Cornille, 'Les volontaires nationaux et le recrutement de l'armée pendant la Révolution dans l'Yonne', *Bulletin de la Société des sciences historiques et naturelles de l'Yonne*, 66 (1912), p. 592.

9. Pierre Debeauvais, 'Un grognard malgré lui: lettres de guerre de Nicolas Bognier, 1806–14', in *Soldats et armées en Savoie: actes du 28e congrès des Sociétés Savantes de Savoie* (Chambéry, 1981), p. 196.

10. Jacques Staes, 'Lettres de soldats béarnais de la Révolution et du Premier Empire', 2, *Revue de Pau et du Béarn*, 8 (1980), p. 160.

11. Jean Barada, 'Lettres d'Alexandre Ladrix, volontaire de l'an II', *Carnet de la Sabretache*, third series, 9 (1926), p. 68.

12. Marcel Deible, 'Lettres du grognard Michaud, natif de Villognon (Charente)', *Revue de l'Institut Napoléon*, 135 (1979), p. 53.

13. AD Vosges, 18R4, letter from Jérôme, grenadier in the Regiment of the Ile-de-France, to his father, 7 July 1809.

14. Staes, 'Lettres de soldats béarnais', 2, p. 153.

15. AD Lozère, F424, correspondence of Joseph Vachin with his uncle in Mende, especially letter of 13 Thermidor XI.

16. AD Vosges, 18R4, letter from Baumon to his father at La Chapelle-au-Bois, near Epinal, 7 February 1811.

17. J.-R. Coignet, *Souvenirs d'un vieux grognard* (Paris, 1912), pp. 40–41.

18. AD Savoie, L1137, letter from Basile Costery to his father in Beaune (Saint-Michel-de-Maurienne), 21 September 1807.

19. Palluel-Guillard, 'Correspondance et mentalité des soldats savoyards de l'armée napoléonienne', p. 200.

20. Ibid., p. 200.

21. Archives de la Guerre (AG) Vincennes, Xw57, letter from Dochy with the 10th Battalion of Mountain Chasseurs to his mother in Orléans, 2 Prairial II.

22. See above, pp. 41–42.

23. Jean-Paul Bertaud, 'Réflexion sur la conscription sous le Premier Empire', *Rivista Napoleonica*, 1–2 (2000), pp. 267–69.

24. Jean-Paul Bertaud, *Guerre et société en France de Louis XIV à Napoléon 1er* (Paris, 1998), pp. 192–97.

25. AD Mayenne, 108Jcj, leter from Daniel Griveau in Lille to his parents in Courveille, 20 March 1809.

26. M. Demay, 'Les volontaires auxerrois de 1792 aux armées de la République', *Bulletin de la Société des sciences historiques et naturelles de l'Yonne*, 28 (1874), p. 574.

27. Lorédan Larchey, *Journal de marche d'un volontaire de 1792: le journal du sergent Fricasse* (Paris, 1911), p. 8.

28. Fairon and Heuse, *Lettres de grognards*, p. 350.

29. Archives de l'Etat, Liège, Fonds Français 1042, letter from Gérard Jacquet to his parents.

30. Guy Citerne, 'Les soldats de l'an II: lettres de conscrits auvergnats', *Gavroche: revue d'histoire populaire*, 13 (1984), p. 14.

31. AD Oise, R (non-classée), letter from Berra in Nijmegen to his brother and sister at Noyon (Oise), 11 March 1808.

32. AD Mayenne, 1J409, letter from René Vilain to his parents in Arras, 19 April 1813.

33. AD Oise, R (non-classée), letter from Lépine to his father at Thury near Senlis, 23 September 1806.

34. J. Bernet, 'Document inédit: lettres de soldats compiègnois à leurs familles sous la Révolution', *Annales historiques compiègnoises modernes et contemporaines*, 2 (1978), p. 48.

35. Fairon and Heuse, *Lettres de grognards*, p. 346.

36. AD Savoie, 49F48, letter from Telan to his parents in Aiguebelle, 4 Germinal XIII.

37. Fairon and Heuse, *Lettres de grognards*, p. 359

38. AD Oise, R (non-classée), letter from Fontaine to his parents in Compiègne, 6 February 1809.

39. AD Mayenne, 1J409, letter from Louis Goddos to his parents in Larchamp (Mayenne), 1813.

40. AD Mayenne, 108Jcj, letters from Daniel Griveau to his parents, on 20 January 1810 from Antwerp and 5 June 1810 from Ostend.

41. AD Loir-et-Cher, L615, letter from Augustin Bardon to his brother, 23 Fructidor II.

42. Barada, 'Lettres d'Alexandre Ladrix, volontaire de l'an II', p. 13.

43. AD Lozère, F2258, letter from Charles Ignon to his brother, undated, from Privas, but received on 28 Floréal XII.

44. AD Oise, R (non-classée), letter from Marie-Antoine Lemaire to his mother, 28 June 1811.

45. Barada, 'Lettres d'Alexandre Ladrix', p. 143.

46. AD Loir-et-Cher, F2196, letter from Louis Godeau to his parents, 25 Thermidor VIII.

47. AG Vincennes, Xw7, letter from Jean Floizac to his parents in Saint-Ybars (Ariège), 10 Ventôse III.

48. AD Loir-et-Cher, F2196, letter from Louis Godeau to his parents, 27 Vendémiaire VIII.

49. AD Haute-Loire, R5973, letter from Molliere to his sister in Lantriac, 20 November 1808.

50. AD Gironde, 2R861, correspondence between Jean Costedouat and his father in Banos (Landes), 9–15 Vendémiaire VIII.

51. AG Vincennes, Xw30, letter from Antoine Lapassa in Piedmont to his father in Romans (Drôme), undated.

52. AG Vincennes, Xw66, letter from Rémy Thirion to his parents at Beuvezain (Meuse), 13 Germinal II.

53. F.-X. Joliclerc, *Ses lettres, 1793–96* (Paris, 1905), pp. 228–29.

54. AD Drôme, 20R1–2, letter from *veuve* Cany to her cousin, undated.

55. AD Savoie, L1137, letters from prisoners arrested for desertion, from Sélestat (3 February 1805), Châlon-sur-Saône (18 November 1809), and Saint-Quentin (7 May 1810).

56. AD Cher, Z559, letters from Jean-Claude Crochet from prison in Lyon, 18 May and 14 August 1808, and from Michel Guaguin from prison in Besançon, 15 May 1813.

57. Joliclerc, *Ses lettres*, p. 98.

58. AD Savoie, L1137, letter from Jacques Vairat to his mother, written from near Milan, 7 July 1809.

59. AD Lozère, F2258, letter from Guillaume Brunel to his parents at Malasagne (Lozère), 1 August 1806.

60. AD Lozère, F428, letter from Jean-Baptiste Gely to his parents, from Alessandria in Piedmont, 7 June 1809.

Notes to Chapter 8: From One War to Another

1. Isser Woloch, *Jacobin Legacy: The Democratic Movement under the Directory* (Princeton, 1970), pp. 70–76.

2. Pierre Nora, 'Lavisse, instituteur national', in Pierre Nora (ed.), *Les lieux de mémoire*, i, *La République* (Paris, 1984), pp. 247–89.

3. Richard Holt, *Sport and Society in Modern France* (London, 1981), pp. 11–12.

4. Richard Cobb, 'France and the Coming of War', in R. J. W. Evans and Hartmut Pogge von Strandmann (eds), *The Coming of the First World War* (Oxford, 1988), p. 125.

5. Maurice Agulhon, 'Marianne en 14–18', in Jean-Jacques Becker, Jay

M. Winter, Gerd Krumeich, Annette Becker and Stéphane Audoin-Rouzeau (eds), *Guerre et cultures, 1914–1918* (Paris, 1994), p. 374.

6. Marc Ferro, 'Cultural Life in France, 1914–1918', in Aviel Roshwald and Richard Stites (eds), *European Culture in the Great War: The Arts, Entertainment and Propaganda, 1914–18* (Cambridge, 1999), p. 295.

7. Jean-Pierre Guéno, 'Les saisons de l'âme', in Jean-Pierre Guéno and Yves Laplume (eds), *Paroles de poilus: lettres et carnets du front, 1914–1918* (Paris, 1998), pp. 7–8.

8. Guillaume Leveque, 'L'image des héros dans la presse périodique photographique française de la Première Guerre Mondiale' (mémoire de DEA, Université de Paris-I, 1989), pp. 14–24.

9. Gérard Bacconnier, André Minet and Louis Solet, *La plume au fusil: les poilus du Midi à travers leur correspondance* (Toulouse, 1985), p. 29.

10. Ibid., p. 109.

11. Ibid., p. 19.

12. Paul Raybaut, *Correspondance de guerre d'un rural, 1914–17* (Paris, 1974), p. 26.

13. Ibid., p. 157.

14. Frédéric Rousseau, *La guerre censurée: une histoire des combattants européens de 14–18* (Paris, 1999), p. 40.

15. Daniel Mornet, *Tranchées de Verdun* (Nancy, 1990), p. 45.

16. Henri Castex, *Verdun, années infernales: lettres d'un soldat au front, août 1914 à septembre 1916* (Paris, 1996), p. 117.

17. Pierre Albin (ed.), *Tous les journaux du front* (Paris, 1916), pp. 6–10.

18. Stéphane Audoin-Rouzeau, *Cinq deuils de guerre, 1914–1918* (Paris, 2001), pp. 97ff.

19. Joanna Bourke, *An Intimate History of Killing: Face-to-Face Killing in Twentieth-Century Warfare* (London, 1999), esp. pp. 1–8.

20. Rémy Cazals (ed.), *Les carnets de guerre de Louis Barthas, tonnelier, 1914–1918* (Paris, 1997), p. 10.

21. Leonard V. Smith, *Between Mutiny and Obedience: The Case of the French Fifth Infantry Division during World War I* (Princeton, 1994), pp. 79–89.

22. Henri Barbusse, *Le feu* (Paris, 1916); for an appraisal of Barbusse's antimilitarist stance see Frank Field, *Three French Writers and the Great War* (Cambridge, 1975), pp. 19–78.

23. Anick Cochet, 'L'opinion et le moral des soldats en 1916, d'après les archives du Contrôle Postal' (thèse de doctorat, Université de Paris-X, 1986), p. 91.

24. Jean Nicot, *Les poilus ont la parole: lettres du front, 1917–18* (Paris, 1998), p. 386.

25. Anick Cochet, 'L'opinion et le moral', p. 492.

26. John Norton Cru, *Du témoignage* (Paris. 1997), p. 132. When his work first appeared, as *Témoins*, in 1929, it caused widespread outrage and controversy amongst both politicians and veterans of the Great War.

27. Stéphane Audoin-Rouzeau and Annette Becker, *14–18: retrouver la Guerre* (Paris, 2000), p. 36.

28. Leonard V. Smith, 'John Norton Cru and the Combatants' Literature of the First World War', *Modern and Contemporary France*, 9 (2001), pp. 165–66.

29. Audoin-Rouzeau and Becker, *14–18*, p. 32.

30. Jean-Jacques Becker, *The Great War and the French People* (Leamington Spa, 1985), p. 327.

31. Antoine Prost, 'Les monuments aux morts', in Pierre Nora (ed.), *Les lieux de mémoire*, i, *La République*, pp. 195–225.

Bibliography

MANUSCRIPT SOURCES

1. Archives Départementales (AD)

Collections of soldiers' letters of the Revolution and Empire, of widely varying interest, are to be found scattered in a number of departmental archives. Some are exceptionally rich – most notably, perhaps, in those of the Oise and Savoie. But since they do not represent the papers of any particular administration and entered the public domain by a great variety of routes, these letters are catalogued in very different ways. Most often they are to be found in series L (*Révolution*), for letters written before 1800, and R (*Affaires militaires*, post-1800), for those written under the Consulate and Empire. More occasionally there are small deposits to be found in either Z (*Fonds des sous-préfectures*) or Efs-dépôt (*Dépôts des communes*). But letters also turn up elsewhere, notably in series F (*Fonds divers*) and J (*Documents entrés par voies extraordinaires*), series composed of documents whose origin is not from regular administrative deposits but which came as a gift or as a special deposit. Needless to say, I am much indebted to the archivists and staff of the departments concerned, who often provided references which would have been very difficult to uncover in the published catalogues.

AD Alpes-Maritimes
    R32   Fonds Consulat et Empire, Conscription, 1808
AD Cher
    Z559   Fonds de la sous-préfecture de Sancerre: lettres de soldats, 1800–14
AD Corrèze
    2F81   Lettres de soldats de la Corrèze
AD Côte d'Or
    L3005   Sociétés populaires de Dijon, correspondance, 1792-an III

L3023   Sociétés populaires de Nuits-Saint-Georges, correspondance, 1792-an III

L3033   Correspondance reçue de divers particuliers, commune de Saint-Jean-de-Losne, 1791-an IV

AD Drôme

6R3–3   Divers: lettres de soldats, 1791–1870

20R1–2   Lettres de soldats en campagne, Consulat-Deuxième Restauration

AD Eure

VF 84   Lettres de Pierre Besnard de Beaumesnil (Eure)

AD Finistère

35J11   Lettres de F. Avril à ses parents, 1804–1810

60J99   Lettres de militaires, 1809–11

AD Gironde

12L35   Sociétés populaires de Bordeaux: correspondance avec les armées

2R289   Colonne mobile

2R861   Procédures jugées pour désertion

AD Indre

L778   Affaires militaires: lettres de soldats, 1792-an VI.

AD Indre-et-Loire

E dépôt   Chinon 1 H 12 Lettres de conscrits de Chinon

AD Loir-et-Cher

L615   Lettres de soldats à leurs parents

L2196   Correspondance de Louis Godeau, 1793–1801

AD Haute-Loire

L1032   Lettres de militaires à leur famille, 1793-an VII

R5973   Lettres de soldats à leur famille, an XIII – 1822

AD Lozère

F424   Lettres de Joseph Vachin, soldat et officier, an XI – 1816

F428   Lettres diverses adressées à Joseph Vachin, 1789–1815

F2258   Lettres de Charles Ignon à sa mère et à son frère, an VI – 1814

R7814   Lettres de militaires à leurs parents, 1806–14

AD Mayenne

1J293   Lettres de conscrits, an II – 1810

1J409   Lettres de conscrits, 1793–1819
108Jcj   Documents de familles – Dossier Griveau
108Jep   Documents de familles – Dossier Lepron
L1028   Lettres de conscrits de la Mayenne, an II – an III

AD Meuse

R100   Recueil des lettres de Nicolas Sommière, 1807–10

AD Nièvre

Ls/sR   Militaires de la Nièvre pendant la République,
               lettres, 1793-an III

AD Nord

1R212   Réfractaires et déserteurs, 1808–09
1R213   Réfractaires et déserteurs, 1810–11

AD Oise

R (non-classée) Lettres de soldats de l'Empire, an VIII – 1823

AD Pas-de-Calais

1J625   Lettres de soldats impériaux, 1806–11
1J1237   Lettres du caporal Ambroise Forentiez de Farbus

AD Haute-Saône

34L 7   Lettre adressée au District de Vesoul

AD Savoie

49F48   Fonds Gros: correspondance, lettres non officielles
L1137   Lettres adressées à leurs parents par des militaires,
               an XI – 1815

AD Seine-et-Oise

1F256   Lettres de soldats du Premier Empire
IV. M. 1–6 Premier Empire: lettres de soldats de la Seine-et-Oise

AD Vaucluse

1J161   Premier Empire: lettres de soldats

AD Vosges

18R4   Dernières lettres écrites à leurs parents par
               des militaires, 1799–1825

2. Archives de la Guerre, Vincennes (AG)

Also invaluable are the many soldiers' letters which were copied by hand as part of the task of building up an archive of the revolutionary period in the Archives de la Guerre at Vincennes. These documents, which were uncovered in the departmental archives, have been catalogued by department in the series Xw. The following cartons proved especially useful.

Xw7	Ariège
Xw29	Deux-Sèvres
Xw30	Drôme
Xw49	Indre
Xw57	Loiret
Xw61	Maine-et-Loire
Xw66	Meuse
Xw73	Nord

In the series 'Mémoires et Reconnaissances' (MR), I also consulted some of the petitions and addresses of the troops to the National Assembly in 1789 (MR 1718).

3. Archives de l'Etat, Liège

Besides the excellent collection of soldiers' letters from Liège edited by Fairon and Heuse, the Fonds Français contains two interesting cartons which throw a slightly different light on the soldiers' communications.

> 1042 Lettres de grognards produits pour prouver l'existence aux armées d'un frère plus âgé: lettres venant de soldats des régiments de ligne.

> 1045 Lettres provenant de gendarmes, de prisonniers en Angleterre, de déserteurs et d'ouvriers.

PRINTED PRIMARY SOURCES

1. Letters and Memoirs of the Revolution and Empire

Barada, Jean, 'Lettres d'Alexandre Ladrix, volontaire de l'an II', Carnet de la Sabretache, third series, 9 (1926).

Barada, Jean, 'Lettres de Joseph Ladrix, soldat de la Révolution', Carnet de la Sabretache, third series, 8 (1925).

Bernet, Jacques, 'Document inédit: lettres de soldats compiègnois à leurs familles sous la Révolution', Annales historiques compiègnoises modernes et contemporaines, 2 (1978).

Blaze, Elzéar, La vie militaire sous le Premier Empire (Paris, 1888).

Bontin, Capitaine de and Lieutenant Cornille, 'Les volontaires nationaux et le recrutement de l'armée pendant la Révolution dans l'Yonne', *Bulletin de la Société des sciences historiques et naturelles de l'Yonne*, 66 (1912).

Boulle, Maurice (ed.), 'Un ardéchois soldat de la République: André Amblard de Lussas à Mayence, en 1793', *Revue de la Société des enfants et amis de Villeneuve-de-Berg*, 40 (1980).

Boulle, Maurice (ed.). 'Journal du Capitaine Amblard, sur les routes d'Europe', *Revue de la Société des enfants et amis de Villeneuve-de-Berg*, 42 (1982).

Bouscayrol, René, *Cent lettres de soldats de l'An II* (Paris, 1987).

Bricard, L.-J., *Journal du canonnier Bricard, 1792–1802* (Paris, 1891).

Chatry, Michel (ed.), *Turreau en Vendée: mémoires et correspondance* (Cholet, 1992).

Chauvigny, Louis de, *Lettres inédites de Choderlos de Laclos* (Paris, 1904).

Chevalier, Jean-Michel, *Souvenirs des guerres napoléoniennes* (Paris, 1970).

Citerne, Guy, 'Les soldats de l'an II: lettres de conscrits auvergnats', *Gavroche: revue d'histoire populaire*, 13 (1984).

Coignet, J.-R., *Souvenirs d'un vieux grognard* (Paris, 1912).

Coutansais, Françoise, 'La Guerre des Géants vue par des Bleus', *Revue du Bas-Poitou et des provinces de l'Ouest*, 74 (1963).

Darimon, Alfred (ed.), *Mémoires de François Lavaux, sergent au 103e de Ligne, 1793- 1804* (Paris, 1894).

Debeauvais, Pierre, 'Un grognard malgré lui: lettres de guerre de Nicolas Bognier, 1806–14', in *Soldats et armées en Savoie: actes du 28e congrès des Sociétés savantes de Savoie* (Chambéry, 1981).

Deible, Marcel, 'Lettres du grognard Michaud, natif de Villognon (Charente)', *Revue de l'Institut Napoléon*, 135 (1979).

Demay, M., 'Les volontaires auxerrois de 1792 aux armées de la République', *Bulletin de la Société des sciences historiques et naturelles de l'Yonne*, 28 (1874).

Dumey, François, 'Lettres de campagne du sergent-major Dumey de la 8e demi-brigade', *Carnet de la Sabretache*, third series, 1 (1913).

Dupont-Ferrier, Gustave, 'Trois lettres inédites d'un caporal-fourrier aux Armées des Alpes et d'Italie (1795–97), *Annuaire-bulletin de la Société de l'histoire de France* (1929).

Ermisse, G., 'Lettre d'un soldat de l'an II', *Société d'archaéologie et de statistique de la Drôme*, 79 (1974).

Ernouf, Baron, *Souvenirs d'un jeune abbé, soldat de la République, 1793–1801* (Paris, 1881).

Fairon, Emile and Henri Heuse, *Lettres de grognards* (Liège, 1936).

Foubert, Bernard, 'Lettres de combattants aubois (1792–1793) écrivant de Saint-Domingue', *La vie en Champagne* 27 (1979).

Girault, Philippe-René, *Mes campagnes sous la Révolution et l'Empire* (Paris, 1983).

Guigal, 'Correspondance d'un officier de l'armée républicaine', *Revue du Vivarais*, 85 (1981).

Hénault, M., 'Lettre d'un volontaire de Tagnon (Ardennes), *Revue historique ardennaise*, 5 (1898).

Hennet, L. and E. Martin (eds), *Lettres interceptées par les Russes durant la campagne de 1812* (Paris, 1913).

Huetz de Lemps, R., 'Un témoignage sur les Guerres de Vendée: le journal de Nicolas Poincenet', *Revue du Bas-Poitou*, 71 (1960).

Joliclerc, F.-X., *Ses lettres, 1793–96* (Paris, 1905).

Larchey, Lorédan, *Journal de marche d'un volontaire de 1792: le journal du sergent Fricasse* (Paris, 1911).

Levé, Charles, 'Souvenirs: un prisonnier des Blancs et des Bleus', *L'Anjou historique*, 96 (1916).

Marnier, Jean, *Souvenirs de guerre en temps de paix, 1793 – 1806 – 1823 – 1862* (Paris, 1867).

Maury, Eugène (ed.), *Lettres de volontaires républicains, 1791–94* (Troyes, 1901).

Noël, Gabriel, *Au temps des volontaires* (Paris, 1912).

Pages, G., 'Lettres de requis et volontaires de Coutras en Vendée et en Bretagne', *Revue historique et archéologique du Libournais*, 190 (1983)

Paris, Pierre-Auguste, 'Souvenirs du 14e Léger, 1805–12, par un officier du corps', *Carnet de la Sabretache* (1904), pp. 104–5.

Pélissier, L.-G., 'Lettres de soldats, 1792–93', *Revue alsacienne*, 1891.

Picard, Ernest, *Au service de la Nation: lettres de volontaires, 1792–98* (Paris, 1914).

Pioger, A., 'Lettres de Pierre Cohin, volontaire à l'Armée du Nord, à des membres de sa famille', *Annales historiques de la Révolution Française*, 27 (1955).

Prot, E., 'Lettres du sergent Jean Bernier, volontaire à la première compagnie du premier bataillon du Bec d'Ambès', *Revue historique et archéologique du Libournais* (1959).

Reible, Marcel, 'Lettres du grognard Michaud, natif de Villognon (Charente), *Revue de l'Institut Napoléon*, 135 (1979).

Ritter, Jean, 'Un jeune Strasbourgeois en Vendée: lettres d'un volontaire au 8e Bataillon du Bas-Rhin, 1793–96', *Actes du 103e congrès national des Sociétés savantes, Nancy-Metz 1978*, i (Paris, 1979).

Staes, Jacques, 'Lettres de soldats béarnais de la Révolution et du Premier Empire', 2, *Revue de Pau et du Béarn*, 8 (1980).

Tholin, G., 'Mémoires et pièces diverses pour servir à l'histoire des volontaires du Lot-et-Garonne, engagés de l'an II', *Revue de l'Agenais*, 22 (1895).

Vallée, Gustave and Georges Pariset (eds), *Carnet d'étapes du dragon Marquant: démarches et actions de l'Armée du Centre pendant la campagne de 1792* (Paris, 1898).

Vermale, F., 'Lettres à un soldat de l'an II', *Annales historiques de la Révolution Française*, 8 (1931).

Vermale, F., 'Lettres inédites d'un sous-lieutenant de l'Armée des Alpes', *Annales historiques de la Révolution Française*, 6 (1929).

Vigo-Roussillon, François, *Journal de campagne, 1793–1837* (Paris, 1981).

2. Other Printed Primary Sources

Military Newspapers:

> *Bulletin de la Grande Armée.*
> *Journal de l'Armée des Côtes de Cherbourg.*
> *Journal de Bonaparte et des Hommes Vertueux.*
> *La Soirée du Camp.*

Albin, Pierre (ed.), *Tous les journaux du front* (Paris, 1916).

Bacconnier, Gérard, André Minet and Louis Solet, *La plume au fusil: les poilus du Midi à travers leur correspondance* (Toulouse, 1985).

Barbusse, Henri, *Le feu* (Paris, 1916).

Castex, Henri, *Verdun, années infernales: lettres d'un soldat au front, août 1914 – septembre 1916* (Paris, 1996).

Cazals, Rémy (ed.), *Les carnets de guerre de Louis Barthas, tonnelier, 1914–1918* (Paris, 1997).

Clausewitz, Carl von, *On War* (London, 1968).

Guéno, Jean-Pierre and Yves Laplume (eds), *Paroles de poilus: lettres et carnets du front, 1914–1918* (Paris, 1998).

Guibert, Jacques-Antoine-Hyppolite de, *Essai général de tactique* (Paris, 1772).

Las Cases, Emmanuel de, *Mémorial de Sainte-Hélène* (2 vols, Paris, 1962).

Lemaire, Antoine-François, *L'Ami des Soldats: par l'auteur des lettres bougrement patriotiques* (Paris, 1790).

Nicot, Jean, *Les poilus ont la parole: lettres du front, 1917–18* (Paris, 1998).

Norton Cru, John, *Témoins* (Paris, 1929).

Raybaut, Paul, *Correspondance de guerre d'un rural, 1914–17* (Paris, 1974).

Robespierre, Maximilien, *Oeuvres complètes*, ed. E. Déprez and others (10 vols, Paris. 1910–67).

Servan, Joseph, *Le Soldat-citoyen* (Paris, 1781).

Stewart, J. M., *A Documentary Survey of the French Revolution* (New York, 1951).

Vingtrinier, Joseph, *Chants et chansons des soldats de France* (Paris, 1902).

SECONDARY WORKS

Audoin-Rouzeau, Stéphane, *Cinq deuils de guerre, 1914–1918* (Paris, 2001).

Audoin-Rouzeau, Stéphane and Annette Becker, *14–18: retrouver la Guerre* (Paris, 2000).

Baker, Keith Michael, 'Defining the Public Sphere in Eighteenth-Century France: Variations on a Theme by Habermas', in Craig Calhoun (ed.), *Habermas and the Public Sphere* (Cambridge, Massachusetts, 1992), pp. 181–211.

Bastide, Capitaine de la, 'Lettres de soldats (an II)', *Carnet de la Sabretache*, 7 (1908).

Baticle, René, 'Le plébiscite sur la constitution de 1793', *Révolution Française* 58 (1910).

Becker, Jean-Jacques, *The Great War and the French People* (Leamington Spa, 1985).

Becker, Jean-Jacques, Jay M. Winter, Gerd Krumeich, Annette Becker and Stéphane Audoin-Rouzeau (eds), *Guerre et Cultures, 1914–1918* (Paris, 1994).

Bergeron, Louis, *France under Napoleon* (Princeton, 1981).

Bergès, Louis, 'Le civil et l'armée au début du dix-neuvième siècle: la résistance à la conscription dans les départements aquitains, 1798–1814' (thèse de l'Ecole des Chartes, 1980).

Bertaud, Jean-Paul, *Guerre et société en France de Louis XIV à Napoléon Ier* (Paris, 1998).

Bertaud, Jean-Paul, *La presse et le pouvoir de Louis XIII à Napoléon Ier* (Paris, 2000).

Bertaud, Jean-Paul, 'Réflexion sur la conscription sous le Premier Empire', *Rivista Napoleonica*, 1–2 (2000).

Bertaud, Jean-Paul, *La Révolution armée: les soldats-citoyens et la Révolution Française* (Paris, 1979).

Bertaud, Jean-Paul, *La vie quotidienne des soldats de la Révolution, 1789–99* (Paris, 1985).

Bertaud, Jean-Paul and Daniel Reichel (eds), *Atlas de la Révolution Française*, iii, *L'armée et la guerre* (Paris, 1989).

Black, Jeremy, *European Warfare, 1660–1815* (London, 1994).

Blanning, T. C. W., *The French Revolutionary Wars, 1787–1802* (London, 1996).

Blond, Georges, *La Grande Armée* (Paris, 1979).

Bourke, Joanna, *An Intimate History of Killing: Face-to-Face Killing in Twentieth-Century Warfare* (London, 1999).

Brécy, Robert, 'La chanson révolutionnaire de 1789 à 1799', *Annales historiques de la Révolution Française*, 53 (1981), pp. 279–303.

Castel, J.-A., 'L'application de la Loi Jourdan dans l'Hérault' (mémoire de maîtrise, Université de Montpellier, 1970).

Chabrol, André, 'La poste aux armées', in Maurice Bruzeau (ed.), *La poste durant la Révolution, 1789–1799* (Paris, 1989).

Chagniot, Jean, *Paris et l'armée au dix-huitième siècle: étude politique et sociale* (Paris, 1985).

Challener, Richard, *The French Theory of the Nation-in-Arms, 1866–1939* (New York, 1955).

Chandler, David (ed.), *Napoleon's Marshals* (London, 1987).

Chartier, Roger, *The Cultural Uses of Print in Early Modern France* (Princeton, 1987).

Chartier, Roger, Alain Boureau and Cécile Dauphin, *Correspondence: Models of Letter-Writing from the Middle Ages to the Nineteenth Century* (Cambridge, 1997).

Cochet, Anick, 'L'opinion et le moral des soldats en 1916, d'après les archives du Contrôle Postal' (thèse de doctorat, Université de Paris-X, 1986).

Connelly, Owen, *Blundering to Glory: Napoleon's Military Campaigns* (Wilmington, Delaware, 1987).

Crépin, Annie, *La conscription en débat: ou le triple apprentissage de la nation, de la citoyenneté, de la république, 1798–1889* (Arras, 1998).

Crook, Malcolm, *Napoleon Comes to Power: Democracy and Dictatorship in Revolutionary France, 1795–1804* (Cardiff, 1998).

Delarue, M., 'L'éducation politique à l'armée du Rhin' (mémoire de maîtrise, Université de Paris-Nanterre, 1968).

Deplace, Françoise, 'L'assistance aux militaires et aux familles des militaires à Paris sous la Convention' (mémoire de maîtrise, Université de Paris-I, 1987).

Devleeshouwer, Robert, *L'arrondissement du Brabant sous l'occupation française, 1794–95* (Brussels, 1964).

Dhombres, Jean et Nicole, *Lazare Carnot* (Paris, 1997).

Duchet, L., *Deux volontaires de 1791: les frères Favier de Montluçon* (Montluçon, 1909).

Edelstein, Melvin, 'Le militaire-citoyen, ou le droit de vote des militaires pendant la Révolution Française', *Annales historiques de la Révolution Française*, 310 (1997).

Elting, John R., *Swords Around a Throne: Napoleon's Grande Armée* (London, 1989).

Epstein, Robert M., *Napoleon's Last Victory and the Emergence of Modern War* (Lawrence, Kansas, 1994).

Esdaile, Charles J., *The Spanish Army in the Peninsular War* (Manchester, 1988).

Esdaile, Charles J., *The Wars of Napoleon* (London, 1995).

Evans, R. J. W., and Hartmut Pogge von Strandmann (eds), *The Coming of the First World War* (Oxford, 1988).

Ferrier, Maurice (ed.), *La poste aux armées: textes, documents, souvenirs et témoignages* (Paris, 1975).

Field, Frank, *Three French Writers and the Great War* (Cambridge, 1975).

Foissy-Aufrère, Marie-Pierre (ed.), *La mort de Bara*, exhibition catalogue from the Musée Calvet (Avignon, 1989)

Forrest, Alan, *Conscripts and Deserters: The Army and French Society during the Revolution and Empire* (New York, 1989).

Forrest, Alan, *The French Revolution and the Poor* (Oxford, 1981).

Forrest, Alan, *The Soldiers of the French Revolution* (Durham, North Carolina, 1990).

Frank, Ph.-F. de, *Les marques postales de la Grande Armée, par son histoire, 1805–08* (Paris, 1948).

Furet, François and Jacques Ozouf, *Reading and Writing: Literacy in France from Calvin to Jules Ferry* (Cambridge, 1982).

Fussell, Paul, *The Great War and Modern Memory* (Oxford, 1975).

Garnier, Nicole, *Catalogue de l'imagerie populaire française* (2 vols, Paris, 1990 and 1996).

Gates, David, *The Napoleonic Wars, 1803–1815* (London, 1997).

Gildea, Robert, *The Past in French History* (New Haven and London, 1994).

Goodman, Dena, *The Republic of Letters: A Cultural History of the French Enlightenment* (Ithaca, New York, 1994).

Griffith, Paddy, *The Art of War of Revolutionary France, 1789–1802* (London, 1998).

Gross, Jean-Pierre, *Saint-Just: sa politique et ses missions* (Paris, 1976).

Habermas, Jürgen, *The Structural Transformation of the Public Sphere: An Enquiry into a Category of Bourgeois Society* (Cambridge, Massachusetts, 1989).

Haydon, Colin and William Doyle (eds), *Robespierre* (Cambridge, 1999).

Heim, Jean-François, Claire Béraud and Philippe Heim, *Les salons de peinture de la Révolution Française, 1789–99* (Paris, 1989).

Holt, Richard, *Sport and Society in Modern France* (London, 1981).

Hopkin, David M., 'Changing Popular Attitudes to the Military in Lorraine and the Surrounding Regions, 1700–1870' (Ph.D. thesis, University of Cambridge, 1997).

Hopkin, David M., 'La Ramée: The Archetypal Soldier', *French History* 14 (2000).

Horne, John, 'From *Levée en Masse* to "Total War": France and the Revolutionary Legacy, 1870–1945', in Robert Aldrich and Martyn Lyons (eds), *The Sphinx in the Tuileries and Other Essays in Modern French History* (Sydney, 1999).

Houston, Rab, *Literacy in Early Modern Europe: Culture and Education, 1500–1800* (London, 1988).

Hunt, Lynn, *Politics, Culture and Class in the French Revolution* (Berkeley, California, 1984), p. 20n.

Hynes, Samuel, 'Personal Narratives and Commemoration', in Jay Winter and Emmanuel Sivan (eds), *War and Remembrance in the Twentieth Century* (Cambridge, 1999).

Hynes, Samuel, *The Soldiers' Tale: Bearing Witness to Modern War* (London, 1997).

Jones, Peter, *The Peasantry in the French Revolution* (Cambridge, 1988).

Leclercq, Jean-Yves, 'Le mythe de Bonaparte sous le Directoire, 1796–99' (mémoire de maîtrise, Université de Paris-I, 1991).

Lefebvre, Georges, *Napoleon: From 18 Brumaire to Tilsit, 1799–1807* (London, 1969).

Leith, James A., *Art as Propaganda in France, 1750–99* (Toronto, 1965).

Leleu, Edmond, *La société populaire de Lille* (Lille, 1919).

Lemarchand, Lionel, *Lettres censurées des tranchées, 1917* (Paris, 2001).

Léonard, E.-G., *L'armée et ses problèmes au dix-huitième siècle* (Paris, 1958).

Leveque, Guillaume, 'L'image des héros dans la presse périodique photographique française de la Première Guerre Mondiale' (mémoire de DEA, Université de Paris-I, 1989).

Leverrier, Jules, *La naissance de l'armée nationale, 1789–94* (Paris, 1939).

Lockhart, Greg, *Nation in Arms: The Origins of the People's Army of Vietnam* (Sydney, 1989).

Luzzatto, Sergio, *Mémoire de la Terreur* (Lyon, 1988).

Lynn, John, 'Toward an Army of Honor: The Moral Evolution of the French Army, 1789–1815', *French Historical Studies*, 16 (1989).

Lynn, John, *The Bayonets of the Republic: Motivation and Tactics in the Army of Revolutionary France, 1791–94* (Urbana, Illinois, 1984).

Lyons, Martyn, *Napoleon Bonaparte and the Legacy of the French Revolution* (London, 1994).

McPherson, James M., *For Cause and Comrades: Why Men Fought in the Civil War* (New York, 1997).

Maeght, Xavier, 'La presse dans le département du Nord sous la Révolution Française, 1789–1799' (thèse de troisième cycle, Université de Lille-III, 1971).

Martin, Marc, 'Journaux d'armées au temps de la Convention', *Annales historiques de la Révolution Française*, 44 (1972).

Martin, Marc, *Les origines de la presse militaire en France à la fin de l'Ancien Régime et sous la Révolution, 1770–1799* (Vincennes, 1975).

Ménager, Bernard, *Les Napoléon du peuple* (Paris, 1988).

Monnier, Raymonde, 'Le culte de Bara en l'an II', in *Joseph Bara (1779–1793): pour la deuxième centenaire de sa naissance* (Paris, 1981).

Moran, Daniel and Arthur Waldron (eds), *The People in Arms: Military Myth and Political Legitimacy since the French Revolution* (Cambridge, 2002).

Mornet, Daniel, *Tranchées de Verdun* (Nancy, 1990).

Nora, Pierre (ed.), *Les lieux de mémoire*, i, *La République* (Paris, 1984).

Ozouf, Mona, *La fête révolutionnaire, 1789–99* (Paris, 1976).

Palluel-Guillard, André, 'Correspondance et mentalité des soldats savoyards de l'armée napoléonienne', in *Soldats et armées en Savoie: actes du 28e congrès des Sociétés Savantes de Savoie, Saint-Jean-de-Maurienne, 1980* (Chambéry, 1981).

Paret, Peter, *Clausewitz and the State: The Man, his Theories and his Times* (Princeton, 1985).

Prendergast, Christopher, *Napoleon and History Painting: Antoine-Jean Gros's 'La Bataille d'Eylau'* (Oxford, 1997).

Rapport, Michael, *Nationality and Citizenship in Revolutionary France: The Treatment of Foreigners* (Oxford, 2000).

Reinhard, Marcel, 'Nostalgie et service militaire pendant la Révolution', *Annales historiques de la Révolution Française*, 30 (1958).

Richard, Alain, 'Un journal d'armée sous la Révolution: *L'Ami Jacques, Argus du Département du Nord*' (mémoire de maîtrise, Université de Lille-III, 1978).

Roshwald, Aviel and Richard Stites (eds), *European Culture in the Great War: The Arts, Entertainment and Propaganda, 1914–18* (Cambridge, 1999).

Rothenberg, Gunther E., *The Art of Warfare in the Age of Napoleon* (Bloomington, Indiana, 1978).

Rousseau, Frédéric, *La guerre censurée: une histoire des combattants européens de 14–18* (Paris, 1999).

Schroeder, Paul, *The Transformation of European Politics, 1763–1848* (Oxford, 1994).

Smith, Leonard V., *Between Mutiny and Obedience: The Case of the French Fifth Infantry Division during World War I* (Princeton, 1994).

Smith, Leonard V., 'John Norton Cru and the Combatants' Literature of the First World War', *Modern and Contemporary France*, 9 (2001).

Staes, Jacques, 'Les minutes notariales, source pour l'histoire militaire pendant le Premier Empire', in *Neuvième Rencontre Historiens Gascogne-Adour* (Université de Pau, 1980), pp. 71–105.

Tholin, G., 'Mémoires et pièces diverses', *Revue de l'Agenais*, 20 (1893).

Thomas, Jack, *Le temps des foires: foires et marchés dans le Midi toulousain de la fin de l'Ancien Régime à 1914* (Toulouse, 1993).

Vovelle, Michel, *La Révolution Française: images et récit* (5 vols, Paris, 1986).

Vovelle, Michel, 'Y a-t-il eu une révolution culturelle au dix-huitième siècle? A propos de l'éducation populaire en Provence', *Revue d'histoire moderne et contemporaine*, 22 (1975), pp. 89–141.

Watelet, Marcel and Pierre Couvreur (eds), *Waterloo, lieu de mémoire européenne, 1815–2000* (Louvain-la-Neuve, 2000).

Wiley, Bell Irvin, *The Life of Johnny Reb: The Common Soldier of the Confederacy* (Baton Rouge, Louisiana, 1943).

Wilson-Smith, Timothy, *Napoleon and his Artists* (London, 1996).

Winter, Jay, *Sites of Memory, Sites of Mourning: The Great War in European Cultural History* (Cambridge, 1995).

Woloch, Isser, *The French Veteran from the Revolution to the Restoration* (Chapel Hill, North Carolina, 1979).

Woloch, Isser, *Jacobin Legacy: The Democratic Movement under the Directory* (Princeton, 1970).

Woolf, Stuart, *Napoleon's Integration of Europe* (London, 1991).

Index